MODULE B

—◦—

MANAGING BEHAVIOR
in Common Areas and With Schoolwide Policies

Module 2 of 6 in *Foundations: A Proactive and Positive Behavior Support System* (3rd ed.)

Randy Sprick
Paula Rich

RANDY SPRICK'S

safe & civil
SCHOOLS

Practical Solutions, Positive Results!

Published in the United States by
Pacific Northwest Publishing
21 West 6th Ave.
Eugene, Oregon 97401
www.pacificnwpublish.com

ISBN: 978-1-59909-070-2

Part of *Foundations: A Proactive and Positive Behavior Support System* (3rd ed.)
ISBN: 978-1-59909-068-9

Cover by Aaron Graham
Book design and layout by Natalie Conaway
Illustrations by Aaron Graham and Tom Zilis

TRENDS is a registered trademark of Pacific Northwest Publishing
in the United States.

Pacific
Northwest
Publishing

Eugene, Oregon | www.pacificnwpublish.com

CONTENTS

CONTENTS

ABOUT THE AUTHORS

Randy Sprick, Ph.D.

Randy Sprick, Ph.D., has worked as a paraprofessional, teacher, and teacher trainer at the elementary and secondary levels. Author of a number of widely read books on behavior and classroom management, Dr. Sprick is director of *Safe & Civil Schools,* a consulting company that provides inservice programs throughout the country. He and his trainers work with numerous large and small school districts on longitudinal projects to improve student behavior and motivation. Efficacy of that work is documented in peer-reviewed research, and *Safe & Civil Schools* materials are listed on the National Registry of Evidence-based Programs and Practices (NREPP). Dr. Sprick was the recipient of the 2007 Council for Exceptional Children (CEC) Wallin Lifetime Achievement Award.

Paula Rich, B.Mus.Ed., M.Mus.

Paula Rich, B.Mus.Ed., M.Mus., has been a substitute teacher in public schools and was a freelance musician and taught private music lessons for many years in the Boston, Massachusetts, area. Since joining Pacific Northwest Publishing in 2006, she has contributed original stories and poems to the *Read Well* curriculum for second-grade readers and has edited several of Randy Sprick's staff development and behavior management books and papers. She was instrumental in developing TRENDS, Pacific Northwest Publishing's online behavioral data management system, as well as Connections, an online check-and-connect program.

SAFE & CIVIL SCHOOLS

THE SAFE & CIVIL SCHOOLS SERIES is a comprehensive, integrated set of resources designed to help educators improve student behavior and school climate at every level—districtwide, schoolwide, within the classroom, and at the individual intervention level. The findings of decades of research literature have been refined into step-by-step actions that teachers and staff can take to help all students behave responsibly and respectfully.

The hallmark of the *Safe & Civil Schools* model is its emphasis on proactive, positive, and instructional behavior management—addressing behavior before it necessitates correction, collecting data before embarking on interventions, implementing simple corrections before moving to progressively more intensive and time-intrusive ones, and setting a climate of respect for all. As a practical matter, tending to schoolwide and classwide policies, procedures, and interventions is far easier than resorting to more costly, time-intrusive, and individualized approaches.

Foundations and PBIS

Positive Behavioral Interventions and Supports (PBIS) is not a program. According to the U.S. Department of Education, PBIS is simply a framework to help provide "assistance to schools, districts, and states to establish a preventative, positive, multi-tiered continuum of evidence-based behavioral interventions that support the behavioral competence of students" (A. Posny, personal communication, September 7, 2010). That framework perfectly describes *Foundations*. *Foundations* provides instructions for implementing such an approach—with detailed processes and hundreds of examples of specific applications from successful schools. Furthermore, *Foundations* provides step-by-step guidance for involving and unifying an entire district staff to develop behavior support procedures that will prevent misbehavior and increase student connectedness and motivation. *Foundations* moves well beyond a simple matrix into how to guide and inspire staff to take ownership of managing and motivating all students, all the time, every day.

SAFE & CIVIL SCHOOLS

Resources in the series do not take a punitive approach to discipline. Instead, *Safe & Civil Schools* addresses the sources of teachers' greatest power to motivate: through structuring for student success, teaching expectations, observing and monitoring student behavior, and, above all, interacting positively. Because experience directly affects behavior, it makes little sense to pursue only the undesired behavior (by relying on reprimands, for example) and not the conditions (in behavioral theory, the antecedent) that precipitate experience and subsequent behavior.

The *Safe & Civil Schools* Positive Behavioral Interventions and Supports (PBIS) Model is listed in the National Registry of Evidence-based Programs and Practices (NREPP) after review by the Substance Abuse and Mental Health Services Administration (SAMHSA).

Inclusion in NREPP means that independent reviewers found that the philosophy and procedures behind *Foundations, CHAMPS, Discipline in the Secondary Classroom, Interventions,* and other *Safe & Civil Schools* books and DVDs have been thoroughly researched, that the research is of high quality, and that the outcomes achieved include:

- Higher levels of academic achievement
- Reductions in school suspensions
- Fewer classroom disruptions
- Increases in teacher professional self-efficacy
- Improvement in school discipline procedures

For more information, visit www.nrepp.samhsa.gov.

The most recent evidence of the efficacy of the *Safe & Civil Schools* PBIS Model appeared in the October 2013 issue of *School Psychology Review.* "A Randomized Evaluation of the *Safe and Civil Schools* Model for Positive Behavioral Interventions and Supports at Elementary Schools in a Large Urban School District," by Bryce Ward and Russell Gersten, shows how the *Safe & Civil Schools* PBIS Model improves student behavior and school climate. Thirty-two elementary schools in a large urban school district were randomly assigned to an initial training cohort or a wait-list control group. Results show reduced suspension rates, decreases in problem behavior, and evidence of positive academic gains for the schools in the training cohort.

Observed improvements persisted through the second year of trainings, and once the wait-list control schools commenced *Safe & Civil Schools* training, they experienced similar improvements in school policies and student behavior.

Download and read the full article at:
www.nasponline.org/publications/spr/index.aspx?vol=42&issue=3

Safe & Civil Schools acknowledges the real power educators have—not in controlling students but in shaping their behavior through affecting every aspect of their experience while they are in school: the physical layout, the way time is structured, arrivals and departures, teaching expected behavior, meaningful relationships with adults, and more. These changes in what adults do can create dramatic and lifelong changes in the behavior and motivation of students.

ACKNOWLEDGMENTS

As lead author, I owe a huge debt to many people who have guided the development and revision of *Foundations* over the past three decades. Betsy Norton, Mickey Garrison, and Marilyn Sprick were instrumental in the development and implementation of *Foundations* long before the publication of the first edition in 1992. Dr. Jan Reinhardtsen received the very first federal grant on the topic of positive behavior support and, with Mickey, implemented the first edition of *Foundations* as the basis for Project CREST in the early and mid-1990s. Jan also came up with *Safe & Civil Schools,* which became the name of our staff development services. Dr. Laura McCullough implemented a brilliant state-level Model School project in Kentucky, followed by the Kentucky Instructional Discipline System (KIDS) project that taught me so much about the importance of training and coaching to assist schools with implementation of both schoolwide and classroom behavior support.

I want to thank my coauthors of the different modules within this edition. Susan Isaacs, Mike Booher, and Jessica Sprick are outstanding trainers of *Foundations,* and their respective expertise has added depth to the content that makes this edition more practical, rich, and fun than previous editions. Paula Rich has provided both organizational skill and writing expertise to weave together a vast amount of content with many school- and district-level examples to create a highly accessible and user-friendly resource.

Thanks to the awesome staff of Pacific Northwest Publishing: Aaron Graham and Natalie Conaway with design, Sara Ferris and K Daniels with editing, Matt Sprick for directing both video and print development, Sam Gehrke for video editing, Robert Consentino and Jake Clifton for camera and sound, and the rest of the Pacific Northwest Publishing and *Safe & Civil Schools* staff—Jackie Hefner, Karen Schell, Sarah Romero, Kimberly Irving, Brandt Schram, Caroline DeVorss, and Marilyn Sprick—for their great work.

Implementation of *Foundations*, *CHAMPS*, and *Interventions* would not have thrived without the skill and dedication of great staff developers and trainers: Tricia Berg, Mike Booher, Phyllis Gamas, Laura Hamilton, Andrea Hanford, Jane Harris, Susan Isaacs, Debbie Jackson, Kim Marcum, Bob McLaughlin, Donna Meers, Carolyn Novelly, Robbie Rowan, Susan Schilt, Tricia Skyles, Pat Somers, Karl Schleich, Jessica Sprick, and Elizabeth Winford as Director of Professional Development.

ACKNOWLEDGMENTS

Fresno Unified School District and Long Beach Unified School District in California allowed us to visit with the Pacific Northwest Publishing video crew to capture the excitement, professionalism, and commitment of school and district personnel. These districts have taught us so much about the importance of common language and district support in creating a sustainable implementation.

Lastly, I want to the thank the schools and districts that have implemented *Foundations* over the years and graciously shared their lessons, posters, staff development activities, forms, and policies that you will find as examples throughout the print and video presentations. These real-world examples will help your implementation process by illustrating how other schools and districts have successfully implemented and sustained *Foundations*.

—R.S.

HOW TO USE FOUNDATIONS

This third edition of *Foundations* is constructed as six modules to accommodate schools that are just beginning their implementation of multi-tiered systems of behavior support (MTSS) as well as schools that already have some, but not all, pieces of behavior support firmly in place. For example, a school may have done great work on improving behavior in the common areas of the school but very little work on intentionally constructing a positive, inviting climate or addressing conflict and bullying in a comprehensive way. This school could go directly to Module C: *Conscious Construction of an Inviting Climate*, and after implementing those strategies, move to Module E: *Improving Safety, Managing Conflict, and Preventing Bullying.*

Each module incorporates multiple resources to assist you: video presentations on DVD, the book you are reading now, and a CD with forms and samples. The videos can guide a building-based leadership team through implementing *Foundations.* The same content is available in print format; we provide eight copies of this book for each module, one for each member of the leadership team. Teams can decide which content delivery form works best for them—video or print.

Each book comes with a CD that contains reproducible forms, examples of policies and procedures from real schools that have implemented *Foundations*, and other implementation resources. The CD also includes PowerPoint presentations that correspond directly to the video and print content. Your leadership team can use these presentations to deliver the most relevant *Foundations* information to the entire staff.

Beginning Behavior Support

For schools and districts that are just beginning with behavior support or are unsure where to begin, we suggest starting with Module A: *Foundations of Behavior Support—A Continuous Improvement Process.* This module is the foundation of *Foundations.* It describes the importance of a well-designed leadership team, a formalized continuous improvement cycle, how to use multiple data sources to drive that cycle, and how to involve and unify the staff in implementation. Without laying this groundwork, any specific work on procedures, such as improving the cafeteria, is unlikely to be effective or sustainable.

Once your team is collecting and analyzing data, you will probably move through Modules B–F (described below) in order. You'll work on the common areas of the school, then positive climate, and so on. Once a module has been implemented, you are not done with that module. For example, after implementing the procedures in Module B for a couple of common areas and a couple of schoolwide policies, such as dress code, you may move on to Module C to work on improving school climate. However, you will concurrently continue to implement Module B procedures for additional common areas and schoolwide policies. Working through all six modules will take about two to five years of development and implementation.

MTSS in Progress

Schools and districts that have been effectively implementing other approaches to PBIS should follow these guidelines when implementing *Foundations*.

You may be able to use the modules in a nonlinear fashion if your school has a highly functional team, uses multiple data sources to involve the entire staff in continuous improvement of behavior support, and has worked to improve several common areas or schoolwide policies. To self-assess where to begin, a resource for each module called the Foundations Implementation Rubric and Summary is included in Appendix A of the book and on the CD. The rubric can help your leadership team assess which modules have information useful to your school at this time and help you make judgments about where to begin. Print the rubric, work through it as a team, and summarize your findings, and you will see patterns emerge. (Instructions are included with the rubric.)

For example, if all the conditions described at the beginning of this paragraph are in place, you will probably find that you are already implementing many of the procedures delineated in Modules A and B. One school may have an urgent need to go directly to Module E because the school has no programs or policies to address conflict and bullying, whereas another school may go directly to Module D because staff are very inconsistent about when and how to use disciplinary referral to the office. Another school may go directly to Module F because their schoolwide structures are relatively well established, but they have yet to address classroom management or the integration of universal, targeted, and intensive interventions.

HOW TO USE FOUNDATIONS

Appendix B of each module presents an Implementation Checklist for that module. The Implementation Checklist details the summarized items on the rubric. You will use this tool as you near completion on any module to ensure that you have fully implemented it, and it's also useful for reviewing the implementation every three years or so. The checklist can identify strengths to celebrate and catch gaps in your implementation that you may be able to fill before a major problem emerges.

OVERVIEW OF MODULES

The modules in *Foundations* are designed to be used sequentially by a school or district that is just getting started with behavior support. However, if a school or district is already implementing a team-based, data-driven approach to continuous improvement of climate, safety, discipline, and motivation, the modules can be used in any order.

This module—**Module B: *Managing Behavior in Common Areas and With Schoolwide Policies***—delineates processes for ensuring that common areas (arrival, cafeteria, hallways, and so on) and schoolwide policies (dress code, electronics use, public displays of affection, and so on) are structured for success and that expectations for behavior are directly taught with clarity and repetition to students. In addition, this module includes detailed information for all staff about how to provide positive and systematic supervision and how to correct misbehavior calmly, consistently, and respectfully.

- Presentation 1: Laying the Groundwork for Consistency in All School Settings
- Presentation 2: Structuring Common Areas and Schoolwide Policies for Success
- Presentation 3: Teaching Expectations to Students
- Presentation 4: Effective Supervision, Part 1—Protect, Expect, and Connect
- Presentation 5: Effective Supervision, Part 2—Correct and Reflect
- Presentation 6: Supervising Common Areas and Schoolwide Policies—for All Staff
- Presentation 7: Adopting, Implementing, and Monitoring Improvements to Common Areas and Schoolwide Policies
- Appendix A: Foundations Implementation Rubric and Summary
- Appendix B: Module B Implementation Checklist
- Appendix C: Guide to Module B Reproducible Forms and Samples

Other modules in *Foundations: A Proactive and Positive Behavior Support System* are:

Module A: *Foundations of Behavior Support—A Continuous Improvement Process* covers the essential processes for involving the entire staff in developing, implementing, and sustaining positive behavior support. It includes detailed information about establishing a building-based leadership team (Foundations Team) to represent the entire staff. This module advises the team on how to collect and analyze data, identify and rank a manageable number of priorities for improvement, and guide the staff in revising, adopting, and implementing new policies and procedures for each priority. This process creates a cycle of continuous improvement that empowers and unifies the entire staff.

- Presentation 1: Foundations—A Multi-Tiered System of Behavior Support
- Presentation 2: Team Processes
- Presentation 3: The Improvement Cycle
- Presentation 4: Data-Driven Processes
- Presentation 5: Developing Staff Engagement and Unity
- Appendix A: Foundations Implementation Rubric and Summary
- Appendix B: Module A Implementation Checklist
- Appendix C: Guide to Module A Reproducible Forms and Samples

Module C: *Conscious Construction of an Inviting School Climate* guides the entire staff in creating and sustaining a school environment that makes all students feel welcomed and valued. This process includes developing Guidelines for Success, a set of behaviors and traits that provides a common language and common values among staff, students, and parents. This module explains how and why to maintain at least 3:1 ratios of positive interactions and covers the importance of regular attendance and strategies for improving attendance. Strategies for meeting the basic human needs of all students are also discussed. Finally, the module outlines how to welcome and orient staff, students, and families who are new to the school in a way that connects them to the school community.

- Presentation 1: Constructing and Maintaining a Positive Climate
- Presentation 2: Guidelines for Success
- Presentation 3: Ratios of Positive Interactions
- Presentation 4: Improving Attendance
- Presentation 5: School Connectedness—Meeting Basic Human Needs
- Presentation 6: Programs and Strategies for Meeting Needs
- Presentation 7: Making a Good First Impression—Welcoming New Staff, Students, and Families
- Appendix A: Foundations Implementation Rubric and Summary
- Appendix B: Module C Implementation Checklist
- Appendix C: Guide to Module C Reproducible Forms and Samples

Module D: *Responding to Misbehavior—An Instructional Approach* focuses on the vital importance of an instructional approach to correction to reduce future occurrences of the misbehavior. This module covers training and inspiring all staff to correct all misbehavior by providing information on how to behave successfully and by using the mildest consequences that reasonably fit the infractions. Module D describes how to achieve consensus among staff about when (and when not) to use office discipline referral. It provides menus of corrective techniques for mild and moderate misbehavior, from gentle verbal correction to time owed after class to restorative justice strategies. All staff learn strategies for de-escalating emotional situations, and administrators are introduced to a comprehensive game plan for dealing with office referrals and for implementing alternatives to out-of-school suspension. This module includes sample lessons for students on how to interact with people in authority.

- Presentation 1: The Relationship Between Proactive Procedures, Corrective Procedures, and Individual Student Behavior Improvement Plans
- Presentation 2: Developing Three Levels of Misbehavior
- Presentation 3: Staff Responsibilities for Responding to Misbehavior
- Presentation 4: Administrator Responsibilities for Responding to Misbehavior
- Presentation 5: Preventing the Misbehavior That Leads to Referrals and Suspensions
- Appendix A: Foundations Implementation Rubric and Summary
- Appendix B: Module D Implementation Checklist
- Appendix C: Guide to Module D Reproducible Forms and Samples

Module E: *Improving Safety, Managing Conflict, and Reducing Bullying* guides the Foundations Team in assessing school strengths and weaknesses related to safety, conflict, and bullying. The module begins by examining the attributes of safe and unsafe schools and offers suggestions for moving your school toward the evidence-based attributes that contribute to safety. One potential risk to safety is poor conflict management, so this module includes a simple conflict resolution strategy that students can use to manage conflict in peaceful and mutually beneficial ways. Bullying is another serious risk to safety. Module E provides a step-by-step process for analyzing strengths and gaps in your school's bullying policies and procedures as well as suggestions and examples for turning gaps into strengths. This module includes lessons for students on safety, conflict, and bullying prevention and intervention.

- Presentation 1: Ensuring a Safe Environment
- Presentation 2: Attributes of Safe and Unsafe Schools
- Presentation 3: Teaching Conflict Resolution
- Presentation 4: Analyzing Bullying Behavior, Policies, and School Needs
- Presentation 5: Schoolwide Bullying Prevention and Intervention
- Appendix A: Foundations Implementation Rubric and Summary
- Appendix B: Module E Implementation Checklist
- Appendix C: Guide to Module E Reproducible Forms and Samples

Module F: *Establishing and Sustaining a Continuum of Behavior Support* outlines how the Foundations Team can analyze and guide an integration of universal prevention, targeted support, and intensive support for students. This process includes adopting and supporting a schoolwide or district approach to classroom management that creates a common language and ensures that teachers, administrators, and support staff are on the same page about classroom organization and management. For students who need individual support, this module provides staff training in early-stage interventions and a variety of problem-solving structures that match the intensity of student need to the intensity of school- and district-based resources. Finally, Module F provides guidance in sustaining *Foundations* at the building and district level so that effective procedures are maintained and improvement continues, even when school administration changes.

- Presentation 1: The Vision of a Continuum of Behavior Support
- Presentation 2: Supporting Classroom Behavior—The Three-Legged Stool
- Presentation 3: Articulating Staff Beliefs and Solidifying Universal Procedures
- Presentation 4: Early-Stage Interventions for General Education Classrooms
- Presentation 5: Matching the Intensity of Your Resources to the Intensity of Your Needs
- Presentation 6: Problem-Solving Processes and Intervention Design
- Presentation 7: Sustainability and District Support
- Appendix A: Foundations Implementation Rubric and Summary
- Appendix B: Module F Implementation Checklist
- Appendix C: Guide to Module F Reproducible Forms and Samples

Laying the Groundwork for Consistency in All School Settings

CONTENTS

DOCUMENTS*

- Foundations Continuum of Behavior Support (B-14)
- Common Area Concerns Worksheet (B-04)
- Schoolwide Policy Concerns Worksheet (B-05)
- Revision Checklist and STOIC Worksheet (B-06)

* All documents listed are available on the CD.

INTRODUCTION
Module B Overview

Module B is designed to help you implement and improve common areas and school-wide policies.

- Presentation 1 introduces the concepts of common areas and schoolwide policies and outlines the improvement process.

- Presentation 2 is all about structuring for success.

- Presentation 3 gives suggestions for teaching expectations to students and designing appropriate lessons.

- Presentations 4 and 5 can be used in training noncertified personnel to supervise common areas such as playgrounds, cafeterias, and secondary school hallways.

- Presentation 6 provides information for classroom teachers and others who do not supervise areas such as playgrounds or cafeterias but might have responsibilities for arrival, dismissal, or hallways.

- Presentation 7 is about adopting, implementing, and monitoring the improvements you've made and integrating multiple common area and schoolwide policies into a continuous improvement cycle.

- Appendix A contains the Foundations Implementation Rubric for use in assessing implementation of each *Foundations* module.

- Appendix B provides a detailed Implementation Checklist for tasks in this module.

- Appendix C presents the contents of the Module B CD for easy reference.

- The *Foundations* Module B CD provides electronic copies of a variety of reproducible forms and sample policies and lessons.

We recommend to most schools that they begin their improvement efforts by working on one or two common areas or schoolwide policies. When common areas are safe, civil, and productive, and schoolwide policies are enforced with clarity and consistency, schools tend to be safe, civil, and productive. If you are already implementing *Foundations*, you can use the information in this module to extend your *Foundations* practices to all common areas and schoolwide policies, leading to the ultimate goal of continuous improvement.

Figure 1a   *The Foundations continuum of behavior support (B-14)*

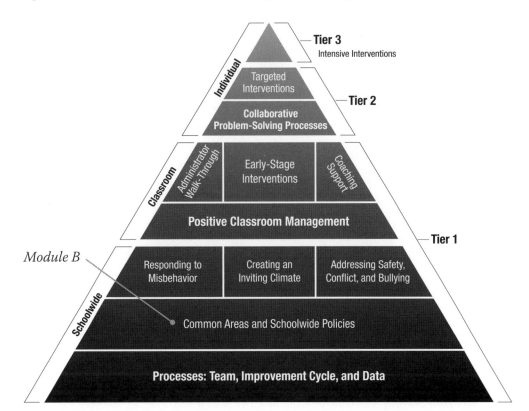

Figure 1a shows the *Foundations* process represented as a triangle in which the implementation and success of all improvements rest on the Foundations Team's efforts, the continuous use of the Improvement Cycle, and effective data collection and analysis. Module A discusses this infrastructure in detail. The *Foundations* process graphic can be printed from the Module B CD.

Once the team is in place and everyone understands how to work within the Improvement Cycle, they can begin to address the next layer up, Common Areas and Schoolwide Policies. Improvements in that second layer will result in better supervision practices, students who understand expectations, and a safer, more positive, and respectful climate in the common areas of the school. Improvements in the third layer up—discipline, inviting climate, bullying prevention, conflict, and safety—depend on the qualities developed to maintain well-managed common areas and schoolwide policies. They won't work unless all staff have been trained in effective supervision practices and students feel safe and understand how to follow expectations.

The pattern continues because the Tier 1: Classroom improvements depend on the supporting structure of Tier 1: Schoolwide, and the Tier 2 and 3 programs hinge on the foundation of Tier 1.

All of these improvements won't take place in one year—or even two. It is essential to work upward from the bottom of the triangle and take the time you need to ensure that the foundation is set. The triangle shape correlates to the number of students affected. The wider area at the bottom of the triangle indicates that all students and staff are positively affected by improved common areas and schoolwide policies. That's one of the reasons we recommend beginning your *Foundations* improvement process there—you get a lot of bang for your buck, including staff buy-in and better overall student behavior.

ଚ FOUNDATIONS RECOMMENDATION ଔ

Consider starting your Foundations *improvement process by working on just one or two common areas or schoolwide policies.*

This module will guide you through selecting and then improving one common area or schoolwide policy. Ideally, you will repeat the selection and improvement process with all major common areas and policies until you've analyzed each one for efficacy. You'll also archive the effective procedures and policies you've developed to make it easier to sustain and enforce them in subsequent years.

School culture can be defined as the beliefs, perceptions, relationships, attitudes, and written and unwritten rules that shape and influence every aspect of how a school functions. The term also encompasses more concrete issues, such as the physical and emotional safety of students, the orderliness of classrooms and public spaces, and the degree to which the school embraces and celebrates racial, ethnic, linguistic, and cultural diversity (Glossary of Education Reform, n.d.).

Common areas and schoolwide policies are effective vehicles for communicating the school culture; that is, students, staff, and families can learn and understand the school culture by learning and understanding the expectations, attitudes, emphasis on safety, and so on of the common areas and schoolwide policies. And when the school culture is developed with coherent and cohesive policies, procedures, and rituals, it will endure long beyond the tenure of the current staff. The safe, welcoming, and respectful environment will have been built to last.

Following are some key reasons why smoothly functioning common areas and schoolwide policies are important.

Common areas greatly influence the climate of the whole school. The hallways of a secondary school are much like the arteries of the human body—if the arteries aren't healthy, the entire organism suffers. In elementary schools, the atmosphere of the playground is often responsible for setting the tone for student behavior for the entire rest of the day. Poorly structured areas create opportunities for misbehavior and bullying.

Student behavior in common areas affects student behavior in classrooms. If hallways are chaotic, middle and high school teachers often must spend many precious minutes of each class period calming students down instead of teaching. In some elementary schools, teachers must spend 10 to 15 minutes after each recess dealing with playground squabbles and hurt feelings and settling the unbridled energy that students bring back to the classroom.

Student behavior related to schoolwide policies can affect student behavior in classrooms. If a particular policy, such as the dress code, is unclear or implemented inconsistently, it can lead to arguments among students, students who feel they are being treated unfairly, and even insubordinate behavior from unskilled students.

The improvement of just one problematic common area or schoolwide policy can make a huge difference in school climate and student behavior. In addition (and equally important), the staff become more energized and unified through the process of constructively working together and realizing the important positive goal of improving the school experience for students and staff—in other words, the staff *buy in* to the *Foundations* process.

Creating staff buy-in: Staff must implement all common area procedures and schoolwide policies, so it is essential that the Foundations Team continually strive to have staff actively buy in to the procedures and policies that are developed. Task 1 of this presentation focuses on the importance of educating staff about the problems of common areas and schoolwide policies and the benefits of improving those areas and policies. It also provides guidance for how the staff can identify which schoolwide policies or common areas they want the team to work on first. If the first area chosen is one that is particularly problematic for staff, successfully improving student behavior related to that area or policy can enable staff to see the benefits of the entire *Foundations* process. One high school that serves a tough community improved hallway, restroom, and tardiness procedures so successfully that tardiness was reduced by 96%. The changes in the school climate and student behavior were so dramatic that some of the most skeptical teachers said to the team, "What do we get to work on next?"

Presentation 1 Overview

This presentation introduces the concept of common areas and schoolwide policies and outlines the improvement process. It will help you use all of Module B effectively.

Task 1: Understand Common Areas, Schoolwide Policies, and the Factors That Contribute to Student Misbehavior discusses the definition of common areas and some reasons why misbehavior can occur there. It also provides information about selecting one or more common areas or schoolwide policies to focus on as improvement priorities. The entire staff might view this task, or the Foundations Team might view Task 1 and then prepare an agenda item to review the information with the entire staff.

The rest of this presentation and most of Module B addresses how you will work on a common area or schoolwide policy that you've identified as a priority.

Task 2: Determine Whether More Information Is Needed to Begin Work on the Prioritized Area or Policy provides guidance for getting started on the revision. If the task force find that they need more information, we suggest ways to gain more input from key stakeholders affected by the common area or policy.

Task 3: Design the Steps of Your Revision Process introduces the Revision Checklist and STOIC Worksheet (Form B-06) and outlines the step-by-step sequence for revising, adopting, and eventually implementing the new common area procedures or schoolwide policy.

Note that we refer to the group who will be developing revised policies, procedures, and lessons for a common area or schoolwide policy as the *task force*. In your school, the Foundations Team, the entire staff, a special task force, or some variation may actually do this work.

In summary, use Task 1 of this presentation to involve your entire staff in developing a prioritized list of common areas and schoolwide policies and to identify who will work on the improvement efforts. The rest of Module B will guide the task force as they work to improve the identified area or policy. Through the improvement process, a school culture will develop. The beliefs, perceptions, relationships, attitudes, and written and unwritten rules that shape and influence every aspect of how your school functions will bloom. When you improve the common areas and schoolwide policies, you improve the entire school.

TASK 1

Understand common areas, schoolwide policies, and the factors that contribute to student misbehavior

In Task 1, we discuss the definition of common areas and some reasons why misbehavior can occur there, and we provide information about selecting one or more common areas or schoolwide policies to focus on as improvement priorities.

What are common areas and schoolwide policies?

A *common area* is a school setting or situation in which students are supervised by a variety of different staff members or by one or more paraprofessionals. Settings that are common areas include:

- Hallways and restrooms
- Cafeterias
- Courtyards and commons (i.e., school locations where secondary-level students congregate during nonclassroom time, such as after lunch)
- Playgrounds
- Buses (to and from school, loading and unloading areas)
- Outside entry areas before and after school
- Parking lots
- Classrooms that do not have dedicated supervisors—different teachers bring and supervise their own students (e.g., computer labs)
- Front office

Common area *situations* are more dependent on circumstances than on a particular location. A unified, consistent approach to supervision is still needed, however. Common area situations include:

- Assemblies
- Behavior with substitute teachers
- Arrival
- Dismissal

Settings and situations that are under the direct and consistent supervision of a single certified staff member are *not* considered common areas. The following examples are not common areas:

- Classrooms
- Computer labs with certified computer lab teachers
- Library/media centers with certified library/media specialists

Note that although the expectations in the above settings should be under the control and supervision of the certified staff person, some limited schoolwide policies related to student behavior with specialists can be beneficial. We address this topic in Module B, Presentation 2, Task 2.

Schoolwide policies are any policies or procedures that students are expected to follow in all school settings. Examples are policies for:

- Attendance
- Tardiness
- Cell phones and other electronic devices
- Dress code
- ID badges
- Appropriate language
- Bullying and harassment
- Elementary specialists (music, library, PE, art, and computer)

What factors contribute to student behavior problems in common areas and with schoolwide policies?

Think about a moderately or severely problematic area or policy in your school as you consider the information below. Are some or all of the following points contributing factors?

Structural variables (physical setting, organization, and procedures) and/or supervision arrangements sometimes do not facilitate student success. For example, 200 students who have been taught expectations for playground behavior behave appropriately in an unstructured setting for about 15 minutes, but after that the level of chaos seems to increase exponentially. Scheduling a 25- or 30-minute recess sets students up for behavior problems. Another example is high school passing periods—if they are either too long or too short, misbehavior tends to increase.

When expectations for student behavior are undefined or unclear, behavior problems are bound to occur. All students and all staff need to know what the behavioral rules and expectations are for each common area. You can't expect students to behave responsibly if you haven't taught them, in detail, what constitutes responsible behavior. For example, students need to be taught how to enter the auditorium for assembly, how to find a seat, the acceptable voice level to use until the assembly begins, the signal that staff will give for quiet, and so on. The greater the level of detail in the instructions, the greater the probability that behavior problems in the setting will be reduced.

Example From the Field

Many years ago, I was working with a school to improve the common areas, including the playground. I sat down with the task force charged with improving playground behavior and said, "Before we discuss what we might do to improve student behavior on the playground, let's start with one question: Do you have playground rules?"

Everyone nodded and said, "Oh, yes, we sure do."

I said, "Great. Let's start with those. Where are they?" Silence. No one knew where the rules were written down. So I said, "Don't worry about where they are. Let's just talk about what they are." Again, embarrassed silence.

Finally, one person said, "Well, I know one of the rules. Only one student at a time is allowed on the ladder of the slide."

Two other people in the group responded, "Really?" "Am I supposed to enforce that rule when I'm on playground duty? I don't."

Imagine the inconsistent supervision and corrections that the staff were providing on the playground. Everybody thought they had playground rules, but in fact they didn't, because nobody knew *where* or *what* the rules were. —R.S.

Ineffective supervisory practices are common factors in student misbehavior and can take many forms. *Note:* Presentations 4 and 5 in this module cover effective supervisory practices and can be used to train supervisors.

- **Ineffective supervisors are not active.** They do not listen to, circulate among, and interact with students enough and do not scan the setting often enough. A common sight on school playgrounds is the supervisors huddled together talking instead of interacting with students.

Example From the Field

A substitute teacher was working in a second-grade classroom on a day when a schoolwide assembly was scheduled. She discussed behavioral expectations for the assembly with the students, and she found that they were well versed in assembly behavior. The substitute then said, "What am I supposed to do at the assembly?"

The students replied, very seriously, "Teachers stand against the wall and talk to each other, holding papers in front of their faces."

The staff at this school said this substitute teacher's anecdote gave them a wake-up call about their supervisory practices. They had trained the students to pay attention to the assembly and be quiet. But the staff were modeling the opposite behaviors—talking and not paying attention—which of course affected how well they supervised the students!　　　　　—R.S.

- **Ineffective supervisors respond inconsistently to student misbehavior.** Responses vary from supervisor to supervisor, student to student, and day to day.

    Supervisor-to-supervisor inconsistency: Imagine a student who goes to the school computer lab three times a day, but each time with a different teacher. One teacher allows low-level talking and snacks while students work, while another permits active discussion and movement around the room. The third teacher requires students to be quiet and remain in their seats, and allows no snacks. The third teacher, not surprisingly, has ongoing trouble with student behavior.

    Student-to-student inconsistency: A supervisor who stops one student from running but lets another student run right past her is sending the message that she is biased against the first student. Not only is this inconsistency unfair, but it can incite an emotional and oppositional response from the first student when he questions why he was reprimanded and the other student wasn't.

    Day-to-day inconsistency: Supervisors need to be consistent from one day to the next, no matter their moods. Sometimes it's easy to let students get by with behavior when you are calm and relaxed. But let's say you let a student wander around the library during study period on Monday, and on Tuesday you insist that she stay seated. On Wednesday, the student likely will misbehave just to see what you will do, because to her you've become an interesting experimental subject.

- **Ineffective supervisors respond adversarially or emotionally to student misbehavior.** When a supervisor's demeanor says to students, "I'm just waiting for you to screw up, and I'll make you sorry when you do," she is setting an adversarial tone for all students. And when she corrects by saying sharply and angrily, "Jacob, knock it off! Stop running!" students tend to respond emotionally. For some students, getting emotional increases their oppositional behavior and is highly reinforcing.

- **Ineffective supervisors fail to convey an assumption of student cooperation and compliance.** Supervisors should always use a tone of voice, language, and body language that communicate the expectation that students will behave responsibly and follow directions. (We talk about this concept in more detail in Presentations 5 and 6 later in this module.)

Students fail to respect supervising paraprofessionals. This disrespect might occur because the paraprofessionals lack training and coaching in how to supervise (or be assertive), professional staff members fail to adequately support paraprofessionals, or professional staff members fail to demonstrate adequate respect for paraprofessionals. Professional staff members sometimes inadvertently model disrespect when they refer to paraprofessional supervisors as the "duty." For example, instead of referring to Mr. Jones and Mrs. Smith as the playground supervisors, staff call them the "duty people out on the playground."

What factors contribute to student misbehavior related to schoolwide policies?

Ineffective supervision can contribute to misbehavior. All of the factors described above regarding ineffective supervision in common areas are true for schoolwide policies. Ensuring effective, consistent, and positive supervision can be even more difficult for schoolwide policies because all staff in all settings must follow through on all policies.

Organizational and structural variables can make enforcement of schoolwide policies difficult. For example, some students will inevitably lose their ID badges, so an ID badge policy must include processes for easily getting temporary and replacement badges. If these processes are not in place, enforcement of the ID badge policy is almost impossible. Another example is cell phone policy—if some classrooms use cell phones, but the schoolwide policy says students cannot have cell phones in school, the contradictory organizational variable makes enforcement of the cell phone policy impossible.

When the expectations for a schoolwide policy are undefined or unclear, behavior problems are bound to occur. All students and all staff need to clearly understand the policy. For example, if an aspect of the dress code is unclear, students will likely push the limits, and staff will likely be unable to enforce those limits consistently. If a student wears something during the first two periods of the day without consequence but is corrected during the third period, the inconsistency sets up a high probability that the student will feel she is being treated unfairly. If she is an unskilled student, she may exhibit insubordinate behavior.

What variables should be considered when working to improve a common area or schoolwide policy?

We use the acronym STOIC to describe five variables that can be manipulated to set up students and staff for success. Each of these variables is discussed in more detail in later presentations.

S **Structure for success.** Identify and modify variables that positively influence student behavior. These variables include such things as the physical setting, schedule, routines, procedures, and purpose of the setting, situation, or policy.

T **Teach expectations.** Teach students the specific skills and behavioral expectations that will result in their success.

O **Observe and monitor.** Use effective supervisory techniques such as circulating and visually scanning the area. Use objective data to make decisions and monitor trends across time.

I **Interact positively.** Model the core belief that all students must be treated with respect. Provide positive attention and specific descriptive feedback on behavior when students behave responsibly. Maintain a high ratio of positive to corrective interactions.

C **Correct fluently.** React to misbehavior calmly, consistently, briefly, and immediately.

The acronym STOIC is an easy way to remember these five variables: Structure, Teach, Observe, Interact positively, and Correct fluently. Some people might think the word *stoic* implies someone who is cold and unfeeling. However, *Encarta World English Dictionary* gives a definition of the adjective *stoic* as "tending to remain unemotional, especially showing admirable patience and endurance in the face of adversity." Thus, a stoic teacher or supervisor is one who is unrattled by student misbehavior and who implements research-based strategies (as in *Foundations*).

In Task 3, we present a worksheet based on the STOIC framework that you can use as you work through revising a common area or schoolwide policy.

Have a staff discussion to identify common areas and schoolwide policies as well as the policies left to the discretion of individual staff members.

For example, the dress code is a schoolwide policy, but classroom rules for pencil sharpener use are at the discretion of individual staff members. The following examples are settings, situations, and policies to consider:

- Arrival
- Hallways
- Restrooms
- Playgrounds and courtyards
- Cafeteria
- Assemblies
- Dismissal
- After-school programs
- Front office
- Behavior with substitute teachers
- Attendance
- Tardiness
- Cell phones and other electronic devices
- Dress code
- ID badges
- Appropriate language
- Bullying and harassment
- Elementary specialists (music, library, PE, art, and computer)

Proceed through the Review, Prioritize, and Revise steps of the Improvement Cycle.

Note: Module A describes in more detail how to proceed through the steps of the Improvement Cycle.

Review: Collect and analyze data

Share data from incident reports, surveys, and observations of common areas. Give staff the opportunity to express concerns about areas or policies that may not have data to support the need for improvement but that are nonetheless a concern.

Prioritize: Determine which common area or schoolwide policy to work on first.

Guide the staff in developing a hierarchical list (most to least urgent) of areas and policies in need of improvement. You might create a ballot and have each staff member vote for the top five he or she would like to see improved. Or use a weighted voting process in which each staff member ranks the areas and policies in order of urgency, with a 5 for the most urgent, 4 for the next, and so on. Another way to get staff input is to list the common areas and schoolwide policies on a large piece of butcher paper. Give all staff members three sticky dots and have them place the dots next to the three areas or policies they would like to see improved. The area or policy with the most dots goes to the top of the hierarchical list. A voting activity demonstrates that the *Foundations* process is driven by the entire staff, not just the Foundations Team, and supports and unifies the entire staff.

Report the results to the staff by showing them the hierarchical list. Then ask for opinions about a proposed development process—specifically how many common areas or schoolwide policies you will tackle. Consider the following:

- Availability of staff time (think about inservice days, early release days, etc.)
- Urgency of safety items
- Level of concern of staff and their motivation to participate in the improvement process
- Benefits of including students and parents on the task force

If you identify more than one common area or schoolwide policy, determine how you will address multiple priorities:

- One at a time (determine the order)—best approach if the Foundations Team is solely responsible for all improvements
- Two at a time (determine the order)—two task forces working simultaneously will be needed
- All at one time—multiple tasks forces will be needed

Revise: Identify who will develop the procedures.

Decide who will be responsible for guiding the improvement efforts. Options to consider include:

- The Foundations Team
- A special task force for all common area priorities
- Separate task forces for each common area priority
- The entire staff

More information about forming task forces appears in Module A, Presentation 2.

The next task describes how to continue through the **Revise** step for your selected common area or schoolwide policy.

Task 1 Action Steps & Evidence of Implementation

Action Steps	Evidence of Implementation
1. Educate the staff about the importance of unity and consistency in the management and supervision of common areas and schoolwide policies.	Foundations Process: Staff Presentations
2. Guide staff in generating a complete list of the school's common areas (settings and situations) and schoolwide policies. 3. Share current data (e.g., incident referrals, surveys, and observations) on areas and policies. 4. Guide staff in ranking the common areas and schoolwide policies—from most urgent to least urgent. Decide which area or policy (and how many) to work on first. 5. Decide who will be responsible for guiding the improvement efforts for the items with highest priority.	Foundations Process: Current Priorities

TASK 2

Determine whether more information is needed to begin revising the prioritized area or policy

Task 2 provides guidance for the task force beginning the revision. If the task force need more information, we suggest ways they can gain more guidance from key stakeholders affected by the common area or schoolwide policy. *Note: Foundations Module A discusses the steps in the Improvement Cycle in detail.*

Take initial steps to revise the procedures or policies.

By now you've worked through the **Review** and **Prioritize** steps for common areas and schoolwide policies. The Foundations Team has:

- Collected data about common areas and schoolwide policies, including observations, surveys, and informal feedback from staff and students.

- Reviewed the data and, with staff input, determined the common area or schoolwide policy to work on first.

- Identified who will develop the policies and procedures—the whole staff, the Foundations Team, a task force, or some variation of those approaches.

You are ready to continue with the **Revise** step—developing a detailed proposal for new or modified policies or procedures for the common area. Following are the initial steps that the team or task force should take. *Your main goal at this stage is to ensure that you have sufficient information about the area or policy.*

1. Consider skimming all seven presentations in this module to get an overall idea of what to do.

2. Determine whether written procedures or policies exist for the common area or schoolwide policy. If so, copy them for everyone who will work on the revision.

3. Examine all the data collected during the **Review** step related to the specific setting or situation—surveys, observations, student incident reports, and other existing records.

    The Data/Evaluation Coordinator might conduct the review and present a summary to the team or task force. (See Module A, Presentation 4, "Data-Driven Processes" for detailed information about how to evaluate these data.)

4. If you think additional information is needed, decide whether to conduct more observations, interviews, surveys, focus groups, or some combination of these data collection tools.

Observations. Consider conducting another set of observations in your target setting or situation. If possible, have the people who conducted the initial observations conduct the second observations. (See Module A, Presentation 4, Task 2 for detailed information on conducting common area observations.) For a particularly problematic area or policy, consider having the entire task force conduct one or more observations of the area. (Form B-03, Common Area Observation with directions, is provided on the Module B CD.)

Interviews. Consider interviewing key staff members who supervise the common area, if this wasn't done during the **Review** step. These supervisors will have first-hand information about student behavior in the setting. Also be sure to invite recommendations from any staff roles that will be affected by the policy or procedure. For example, for an ID badge policy, you should seek input from front office staff who help students replace their badges and obtain temporary badges. For restroom policies and procedures, ask the custodial staff for their opinions about any revisions or invite them to participate on the task force.

Focus groups or surveys. Conduct focus groups or brief surveys to gain student and parent input. If an area or policy has been particularly difficult or contentious, invite input from all of the stakeholders—staff, students, and parents. (This step may be unnecessary if the policy or area has not been difficult or contentious.)

Staff feedback. Prepare a presentation or memo to inform staff that the area or policy has been selected as a priority, and invite them to provide suggestions, express concerns, and volunteer to be part of the revision development process. Inform the staff about when and how revision proposals will be developed and give them a sense of when you will present a first draft of the revision proposals.

School visits. Consider arranging visits to other schools of similar size and demographics to observe how they manage their common areas and schoolwide policies.

5. When you are sure all essential information has been collected, schedule a team meeting and plan to complete the following tasks:

Share and discuss the data (e.g., surveys, observations, and incident referrals), faculty input, and existing procedures.

Identify the specific concerns of students, staff, and parents by completing the Common Area Concerns Worksheet (Form B-04, shown in Figure 1b on the next page) or the Schoolwide Policy Concerns Worksheet (Form B-05, shown in Figure 1c on p. 24). A good exercise is for individual team members to complete the student behavior section of the worksheet for 2 or 3 minutes without talking to teammates. Then the team members share what they wrote and try to reach consensus on a set of concerns. Repeat this process for the staff behavior section. Interesting and dynamic discussions usually result! Be sure that the final policy addresses the identified concerns.

Designing solutions without enough information is like a physician diagnosing an illness without running any tests, conducting an exam, or asking the patient for her opinion. Ensure that you have enough information about the problem, especially factors that affect the key staff stakeholders in the common area or schoolwide policy.

Task 2 Action Steps & Evidence of Implementation

Action Steps	Evidence of Implementation
The Foundations Team or task force charged with revising the schoolwide policy or common area procedures should: • Review all data that pertain to the target area or policy. • Conduct observations. • Complete the Common Area Concerns Worksheet (Form B-04) or Schoolwide Policy Concerns Worksheet (Form B-05).	Foundations Process: Current Priorities

Figure 1b   *Common Area Concerns Worksheet (B-04)*

Common Area Concerns Worksheet

Common Area: _____

Student Behavior in the Common Area:

List any concerns that students have about the behavior of other students in the common area:

List any concerns that staff members have about student behavior in the common area:

List any concerns that parents have about student behavior in the common area:

Staff Behavior in the Common Area:

List any concerns that students have about staff behavior in the common area:

List any concerns that staff members have about the behavior of other staff members in the common area:

List any concerns that parents have about staff behavior in the common area:

 This form can be printed from the Module B CD.

Schoolwide Policy Concerns Worksheet

Schoolwide Policy: _____

Student Behavior in Relation to the Schoolwide Policy:

List any concerns that students have about the behavior of other students in relation to the schoolwide policy.

List any concerns that staff members have about student behavior in relation to the schoolwide policy.

List any concerns that parents have about student behavior in relation to the schoolwide policy.

Staff Behavior in Relation to the Schoolwide Policy:

List any concerns that students have about staff behavior in relation to the schoolwide policy.

List any concerns that staff members have about the behavior of other staff members in relation to the schoolwide policy.

List any concerns that parents have about staff behavior in relation to the schoolwide policy.

 This form can be printed from the Module B CD.

TASK 3

Design the steps of your revision process

In this task, we introduce the Revision Checklist and STOIC Worksheet (Form B-06) and outline for your task force the steps involved in revising a policy or procedure, getting staff opinions and recommendations, and adopting and implementing the revised policy or procedure. The items below correspond to tasks found on the first page of the form—the Revision Checklist. Figure 1d on the next page shows a completed form. (The form is available on the Module B CD.)

Revision Checklist

1. Collect enough information and data on the common area or schoolwide policy. See Task 1 of this presentation.

   The numbered items within this task correspond to items on the Revision Checklist and STOIC Worksheet (shown in Figure 1d).

2. Determine a proposed timeline for completing the revision. Include dates for when the task force will:

   - Meet to write the revised procedures.
   - Seek staff feedback on the draft procedures.
   - Complete the proposed procedures.
   - Send the proposed procedures to staff (via email, for example).
   - Present the proposed procedures to the staff for adoption.
   - Develop lesson plans.
   - Teach lesson plans to the staff.
   - Teach and review supervisory expectations for staff.

3. Identify the primary person who will track progress, keep the draft proposals, and organize any needed paperwork, emails, and memos.

   If team or task force members have roles, as suggested in Module A, Presentation 2, "Team Processes," the Recorder will take charge of these tasks. The Materials Manager will also archive key documents in the Foundations Archive.

4. Determine when and how the efficacy of the new procedures will be evaluated after implementation.

5. If the new procedures are effective, identify how they will be archived and institutionalized (included in the Foundations Archive and staff and student handbooks, for example).

Revision Checklist and STOIC Worksheet
For Revising a Prioritized Common Area or Schoolwide Policy (p. 1 of 5)

Common area or schoolwide policy: ___Hallways___

Check off the following tasks as you complete them.

☑ 1. Collect enough information and data on the common area or schoolwide policy.

☑ 2. Determine a proposed timeline for completing the revision. Include dates for when the task force will:

- Meet to write the revised procedures.
- Seek staff feedback on the draft procedures.
- Complete the proposed procedures.
- Send the proposed procedures to staff (via email, for example).
- Present the proposed procedures to staff for adoption.
- Develop lesson plans.
- Teach lesson plans to the staff.
- Teach and review supervisory expectations for staff.

☑ 3. Identify the primary person on the task force who will track progress, keep the draft proposals, and organize any needed paperwork, emails, and memos.

☑ 4. Determine when and how the efficacy of the new procedures will be evaluated after implementation.

☑ 5. If the new procedures are effective, identify how they will be archived and institutionalized (included in the Foundations Archive and staff and student handbooks, for example).

 This form can be printed from the Module B CD.

STOIC Worksheet

The STOIC Worksheet portion of the form presents a summary of the STOIC acronym and then provides areas to work through each of the STOIC elements.

STRUCTURE FOR SUCCESS	**S**TOIC

1. What goal related to the common area or schoolwide policy do you hope to achieve?

   Have the task force ask questions such as, Why does this setting exist? What do we want this setting to be like? You might write, for example, "The cafeteria will provide students with an orderly, respectful setting for eating, relaxing, and socializing." You may choose to reflect the Guidelines for Success in the goal statement.

2. Identify problematic structural and organizational variables of the common area or schoolwide policy. Elements to consider include:

   - Physical setting
   - Entry and exit procedures
   - Schedule
   - Concerns about crowding
   - Procedures

   See Module B, Presentation 2, Task 1 for more information about the structure of common areas and schoolwide policies.

3. Define expectations for adult behavior.

   What adult behaviors will prompt responsible behavior in the common area or in relation to the policy? Consider the following:

   - Model appropriate behavior and respect for others.
   - Provide positive feedback.
   - Encourage students who do not interact.
   - Supervise the line.

TEACH EXPECTATIONS	S**T**OIC

4. Define student behavioral expectations for the common area or schoolwide policy.

   These expectations include all the rules and procedures that students need to know to behave successfully and responsibly. See Module B, Presentation 2, Task 2 for more information about designing rules and procedures.

Revision Checklist and STOIC Worksheet

For Revising a Prioritized Common Area or Schoolwide Policy (p. 2 of 5)

Common area or schoolwide policy: ___Hallways___

Use this worksheet to clarify your revision process.

S **Structure for success.** Identify and modify variables that positively influence student behavior. These variables include the physical setting, schedule, routines, procedures, and purpose of the setting, situation, or policy.

T **Teach expectations.** Teach students the specific skills and behavioral expectations that will result in their success.

O **Observe and monitor.** Use effective supervisory techniques such as circulating and visually scanning the area. Use objective data to make decisions and monitor trends across time.

I **Interact positively.** Model the core belief that all students must be treated with respect. Provide positive attention and specific, descriptive feedback on behavior when students behave responsibly. Maintain a high ratio of positive to corrective interactions.

C **Correct fluently.** React to misbehavior calmly, consistently, briefly, and immediately.

— STRUCTURE FOR SUCCESS —

Read or view Module B, Presentation 2 before developing.

1. What goal related to the common area or schoolwide policy do you hope to achieve? _____

   All staff members supervise effectively to help all students safely arrive to classes on time.

   _____

2. Identify problematic structural and organizational variables of the common area or schoolwide policy:

Structural/Organizational Variable of Concern	Problem/Concern Created	Possible Solutions
Blind corners	Traffic jams, accidents	Mirrors, supervision (create list of unsupervised areas), enforce passing on the right side of hallways
Areas with no class-room (breezeways, etc.)	Student misbehavior, loitering, horseplay	Identify zones of supervision, create schedule of supervision
Narrow hallways	Traffic jams, horseplay, increased noise level	Avoid locker visits except before and after school, class-room sets of books, ensure students have proper supplies
Restrooms	Overcrowding, lack of supervision	Limiting number of students in restroom, create zone for supervision, add shelves to backs of stalls, display poster with expectations

 This form can be printed from the Module B CD.

Revision Checklist and STOIC Worksheet
For Revising a Prioritized Common Area or Schoolwide Policy (p. 3 of 5)

3. Define expectations for adult behavior: What adult behaviors will prompt responsible behavior in the common area or in relation to the policy?

   - Teachers will be at their doorways at least two out of three passing times.
   - Teachers on prep will supervise halls before the period begins and intermittently supervise restrooms.
   - Security and administrative staff will circulate unpredictably and intermittently supervise restrooms.
   - All staff will interact positively with students and make an effort to get to know less outgoing students.
   - All staff will correct misbehavior, usually with quick one-liner reminders.

   ### — TEACH EXPECTATIONS —
   Read or view Module B, Presentations 2 (Task 2) and 3 before developing.

4. Define student behavioral expectations for the common area or schoolwide policy:

   - Travel only on the right.
   - Walk at the designated pace without stopping in the middle of the hallway or causing others to stop.
   - Keep hands, feet, and objects to yourself.
   - Use respectful and appropriate voice level and language.
   - Follow directions given by an adult in the building.
   - _____
   - _____
   - _____
   - _____

5. Teach student behavioral expectations for the common area or schoolwide policy.

   Develop lesson plans for the common area or schoolwide policy. (Review lesson plan templates and samples provided with *Foundations* before developing.) *Note:* If your school has already developed Guidelines for Success (or the equivalent), consider using them to organize your expectations.

5. Teach student behavioral expectations for the common area or schoolwide policy.

    Develop lesson plans for the common area or schoolwide policy. Review lesson plan templates and samples provided with *Foundations* before developing your own.

    See Module B, Presentation 3, Task 1 for detailed information about teaching expectations. If your school has already developed Guidelines for Success (or the equivalent), consider using them to organize your expectations.

    Determine who is responsible for teaching the lessons and when they will be taught. See Module B, Presentation 3, Task 2 for more information. Consider the following phases of teaching:

    - Teaching all students initially
    - Re-teaching all students
    - Teaching new students
    - Re-teaching students who chronically misbehave
    - Substitutes and new teachers (ensure that they know the expectations for students)
    - Other

OBSERVE AND MONITOR STUDENT BEHAVIOR   ST**O**IC

6. Define the rules and procedures for all staff when they are supervising common areas and implementing schoolwide policies. (That is, what are staff members' responsibilities?)

    See Module B, Presentation 2, Task 3 for more information about supervision practices, such as scheduling, placement within common areas, emergency communication procedures, and supervisor training.

INTERACT POSITIVELY WITH STUDENTS   STO**I**C

7. Identify encouragement procedures (include some one-liners that will create common language among staff).

    Module B, Presentations 4 and 5 present valuable information for paraprofessionals whose main job is to supervise common areas. (See Presentation 5, Task 2 for information about one-liners.) Presentation 6 offers supervisory advice for all staff—that is, faculty and others who do not supervise common areas regularly but are sometimes responsible for enforcing common area and schoolwide policies. It covers the O, I, and C of STOIC and discusses what staff can do to create positive and consistent supervision.

Revision Checklist and STOIC Worksheet
For Revising a Prioritized Common Area or Schoolwide Policy (p. 4 of 5)

Determine who is responsible for teaching the lessons and when they will be taught:

- Teaching all students initially: _Teachers show video lessons during 2nd period, lesson plan taught in Advisory._
- Re-teaching all students: _Before and after major vacations, distributed in periods 3-6._
- Teaching new students: _Counselor shows video lessons as part of welcome orientation._
- Re-teaching students who chronically misbehave: _Show video and use learning packet in detention._
- Substitutes and new teachers: _Task force provides Hallway Supervision Job Description._
- Other: _____

— OBSERVE and MONITOR STUDENT BEHAVIOR —
Read or view Module B, Presentation 2 (Task 3) before developing.

6. Define the rules and procedures for all staff when they are supervising common areas and implementing schoolwide policies:

- _Grade-level teams need to divide their portion of the building into specific zones, with each staff member assigned a zone._
- _During each passing period, staff members should go to their specific zones to provide supervision._
- _If a staff member is absent, he or she must inform the substitute about the zone and provide tips on effective supervision._
- _All staff are responsible for student and staff safety._
- _Teams are to arrange a schedule that indicates where and when each team member should be in the hallways during passing times._
- _Staff members are to be at their designated zones at designated times based on the team schedule._

— INTERACT POSITIVELY WITH STUDENTS —
Read or view Module B, Presentations 4, 5, and 6 before developing.

7. Identify encouragement procedures (include some one-liners that will create common language among staff):

- _Engage in continuous scanning of designated zone to look for possible concerns and student misbehaviors._
- _Engage students with positive interactions and noncontingent attention whenever possible (eye contact, saying hello, smiling, nodding, etc.)_
- _Use the words "please" and "thank you" to encourage students to move along to the next class._
- _Question any adult present in the hallways without a pass._
- _Avoid visiting with other staff members to the exclusion of interacting with students._

 This form can be printed from the Module B CD.

Revision Checklist and STOIC Worksheet
For Revising a Prioritized Common Area or Schoolwide Policy (p. 5 of 5)

— CORRECT MISBEHAVIOR FLUENTLY —
Read or view Module B, Presentations 5 and 6 before developing.

8. Identify correction procedures (include some one-liners that will create common language among staff):

- Correct low-level misbehaviors (running, shouting, PDA, etc.) by using a one-liner such as, "Please honor the policy about PDAs."
- Use eye contact or pull students aside to address low-level misbehavior.
- Refer dress-code violations and severe misbehavior (fighting, drugs, alcohol, weapons, etc.) to a member of the administrative staff.
- Avoid shouting instructions or admonishments to students.
-

This form can be printed from the Module B CD.

8. Identify correction procedures (include some one-liners that will create a common language among staff). See Module B, Presentation 5, Task 2 for more information about consequences.

Task 3 Action Steps & Evidence of Implementation

Action Steps	Evidence of Implementation
Begin using the Revision Checklist and STOIC Worksheet (Form B-06) for each identified improvement priority. • Identify tasks that have already been completed. • Identify tasks that need to be done. • Develop and execute a plan for completing the tasks that remain for each identified priority.	Foundations Process: Current Priorities

Structuring Common Areas and Schoolwide Policies for Success

We encourage you to use the STOIC acronym whenever you are planning to improve behavior. STOIC represents a framework for ensuring that common areas and schoolwide policies are addressed in comprehensive and cohesive ways. STOIC stands for:

S **Structure for success.**

T **Teach expectations with clarity.**

O **Observe and supervise.**

I **Interact positively.**

C **Correct fluently.**

DOCUMENTS*

- Indoor Recess Directions (B-24)
- ID Badge Policy (B-61)
- Personal Electronics Policy (B-55)
- Electronic Device Expectations (B-21)
- Sample Expectations Framed Within Guidelines for Success (B-17, B-18, B-23, B-29)
- Proper Use of Playground Equipment (B-27)
- Hallways/Movement, Sample 3 (B-60)
- Red Card (B-07)
- Sample Job Descriptions (B-30, B-31, B-32, B-33)
- Supervisor Training Inservice PowerPoint (B-15)

* All documents listed are available on the CD. Other documents that are not shown in this presentation are also available on the CD (see Appendix C for a complete list).

INTRODUCTION

This presentation focuses on the *S* in STOIC: Structure for success.

Why is the *structure*—the physical design, supervision schedule, and operating procedures—of a common area important? Because you can literally structure a setting either for success or (inadvertently) for failure. Thoughtful, safe physical design, adequate numbers of trained supervisors, and efficient procedures go a long way toward ensuring appropriate student behavior. Poor design, supervision, and procedures can result in crowding, chaotic traffic flow, and long unproductive periods that increase the likelihood of student misbehavior.

Big-picture modifications of common areas can be difficult to initiate in some schools. You might need to think outside the box and fight against *existing regularities*—that is, a "this is the way we've always done it" mindset. Some staff members might not believe that alternative structures are even possible.

> Existing regularities *is a term used by Seymour Sarason (1919–2010), a professor of psychology at Yale University and author of many books, including the landmark text* The Culture of the School and the Problem of Change *(1971).*

Restructuring requires time. Educators typically are pulled in so many different directions all day, every day, that finding time to clear the mind and think creatively about the structure of common areas is difficult. But it's important to ask: If we had the opportunity to build this cafeteria (or playground, courtyard, hallway, etc.) from the ground up, what design would be ideal?

> *A cynic is not merely one who reads bitter lessons from the past; he is one who is prematurely disappointed in the future."*
>
> SYDNEY J. HARRIS (1917–1986), journalist for the *Chicago Daily News* and *Chicago Sun-Times*

You might need to encourage staff to set aside a "that can't work" mentality. Some staff might be pessimistic and cynical. They think that the cafeteria will always be deafeningly noisy because that's just how students are—loud.

The purpose of this presentation is to look at the BIG PICTURE and envision structural change. You may have already selected an area or policy for improvement. The following information will help you identify specific structural and organizational elements that need to be improved. If you haven't yet identified an improvement priority, the information can guide your analysis of all the common areas and schoolwide policies as you decide which to prioritize.

Task 1: Analyze Structural and Organizational Variables explains how to analyze structures, organization, schedules, and procedures of common areas.

Task 2: Design Clear Expectations for Student Behavior clarifies some important considerations for developing behavioral expectations for students.

Task 3: Ensure Adequate Supervision describes what to consider when evaluating supervision arrangements for common areas and situations.

These tasks are geared toward helping the task force responsible for improving a particular area of policy. However, you can also get your entire staff involved in the *Foundations* process by having them view Task 1, then holding a 10-minute brainstorming session on creative structural solutions.

TASK 1
Analyze structural and organizational variables

The structural and organizational features of common areas should be designed to enhance student productivity and facilitate effective adult supervision. For the common areas of your school that you have prioritized for improvement, analyze the:

- Physical setting and materials
- Entry and exit process
- Schedule
- Crowding considerations
- Procedures

Over time, you will want to analyze these factors for all common areas, even those with no behavior problems. Then document the policies and procedures that are working well and include them in the Foundations Archive and the Staff Handbook so that when staff leave the school, the effective procedures do not leave with them. *Note:* In this task, we address common areas first, then we address how the task relates to schoolwide policies.

Analyze the physical setting and materials.

Physical setting includes such things as table layout in the cafeteria, location of playground equipment, and the arrangement of workstations in the computer lab.

Examples of materials include playground equipment, hall passes, and cafeteria trays and utensils. Identify those settings and materials that may need to be changed or improved.

Cafeteria. This example shows how staff can assume that there are no alternatives to the existing regularities of the physical arrangement of a common area and how that assumption can be broken. In a middle school, the cafeteria was identified as a major priority for improvement. The task force noted two major physical design problems. First, the tables were arranged so supervisors could easily circulate around the room—but that arrangement also enabled students to easily evade the supervisors. Second, the salad bar was placed too near the seating area. According to students on the task force, no one wanted to sit at the tables near the salad bar, but the last students to enter the cafeteria were forced to sit there because no other seats were available. (Apparently, salad bar items tended to end up in the hair of nearby students.) Other members of the task force said, "But we can't move the salad bar. It's built into the floor." The custodian happened to be on the task force, too, and responded that he could easily move the salad bar with about an hour's work. So speaking to the right people—the custodian, in this case—allowed the existing regularity of the salad bar placement to be easily modified. The task force also moved the tables closer together and pushed the ends to the wall (with the fire marshal's approval) so that student movement was more restricted. The school's cafeteria was much more manageable after these two physical changes.

Figure 2a   Cafeteria (a) before and (b) after configurations

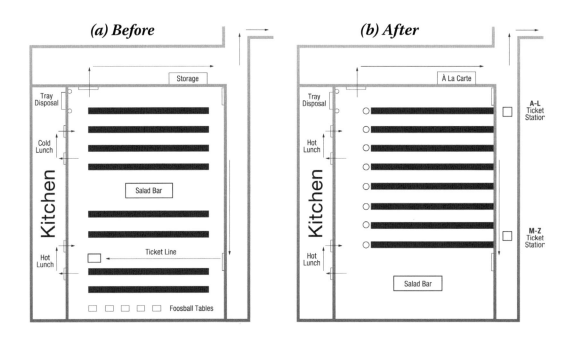

Hall passes. Another example comes from a high school that had a problem with students losing their hall passes. Teachers began using bright orange construction vests as hall passes. The students had to either wear or carry them. The vests were large enough to be visible even when stuffed into a pocket. Hall supervisors could easily notice a student without a vest and take appropriate actions, and they didn't waste time asking students to show them their passes.

Playground. The staff at Roeding Elementary School in Fresno, California, chose the playground as one of their first improvement priorities when they began *Foundations*. They implemented several major structural changes.

- They set up a pattern of mixed grade levels on the playground at the same time. Instead of all intermediate or all primary students at recess, each recess now is made up of some primary and some intermediate classes.

- Checkerboards were painted on some cement tables to create one more outside activity for students.

- Staff instituted a structured reward system. Classes that line up appropriately while waiting for their teacher to pick them up at the end of recess are awarded Straight-Line Stickers. When a class collects 30 stickers, they can invite the principal to have lunch with the class, and when they collect 60, they get a sprinkler party (the opportunity to run through water sprinklers outside in Fresno's fall and spring heat is a big motivator).

- Each playground supervisor receives a prepacked backpack. The backpacks clarify the zone each supervisor is to be in for the day, and they contain all the materials the supervisors may need, including adhesive bandages, antiseptic, latex gloves, report slips on a clipboard with a pen, and Straight-Line Stickers.

These relatively simple changes solved Roeding's playground problems.

High school hall passes. A very large high school with multiple floors and wings needed a better hall pass system. Staff defined specific areas of the school and assigned a color to each area. Students are required to carry colored clipboards that correspond to the areas. When a student is seen with a colored clipboard that does not match the area he is in, it does not necessarily mean that the student is out of bounds, but staff know they should ask to see the student's hall pass.

Analyze entry and exit procedures.

Entry and exit areas and procedures are especially important to consider for cafeterias and playgrounds, where hundreds of students might converge on an area at the same time. Elementary students should be supervised directly by an escort as they enter and exit. Secondary schools need to ensure that enough supervisors are in place to patrol all hallways and common areas during passing periods.

Consider restricting entry to a common area to one door. One supervisor can stand at the door and greet all students as they enter. This procedure sets a friendly tone and at the same time emphasizes to students that they are being supervised from the moment they enter. For playgrounds, have students walk in a line to an established point before they are allowed to have free recess. This mild restriction sends the message that recess is not a free-for-all—there are rules for appropriate behavior and students are expected to follow them.

For the transition from playground to school building, we encourage you to teach students a "freeze in place" procedure. At the supervisor's command to freeze, students stop what they are doing and listen to the supervisor. Then the supervisor can allow small subgroups to leave the playground one at a time rather than make everyone on the playground line up at once: "Everyone who has play equipment may come in. Fourth-grade girls may line up. Now fourth-grade boys."

Analyze the schedule.

Research shows that recess is an important part of the school day. Data on the best length and number of recesses are elusive, but the National Association for Sport and Physical Education recommends that all elementary school children have at least one daily recess of at least 20 minutes. See "Benefits of Recess" on the next page.

See "Indoor Recess Example" below for an example of providing structure to an indoor recess period to minimize conflicts among students and support the recess supervisor.

There's been some interest in recent years in scheduling recess *before* lunch. (Google "play first, then eat" to view articles about this idea.) Proponents cite the following benefits:

- Fewer classroom discipline problems occur because students are full and settled when they return to class after eating.
- Students perform better in the classroom because they are not hungry.
- Students display better lunchroom behavior because they are focused on lunch instead of on getting to the playground.
- Students get better nutrition and a more balanced diet because they take time to eat everything on their plate.
- Less food is wasted because students eat more when they are not in a hurry to get to the playground.

Benefits of Recess

Recess benefits children in cognitive, social-emotional, and physical ways. Research shows that when children have recess, they:

- Fidget less and remain more on task.
- Have improved memory and more focused attention.
- Develop more brain connections.
- Learn negotiation skills.
- Exercise leadership, teach games, take turns, and learn to resolve conflicts.
- Are more physically active before and after school.

A common consequence for behavior problems or not finishing work is to take away recess. But Olga Jarrett, a leading researcher on recess, says, "It's the kids who have trouble concentrating who need recess more than anybody else—and they are the ones who are less likely to get it" (Adams, 2011).

To ensure that a recess-before-lunch schedule runs smoothly, develop a hand-washing regimen after recess and let students deposit their coats in the classroom before going to lunch. Collect and process lunch money before recess.

Besides recess, do students have unstructured time at any other times during the school day? Too much time without adult guidance can be problematic. Experienced playground supervisors know that after about 20 minutes of unstructured play, inappropriate behavior and general chaos seem to increase exponentially. Try to avoid unstructured periods of more than 20 minutes when scheduling the school day.

In secondary schools, consider the length of passing periods. In large schools, 4-minute passing periods might be too short. In small schools, 5-minute passing periods might be too long, allowing students too much time to loiter, socialize, and get into trouble between classes. To determine if the length of your passing periods is about right, follow a small sixth grader in middle school or a small freshman in high school to see how long it takes to cross the campus.

Indoor Recess Example. Linda Slusser, a kindergarten teacher at Cloud Elementary in Wichita, Kansas, has developed a great procedure for organizing indoor recess activities. A different teacher is with her class during the recess period, but on days when recess is held indoors, Linda makes sure that students select their activities earlier in the day. She took photographs of the available play activities (manipulatives)—stuffed animals, plastic building blocks, dry-erase boards, coloring books, Tinkertoys, and so on—and placed them in a basket. Each student has a clothespin with his or her name written on it (Figure 2b). Students choose the activity they want to do during recess by placing their clothespins on a photograph (Figure 2c). Only four clothespins are allowed on each photo (there are about 12 activity photos). Then Linda leaves the photos with the clothespins on a table where the recess teacher can easily find them. Linda also developed some specific expectations for the students that she wrote out for the recess teacher (Figure 2d on the next page), and she has even written directions for substitute teachers so they can ensure that students choose their activities before recess.

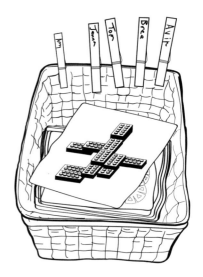

Figure 2b *For indoor recess, each kindergartner has a personalized clothespin.*

Figure 2c *Prior to indoor recess, students attach their clothespins to a photo of the activity they want to do.*

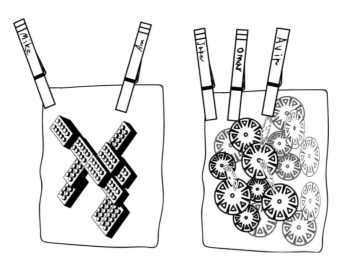

Figure 2d   *Written directions for the recess supervisor (B-24); thanks to Linda Slusser at Cloud Elementary School and Wichita Public Schools in Kansas*

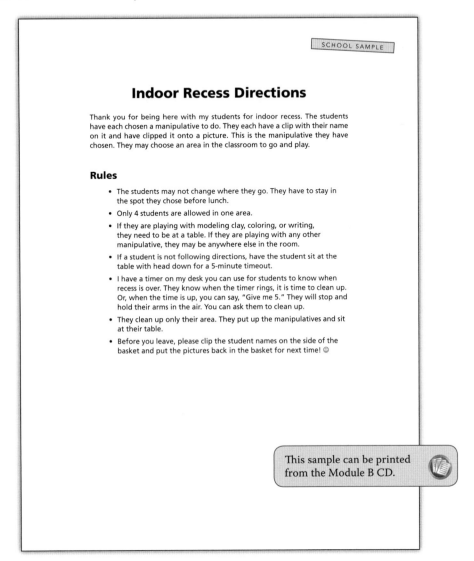

SCHOOL SAMPLE

Indoor Recess Directions

Thank you for being here with my students for indoor recess. The students have each chosen a manipulative to do. They each have a clip with their name on it and have clipped it onto a picture. This is the manipulative they have chosen. They may choose an area in the classroom to go and play.

Rules

- The students may not change where they go. They have to stay in the spot they chose before lunch.
- Only 4 students are allowed in one area.
- If they are playing with modeling clay, coloring, or writing, they need to be at a table. If they are playing with any other manipulative, they may be anywhere else in the room.
- If a student is not following directions, have the student sit at the table with head down for a 5-minute timeout.
- I have a timer on my desk you can use for students to know when recess is over. They know when the timer rings, it is time to clean up. Or, when the time is up, you can say, "Give me 5." They will stop and hold their arms in the air. You can ask them to clean up.
- They clean up only their area. They put up the manipulatives and sit at their table.
- Before you leave, please clip the student names on the side of the basket and put the pictures back in the basket for next time! ☺

This sample can be printed from the Module B CD.

Analyze any concerns about crowding.

Do you have situations where too many students are crowded into a small space? Consider whether you can increase the number of lunch shifts or the number of recesses to reduce the crowding. One middle school we worked with had a courtyard encircled by a hallway. The hallway was quite narrow, so to solve the crowding problem they made the hallway into a one-way route around the courtyard.

Analyze procedures.

Examine your existing procedures to determine whether they are effective and efficient. Sometimes even a small change can yield positive results (see "Consider the Cause" on the next page). Are any situations or circumstances not adequately covered by existing procedures?

- **Emergency procedures.** Is there a way to get the attention of all staff and students in the event of an emergency, even on the playground? Detailed procedures need to be documented and tested, and staff and students need training.

- **Equipment check-out procedures.** Can students check out play equipment and return it efficiently and safely?

- **Quiet-down procedures** (especially in cafeterias). Do you have a way to alert all students to tone down their voice levels?

- **Clean-up and dismissal procedures** (especially in cafeterias). Are they effective and efficient?

Consider the Cause

Sometimes a simple modification to existing procedures can make a big difference. One of our trainers was visiting a school in Texas where the principal was very happy with how the school functioned—except for the cafeteria. He said there was always too much movement and noise, but he couldn't put his finger on what was causing the problem. The trainer observed the cafeteria for a few minutes and then said, "It's the condiments. There aren't enough mustard and ketchup bottles and the like. Most of the movement and noise results from sharing the condiments." The principal had the cafeteria staff triple the number of condiment containers available to the students, and the cafeteria became noticeably calmer.

Remember, fight against existing regularities and consider the big picture: If we had the opportunity to build this cafeteria (or playground, courtyard, hallway, etc.) from the ground up, what would be the ideal design?

Think creatively. Think big.

Structural Elements for Schoolwide Policies

For each schoolwide policy that you have prioritized for improvement, analyze whether any structural elements can be modified to make the policy clearer and easier to enforce. (Eventually, you will want to analyze all schoolwide policies, even if no behavior problems are associated with them, and then document and archive them.)

As part of a secondary school ID badge policy, for example, the school should have procedures to easily correct students who don't have their ID badges. At the Hastings Ninth Grade Center in Alief, Texas, students frequently received detention and in-school suspension for problems related to ID badges. Once the school developed a new policy (Figure 2e), these difficulties were largely eliminated. The new policy makes it easy for staff to correct students when they don't have ID badges, and correction is completely automatic because students are required to purchase a new ID badge when they have used up a predetermined number of temporary ID badges.

Figure 2e   *Sample ID badge policy (B-61); thanks to Hastings Ninth Grade Center and Alief Independent School District in Texas*

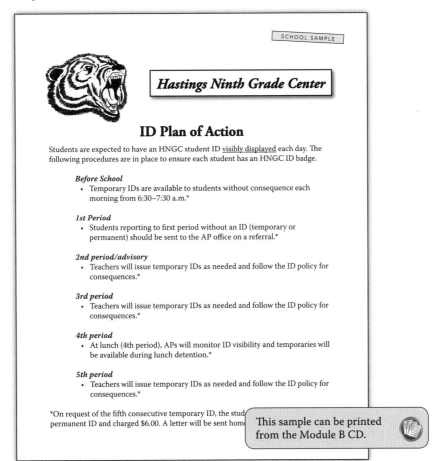

Another example of an effective schoolwide policy improvement is the cell phone policy from Sunnyside High School in Fresno, California. Before the school implemented this policy, cell phones and electronics caused a lot of friction between staff and students. After the new policy (Figure 2f) was instituted, this friction was gone. Students understand the expectations, and staff can easily enforce the expectations.

Figure 2f *Sample personal electronics policy and reporting form for violations (B-55); thanks to Sunnyside High School and Fresno Unified School District in California*

SCHOOL SAMPLE

Sunnyside High School's Electronic Policy & Procedure

Electronic devices are **not allowed** in the library during class time (Regular Schedule: 7:50–11:36 a.m. and 12:22–3:48 p.m.)

This includes: cell phones, iPods, MP3 players, CD players, PDAs, computer games, etc.

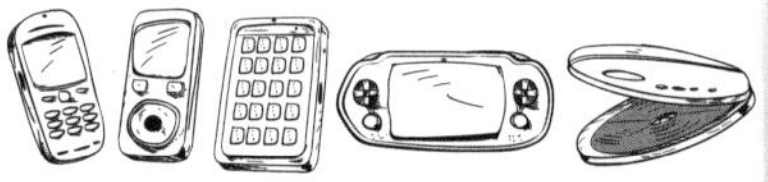

Violators will have their electronic devices confiscated and turned in to the office.

SCHOOL SAMPLE

Sunnyside High School
Home of the Wildcats

Date: _____

Student Name: _____

ID #: _____

Teacher: _____

Period: _____

Incident: _____

_____

_____

_____

☐ **Step 1:** Electronic device confiscated by teacher, parent picks up in university office (7 a.m.–4 p.m.)

☐ **Step 2:** Electronic device confiscated by teacher, 3 days of office lunch detention, parent picks up electronic device in university office (7 a.m.–4 p.m.)

☐ **Step 3:** One-day formal suspension (student to be escorted by CA to university office)

This sample can be printed from the Module B CD.

Task 1 Action Steps & Evidence of Implementation

Action Steps	Evidence of Implementation
1. Evaluate the current structural and organizational variables for each common area improvement priority. Discuss how the following might be contributing to student behavior problems. • Physical setting and materials • Entry and exit procedures • Scheduling • Overcrowding • Procedures	Foundations Process: Current Priorities
2. Evaluate the current structural and organizational variables for each schoolwide policy improvement priority. Can any structural elements be modified to make the policy clearer and easier to enforce?	
3. Brainstorm suggestions for improving the structural and organizational features of the common areas and schoolwide policies. Include suggestions designed to enhance responsible student behavior as well as those intended to minimize irresponsible student behavior. Invite staff input. Consider arranging visits to other schools to get ideas. Think beyond existing regularities!	
4. Plan to eventually analyze structural factors for all common areas and schoolwide policies, even if no behavior problems are associated with them, and document and archive the effective policies and procedures.	

TASK 2

Design clear expectations for student behavior

Common areas are complex, so well-defined and effective common area behavioral expectations for students are important to keep those areas running smoothly. See "What's the Difference Between Rules, Procedures, and Expectations."

Note: Information about teaching behavioral expectations is presented in Module B, Presentation 3.

What's the Difference Between Rules, Procedures, and Expectations?

We sometimes use these terms interchangeably, but to be precise, *rule* refers to general statements such as "No food in the auditorium," "Walk, don't run, in the hallways," and "Sit and stay in your assigned seat on the bus." *Procedure* refers to instructional statements such as "Pick up a single tray, one fork and one spoon, and go through the serving line in single file" and "When the bell rings, wait for your table to be dismissed, then walk to the exit." We use the term *expectations* to encompass both rules and procedures and to imply that students need to be taught and should understand that they are *expected* to follow all the rules and procedures.

To use a driving metaphor, the Guidelines for Success are like the big-picture rules of the road, such as "Drive safely" and "Be aware of traffic around you." Driving *rules* include "Make a full stop at stop signs," "Wear your seat belt," and "Don't pass when climbing a hill." *Procedure* means the actions the driver must take to accomplish her task, such as turning the key to start the car, shifting gears as the car picks up speed, and moving at an appropriate speed when in heavy traffic. The expectations include all the guidelines, rules, and procedures, and the driver must know and follow all the expectations to reach her destination safely.

In general, avoid assigning harsh consequences for students' procedural errors, especially if they are unintentional—this may jeopardize your relationships with the students. Instead, provide gentle reminders of the proper procedures, particularly at the beginning of the year when students are still learning what they are expected to do in many different settings.

Develop detailed written expectations for behavior in the common area.

Once the common area is structured for success, the Foundations Team or task force should analyze whether clear expectations already exist for that area. If not, the first step is to develop detailed written behavioral rules and procedures for the setting. In doing so, make sure that students are not expected to do nothing for long periods. Then ensure that supervisors know and understand the rules and procedures.

Be aware of hidden norms that may exist in your school or in your region of the country. For example, in some parts of the country, children are expected to address all adults as sir or ma'am. A student who transfers to a school like this from a more casual part of the country—say, Southern California—would not know about this cultural norm. She wouldn't understand why she is being corrected when she responds "yes" to a request. If the expectation is for students to say "yes, sir," that expectation should be taught along with all other expectations, even if most students are taught the expectation at home.

Effective common area behavioral expectations are:

- Clear
- Age appropriate
- Detailed
- Reasonable
- Known by all staff members who supervise or may be in the setting or situation

A T-chart such as the one pictured below can help the team think about the big picture of how student behavior in the common area should look and sound. Have individual team members work on both sections of the T-chart for two or three minutes without talking to teammates. Then have team members share what they wrote and try to reach consensus on key expectations. Be sure that the final policy is designed to deliver what the T-chart describes.

Student Behavior Needs to Look Like	Student Behavior Needs to Sound Like

Expectations should be clear. Expectations that are clear to adults may not be clear to students. Ask yourself whether the rules and procedures are detailed enough that students know what to do in all aspects of the setting or situation. For example, many secondary schools teach students to walk on the right side of the hallway—but the hallway rules end there. You should also train students how to close lockers quietly, keep moving during passing periods, congregate in ways that do not block doorways and major passageways, and any other specific behaviors that the students in your school are expected to know.

A&M Consolidated High School in College Station, Texas, came up with an easy, unambiguous way to tell students the expectations for using electronic devices on any given day. Instead of struggling to enforce a complete ban on electronics, which inevitably was broken any time teachers wanted to use technology in the classroom, the school altered the policy to include the three expectations listed on the poster in Figure 2g. The poster is displayed in each classroom, and for each class the teacher places a large clip next to the expectation students are to follow. Students are more compliant and teachers are less frustrated.

***Figure 2g** Electronic Device Expectations poster (B-21); thanks to A&M Consolidated High School in College Station, Texas*

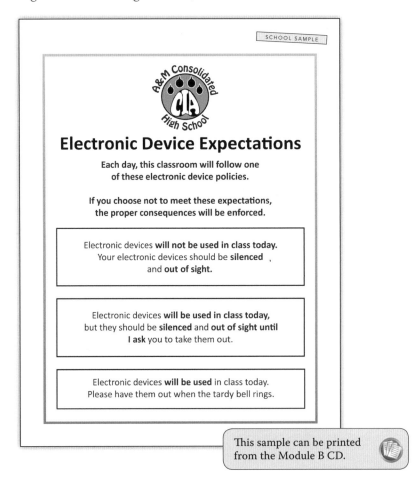

Module B: Managing Behavior in Common Areas and With Schoolwide Policies

Expectations should be age appropriate. Develop some age-appropriate general rules that can be written and displayed.

A technique that can help staff teach and students understand and remember expectations is to organize them around the Guidelines for Success. For example, under the guideline "Be responsible," group playground expectations such as "Return play equipment to where you got it" and "Report bullying and teasing (of you and others) to an adult." Under the guideline "Be safe," include expectations such as "Walk, don't run, from the building to the boundary line" and "One student at a time on the slide." Figure 2h shows some examples of this technique.

Figure 2h *Examples of rules and procedures framed within Guidelines for Success (B-18, B-23)*

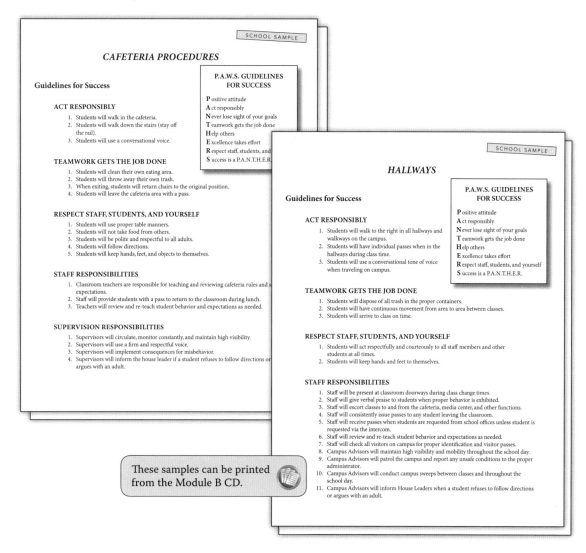

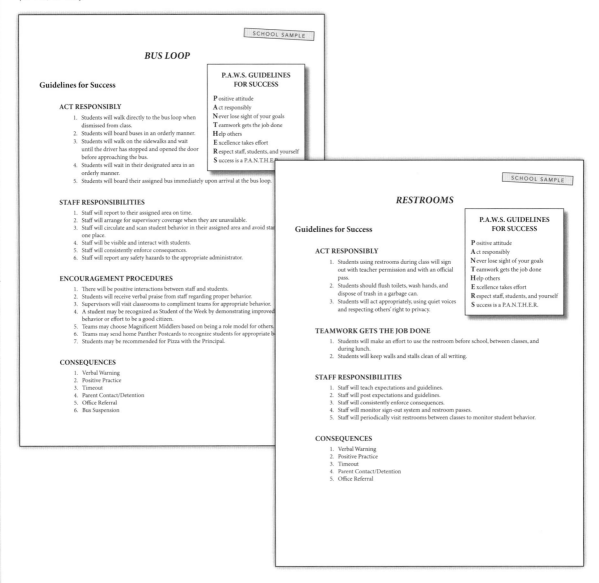

Expectations should be detailed. Written expectations are important, but often do not provide enough detail. Expand on the rules and provide plenty of specific information—enough that a new student, after training, will know exactly how to function successfully in the setting or situation. Common categories of expectations to address are:

- How to enter and exit the common area
- Procedures while in the setting or situation
- Civility—that is, treatment of other students and staff members

The following list provides some examples of specific student behaviors to consider when developing the written rules and procedures.

- Move at the appropriate pace or speed—specify how fast or slow.
- Stay in appropriate areas of the school (hallways, restrooms, stairs, doors, etc.).
- Arrive on time to the designated location.
- Maintain designated voice or noise levels.
- Travel up and down stairways appropriately (one step at a time).
- Maintain appropriate student group size. (How many students can walk together?)
- Be respectful toward peers. (What should that look like?)
- Be respectful toward adults, especially when responding to a reprimand. (What should that look and sound like?)
- Use lockers quietly and appropriately.
- Demonstrate expected behaviors when in line.
- Keep hands, feet, and objects to self.
- Follow the rules for table manners (feet on floor, swallow food before talking, keep utensils on your own tray, etc.) when in cafeteria.

Figure 2i on the next page shows a great example of detailed rules and procedures for the playground developed by Sunnyside Elementary School in Roseburg, Oregon.

Expectations should be reasonable. It is unreasonable to expect students to do nothing. Children do *nothing* very badly. A couple of examples from schools we've worked with illustrate unreasonable expectations for students. At one school, the last class was over at 3 p.m., but the first buses did not arrive until 3:45. As a result, 300 children were expected to wait 45 minutes with nothing productive to do. This situation is a breeding ground for significant misbehavior. No matter how many times students are told to stand in line, keep their hands to themselves, keep the noise down, and so on, 45 minutes with nothing to do is a setup for failure.

At another elementary school, students arrived in the morning 40 minutes before they were allowed to go to their classrooms. Staff expected the students to sit cross-legged on the gym floor in silence for 40 minutes—another recipe for disaster.

If you have significant periods in your school when students are expected to do nothing, you need to either give them something to do or modify the schedule.

Some schools have tried to enforce expectations such as "absolutely no talking in the hallways between classes," or "hands behind your back when walking in the hallway," or "between classes, cheeks must be filled with air ('poofed')" to prevent talking. Consider whether staff would be willing to endure these restrictions, too. If not, it

Figure 2i *Example of detailed rules and procedures for the playground (B-27); thanks to Sunnyside Elementary in Roseburg, Oregon*

Proper Use of Playground Equipment

Swings

- Take turns using swings.
- Remain seated (no seat drops).
- Next student in line counts to 50 (1 equals back and up).
- Alternate the person you count for whenever possible.
- Always swing straight.
- Do not hold on to other swings.
- Do not throw swings over bar to shorten chains.
- If swings have been thrown over, ask an adult to return them to the appropriate position.
- Do not jump out of swings.

Slide

- Sit in the center of the slide and come down feet first with bottom on slide.
- Use only the ladder to reach the top of the slide.
- Only one person on the ladder at a time.
- Do not put rocks on the slide.

Jungle Gym

- Use this equipment for climbing.
- Do not jump off the jungle gym.

Horizontal Ladder

- Begin on the end farthest from the building.
- If you let go of the ladder, go back to the end of the line.
  - After reaching the opposite side, climb down and return to the end of the line.

Horizontal Bars

- Stand in lines and take turns using the bars for sitting, hanging, spinning, and practicing pull-ups.
- No Cherry Drops (twirling by the knees, then dismounting without the use of hands) allowed.

(p. 2 of 3)

Game Rules

Four Square and Two Square Rules

Serve the ball by dropping it and serving it two-handed, underhand from the bounce. If the serve hits a line, the server is out. The server can hit the ball to any of the other three courts. The player receiving the ball must keep it in play by striking the ball after it has bounced once in his or her square. The receiver directs the ball to any other square with an underhand hit. Play continues until one player fails to return the ball or commits a fault. The following are faults:

- Hitting the ball sidearm or overhand.
- Ball landing on a line between the squares (ball landing on an outer boundary is considered good).
- Stepping in another square to play the ball.
- Catching or carrying a return volley.
- Allowing the ball to touch any part of the body except the hands.

When a player misses or commits a fault, he or she goes to the end of the waiting line and all players move up. The player at the head of the waiting line moves into square #4.

Kickball Rules

The batter (kicker) stands in the kicking area, which is marked by a rear and a forward line. The batter kicks the ball, which has been rolled on the ground by the pitcher. The ball should be rolled with moderate speed. If the batter crosses over the forward line to kick the ball, the batter is out. The batter may not start behind the rear line; if he/she does, an out is recorded. No balls or strikes are called. After the fourth ball, the batter is out. Three outs change side. Runners on base may not lead off or steal a base. Runs are scored as in baseball or softball. On a kicked ball, if the ball is carried, thrown, rolled, or otherwise reaches the base being approached by a runner before the runner arrives, and the ball is controlled by a defensive player tagging the base, the runner is out.

Dodgeball Rules

Three fourths of the children form a circle (use painted lines), and the rest are in the center. One ball is used by the outside players. The center players move around trying to avoid being hit by the thrown ball. When a center player is hit, he or she exchanges places with the thrower. Other rules are:

- You must hit below the waist even if the person jumps.
- Person hit or voted out must take their outs.
- Never kick the ball.
- If the ball stops or slows down inside the circle, a center player may take the ball and toss it to a circle player.
- People on the outside must keep their place—no roving around the circle.

(p. 3 of 3)

- Throwers who step inside the circle invalidate their throw. No moving around the circle to throw. Do not step in front of another person when on the outside.
- Do not touch, hit, or block the throws of others. People who throw the ball too hard may not play.
- Persons on the inside who step outside the circle to avoid being hit are out; person who threw the ball is in. There are no timeouts allowed; if you are legally hit, you are out. If a person on the inside of the circle leaves the game, the thrower takes that person's place.
- All disagreements are to be settled by a vote of the people playing. All votes are final.
- People who continually have difficulties will lose their privilege to play.

Football Rules

- Touch only one hand anywhere—no tackling.
- No blocking or pushing.
- Players are not allowed to leave their feet except when trying to catch the ball.
- Three complete passes equal a first down.
- No direct runs—must pass or lateral.
- Organize even teams.
- Grade-level teachers can (if interest is high) organize teams and tournaments.

Basketball Rules

Ten players only on full-court game.

Tetherball Rules

Play: The server's opponent is given the choice of the side of the court to play and the direction the server will serve the ball. The server starts play by throwing the ball into the air and striking it with a hand or fist. As the ball travels around the pole, the server attempts to hit again and again in the direction of the original serve. The opposing player tries to wind the ball around the pole by hitting the ball in the opposite direction. The ball is not considered in play until the server's opponent hits the ball (i.e., the server cannot win the game by winding the rope completely in his/her direction before the opponent has had the opportunity to hit the ball at least once). The player who first winds the rope completely around the pole with the ball touching the pole wins the game. During the game, each player must remain in his/her own playing zone.

The following are fouls:
- Hitting the ball with any part of the body other than the hands or forearms.
- Stopping continuous play by holding or catching the ball.
- Touching the pole with any part of the body.
- Hitting the rope with forearms or hands.
- Hitting the ball while standing outside the playing zone.
- Stepping on the neutral zone lines or out of the circle.
- Throwing the ball.

This sample can be printed from the Module B CD.

is probably unreasonable to expect students to comply, and the expectations might even be perceived as humiliating or disrespectful.

Expectations should be known by the staff. All staff members who supervise or may be present in the setting or situation need to know the rules and procedures thoroughly so they can enforce them consistently.

Consider schoolwide policies to promote appropriate student behavior with specialists.

Specialists in areas such as media, PE, computers, and music may have difficulty teaching their behavioral expectations. In many cases, these specialists see all the students in a school, but only for one or two 20- to 30-minute periods per week. While a classroom teacher might be able to teach expectations for math class every day for a week, a specialist needs five weeks for that same amount of teaching time. Furthermore, because students see the specialist only once or twice a week, they are more likely to forget many of this teacher's expectations from the first meeting to the second.

Although the expectations within the classroom should be under the control and supervision of the certified specialist, some limited schoolwide policies related to specialists can be beneficial. Elementary classroom teachers can help promote good behavior by coordinating with the specialists who see their students. Following are some suggestions for achieving efficient and effective coordination that you might use as a basis for a schoolwide policy about specialists.

Each specialist should provide all classroom teachers with a written explanation of how students should enter her setting (the gym or the computer room, for example) and a written list of two or three important rules for her class. To make this easy for the general education teachers, the specialists could each list their expectations on a different-colored (e.g., PE = red, media = blue, etc.), laminated 4" x 6" card. All the cards can be held together with a metal ring or spiral binding so the teacher does not have to keep track of loose cards (Figure 2j).

Figure 2j   Ring of Expectations

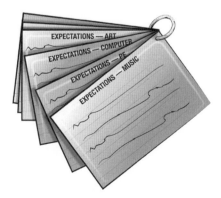

Immediately before a class goes to a particular specialist, the classroom teacher should tell students where they are going and the name of that teacher. The classroom teacher should also go over the written expectations and make it very clear that he expects students to behave responsibly. For example, before the class goes to PE, the classroom teacher might prepare the class as follows:

> *Class, the next thing we are going to do today is go to the gym for Physical Education class. The PE teacher this year is Ms. Simonson. When we go to the gym, we will go quietly in lines, just the way we go to the cafeteria. When we get to the gym, you need to stay in your lines and wait outside the gym with me until Ms. Simonson comes to tell you what you should do and where you should go. Ms. Simonson will go over her rules for safe and responsible gym behavior with you, but she asked me to let you know that her two most important rules are:*
>
> *Keep hands, feet, and objects to yourself.*
>
> *Freeze and listen for directions when you hear her blow the whistle.*
>
> *During PE, Ms. Simonson is the teacher. I fully expect you to give her the same level of respect and cooperation you demonstrate in the classroom. Now I'll excuse you by tables to line up and wait quietly at the door. Everyone at Table 4 is waiting quietly. You may line up. Table . . .*

There should be a formal and public transfer of authority from the classroom teacher to the specialist. Students should see and hear an interaction between the classroom teacher and the specialist that sounds something like the following example:

> **Class Teacher:** *Class, this is Ms. Simonson. Every Monday and Thursday at this time you get to be with her. Ms. Simonson, I told the class that I expect them to behave responsibly during their time with you, and I have told them your two most important rules. Class, I will be back here to meet you in 30 minutes. I look forward to hearing a good report from Ms. Simonson.*
>
> **PE Teacher:** *Thank you, Mr. Hasad. I appreciate your going over my rules. I am looking forward to getting to know such a responsible group of students. Now, class, in just a moment we will enter the gym. Each of you should . . .*

When the time with the specialist is over, the specialist should publicly hand authority back over to the classroom teacher and inform the teacher of how well the class did. For example:

PE Teacher: Mr. Hasad, this class did a wonderful job in PE today. The only thing they should work on is remembering to freeze, even their mouths and voices, when they hear the whistle. I am looking forward to seeing all of you again next Monday.

These procedures should be implemented for at least the first four times the students go to a particular specialist. If students see the specialist twice a week, for example, do this for a minimum of two weeks. If they see the specialist once a week, do it for a minimum of four weeks.

Task 2 Action Steps & Evidence of Implementation

Action Steps	Evidence of Implementation
1. Evaluate the current behavioral expectations for each common area and schoolwide policy improvement priority. Identify whether the expectations are: • Clear • Age appropriate • Sufficiently detailed • Reasonable and humane (for example, students are not expected to do nothing) • Known by all supervising staff members and other adults who might be in the setting or situation	Foundations Process: Meeting Minutes, Current Priorities
2. Identify whether you need schoolwide policies for behavior with specialists.	
3. Brainstorm suggestions for improving behavioral expectations for the common area. Include suggestions designed to enhance responsible student behavior as well as those that will minimize irresponsible student behavior. Think beyond existing regularities!	
4. Plan to eventually evaluate the behavioral expectations for all common areas, even those with no associated behavior problems, and document and archive the expectations.	

TASK 3

Ensure adequate supervision

Adequate common area supervision is a structural consideration because it must be organized and scheduled in advance, and supervisors must be educated about the rules and procedures for student behavior. Effective supervision practices are addressed in Module B, Presentations 4 and 5 for staff with dedicated areas to supervise, such as playground and cafeteria, and in Presentation 6 for the entire staff.

In this task, we discuss six aspects of planning for adequate supervision:

- Number of supervisors
- Schedule for supervisors
- Placement of supervisors
- Emergency communication
- Comprehensive job descriptions
- Supervisor training

Note: We address common areas first, then consider how this task relates to school-wide policies.

Update and clarify expectations.

Update and clarify the expectations for supervisors when any changes in structural elements or expectations for student behavior have been implemented. A T-chart such as the one below can help the team think about how they want staff behavior in the common area to look and sound. Have individual team members work on both sections of the T-chart for two or three minutes without talking to each other. Then have team members share what they wrote and try to reach consensus on key expectations. Be sure that the final policy is designed to deliver what the T-chart describes.

Staff Behavior Needs to Look Like	Staff Behavior Needs to Sound Like

Determine the number of supervisors required for the common area.

Consider the following when determining how many supervisors are needed.

Size and complexity of the common area. For example, a U- or L-shaped playground should have more supervisors than a rectangular playground where all areas are easily visible. Hallways with more turns and stairwells require more supervision than those with fewer hard-to-see areas. An outside drop-off/pick-up zone with blind spots needs more supervisors than one with no blind spots.

History of the common area. For example, sometimes certain restrooms are known as the place to go to smoke or engage in other illegal activities. A stairwell might be perceived as the turf of a particular group of students. Frequent recess disputes might occur on one playing field. These areas need more supervisors, more consistent supervision, or both—the stairwell might need supervision every passing period rather than intermittent supervision, for example.

Degree to which supervisors' attention might be diverted to dealing with injuries, disputes, or serious misbehavior. If only one supervisor is responsible for the playground, for example, she can't adequately supervise the whole setting while she is dealing with two children who are fighting. In fact, we know of one school district that lost a lawsuit regarding this situation. It was demonstrated in court that a lone supervisor couldn't adequately supervise the playground.

Time of the school year. We recommend that during the first week of school (and during the first week of implementing new procedures), common areas should have twice as many supervisors as usual. This procedure is beneficial because it:

- Prompts rule following
- Ensures that misbehaviors will be corrected early
- Increases positive staff-student interactions

❧ FOUNDATIONS RECOMMENDATION ☙

During the first week of school (and during the first week of implementing new procedures), a common area should have twice as many supervisors as usual.

Establish a schedule for supervisors.

Keep the following in mind as you schedule supervisors for the common area.

Account for transition time. Ensure that common area supervisors do not have back-to-back assignments. Let's say a paraprofessional is scheduled to be in the classroom until 9 a.m. and is also scheduled to begin playground duty at 9 a.m. He has to choose between abandoning the classroom teacher or being late to the playground. Either way, he is not able to perform his job as he should.

Coordinate the supervision schedules for common areas. For example, a playground supervisor lines up the students at 10:14 a.m. because the period ends at 10:15 a.m. Another group of students is scheduled to arrive at 10:15 a.m. If the teacher doesn't pick up the first group until 10:20 a.m., the supervisor must deal with the students standing in line in addition to the group that is arriving. All staff need to be aware of potentially unsafe situations that might arise if schedules are not arranged and followed carefully.

Include stairwells and restrooms when assigning hallway coverage. Ensure that both male and female staff members are available during every passing period to conduct intermittent checks in the restrooms.

Consider where to place supervisors in the common area.

Supervisors should be *strategically placed* throughout a setting or situation. Supervisors should *circulate unpredictably* throughout the setting or situation.

Here's a great example of the importance of the above points and of including students on the task force. The task force of an inner-city high school was trying to figure out why they had so much illegal activity in certain hallways, despite full-time campus monitors (armed guards, in this case) who patrolled the hallways every day. A student who was serving on the task force said, "The students know the campus monitors' routes. They know where and when there will be no supervision." The principal said, "The monitors have routes?" She was appalled. But she also suddenly had important knowledge that allowed her to take authoritative action. She immediately went to the campus monitors' supervisor and asked that the monitors supervise unpredictably. When students cannot reliably predict when the coast will be clear, incidents are very likely to decrease.

Figure 2k shows some schoolwide supervision planning documents from Tioga Middle School in Fresno, California. The Foundations Team mapped specific supervisory stations for passing periods, lunch, before school, and after school. Mapping the school in this way defines everyone's role: who needs to be where at what times.

In addition, the map helps the team identify blind corners or hotspots that might require greater supervision and any areas where bullying or gang-related situations might be more likely to occur. More adults should be stationed in those areas.

One rule of thumb, particularly for secondary schools, is to think about whether the smallest, youngest female staff member would feel comfortable supervising in this area and interacting with students—even those she does not know. If the answer is no, you need more adults stationed in that area.

Figure 2k   Tioga Middle School maps showing specific stations for supervisors; thanks to Tioga Middle School and Fresno Unified School District in California

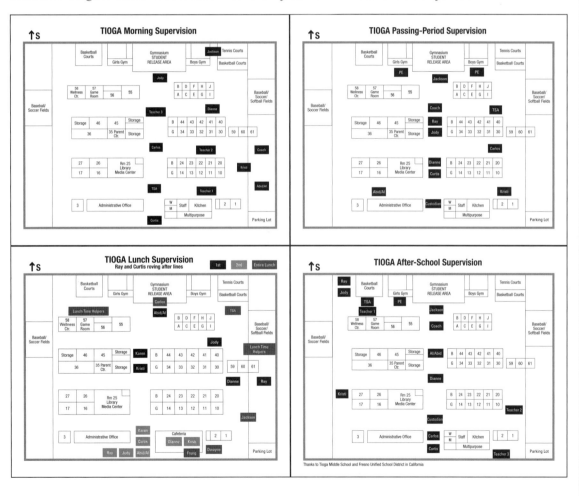

On the playground, consider establishing zones. For example, in the Pacific Northwest, children are used to playing outside on drizzly days. To keep supervisors circulating around the playground instead of huddling together in a covered area out of the rain, some schools establish zones and call the covered area Zone 1, the swings Zone 2, and so on. Supervisors rotate spending time in the covered area and patrolling the zones. (See Figure 2l on the next page for sample maps.)

Figure 2l *Playground maps show supervisory zones. Map A would work with three supervisors, and Map B is a plan for two supervisors.*

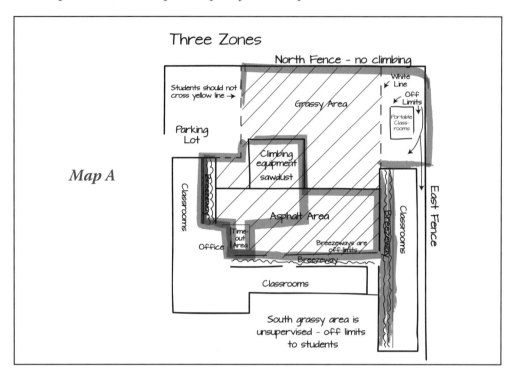

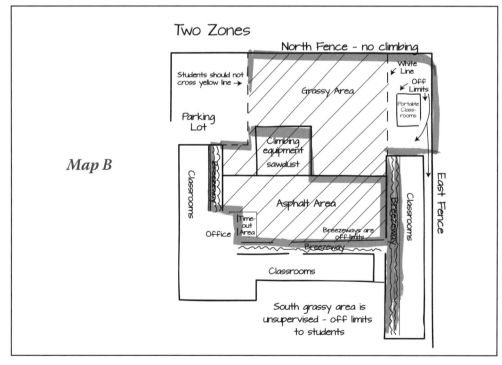

Module B: Managing Behavior in Common Areas and With Schoolwide Policies

You can apply the concept of zones to any area of the school. Figure 2m shows a hallway zones policy from Jardine Middle School in Wichita, Kansas. This policy is available on the Module B CD along with Jardine's corresponding supervisory expectations, student lesson plan, and final adopted policy.

Figure 2m   *Hallway zones policy (B-60); thanks to Jardine Middle School and Wichita Public Schools in Kansas*

SCHOOL SAMPLE

Hallway "Zones" Policy

On March 9, 2007, the Jardine Middle School staff voted to adopt and implement hallway zone supervision as part of a comprehensive hallway management policy. The Jardine PRIDE (Foundations) team knows that some teams have already begun implementing zone management. By **April 5**, the PRIDE team is asking all teams to finalize and begin zone supervision. During the week of **April 9**, the PRIDE team will be informally observing the hallways for discussion purposes at our next meeting. As a reminder, the components of the policy are listed below:

- Buildings will be divided into zones. These zones are to be established by each grade-level team and a team consisting of administration and other support staff.
- Each staff member and other involved adults will be assigned a zone for which they are responsible.
- A schedule of supervision times will be set up by each team. This schedule will show assigned zones and assigned times for supervision.
- Administration and other support staff will also be assigned to zones to assist in areas that grade-level and related arts teams can't cover (e.g., breezeways between buildings, commons area, etc.).
- If you are ever unable to be at your designated zone at the assigned time, you should arrange for coverage of your area.

Please see a PRIDE team member if you have any questions about the new policy.

Remember, this is part of a comprehensive policy the PRIDE team hopes to give to the staff for final approval by the end of this school year. The PRIDE team thanks you in advance for your commitment to ensuring our students' safety in the hallways.

This sample can be printed from the Module B CD.

Develop emergency communication procedures.

Organize emergency communication procedures for common area supervisors in advance, and make sure you have both a basic and a backup plan. Walkie-talkies, cell phones for calling and texting, intercom systems, and internal telephone systems are commonly used for the basic emergency communications plan. These technologies are wonderful, but like anything that is dependent on batteries or electrical circuits, they can instantly become useless without power. You should have a backup plan.

Consider establishing a Red Card System. Every supervisor carries a card of brightly colored paper that may say something like Emergency (Figure 2n; available as Form B-07 on the CD). Students are instructed, perhaps as part of regular fire drill or lockdown instruction, what to do if an adult hands them a card. In a situation where a supervisor needs help and can't use the main communication system or leave the situation, she can hand the card to a student. The student runs to the office or the nearest staff member, shows the card, and tells the adult what happened.

Figure 2n   Sample Red Card (B-07)

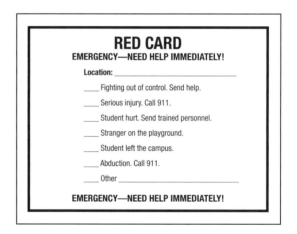

All staff members should be thoroughly trained in emergency communication procedures.

The following true story illustrates the importance of emergency communication procedures. The playground was supervised by a single staff member, who had no walkie-talkie or telephone, when a student collapsed. The supervisor immediately checked for pulse and respiration and determined that the student needed CPR. Between rescue breaths he said to the shocked students, "Go get help." A few minutes later he realized that no student had gone for help, so he then addressed a specific student and said, "Elaine, go to the office and tell them to call 911."

Elaine ran to the office and began to speak. "On the playground, something hap . . ." The office clerk said, "Wait a minute. I'm on the phone," and made the student wait. Elaine was a polite, tractable child, and she waited.

This school should have had a communication system such as walkie-talkies or cell phones as well as a backup system such as the Red Card System. If Elaine had waved a red emergency card as she entered the office, the staff could have recognized immediately that someone needed help.

Develop job descriptions for supervisors of complex settings, such as playgrounds and cafeterias.

Arrange a team (or task force) meeting to create written job descriptions for common areas such as the playground and cafeteria. It is critical to actively include current common area supervisors. Not only will the supervisors have insights into the job, but by including them you will gain a lot of buy-in to the *Foundations* program and the importance of structure and consistent supervision.

Before the meeting, have all attendees read or view Module B, Presentation 1 and Presentations 4 and 5 (Effective Supervision) and take notes on ideas or concepts that can be helpful to your situation.

During the meeting, complete the following tasks:

1. Review any existing job descriptions for supervisors and review the sample job descriptions we provide in this module (see Figure 2o on the next two pages and the Module B CD). How do they compare? Make note of ideas in the samples that might be useful.

2. Discuss the collected data (surveys, observations, incident referrals, and staff and student feedback) that pertain to the common area. The team Data/Evaluation Coordinator should be able to supply data summaries.

3. Discuss your shared vision and goals for the common area (What should it look and sound like?) and the major problems you need to tackle.

4. Brainstorm a list of expectations for supervisors and write the list on the board or a flip chart. Then have the group reach consensus through one of the following methods:

   • Have everyone rate the items on a scale of 1–5, with 1 = *not necessary* and 5 = *must have*. Attendees can write their ratings privately on individual pieces of papers.

   • Go through the items one by one and vote with thumbs up or thumbs down. Discuss the items and vote more than once, as needed.

Cafeteria

Goal

The lunch line and lunch area will be a safe and clean environment where people interact with courtesy and respect.

Responsible Cafeteria Behavior

Items marked with ** indicate expectations that students must understand fully and immediately.

COMING TO LUNCH AND LUNCH LINE

** 1. While in line, students will keep hands, feet, and objects to themselves.
** 2. Students will use quiet voices in the lunch line.
3. Students are to be escorted to the lunch area in two lines.
4. Students will buy lunch or milk before they sit down.
5. Students may sit by friends, but all students will be seated with their respective class.
6. Students should stay away from all stray animals on school premises.

LUNCH AREA PROCEDURES

** 1. Students will use quiet voices when talking.
** 2. Students will keep hands, feet, and objects to themselves.
3. Students will stay in their seats and raise their hands to get help.
4. Students will eat quietly and use good manners.
5. Students will walk in the lunch area.
6. Everyone will treat others with respect.

DISMISSAL

** 1. Students will clean up their own areas.
** 2. When dismissed, students will walk quietly to the playground.
3. Lunch boxes will be left in the playground area where classes line
4. Students are to remain on the playground unless they are given a p

Consequences for Infractions

When a student misbehaves, calmly and consistently implement the mi
might be appropriate.

1. Verbal reprimand
2. Positive practice—have student try it again.
3. Misbehavior in lunch line—have student go to end of line.
4. Misbehavior at table:
   • One-minute timeout against the wall
   • Three-minute timeout against the wall
   • Student accompanies the supervisor for 3 minutes
   • Student is held for 2 minutes after class is dismissed
5. Excessive noise from any given class—report to the classroom te
6. Use office referral only for physically dangerous behavior, illegal b
   insubordination.

Figure 2o Sample job descriptions for common area supervisors (B-30, 31, 32, 33)

The Art of Supervising Secondary School Hallways

OBSERVE ACTIVELY

• Stand at your doorway for as much of the passing period as possible.

• If you have class following the passing period, stay close to your doorway so you can supervise both your classroom and the hallway outside your classroom.

• If you have preparation time following the passing period, circulate throughout your assigned area intentionally and somewhat unpredictably so that students cannot detect a pattern. Pay particular attention to blind corners and potential trouble spots.

• Listen and visually scan for unusual activity (for example, an increase or a decrease in noise level or a group of students looking around furtively). Move close to students who are beginning to have difficulties and stay longer in problem areas so students are aware that you are monitoring.

• If you ever feel unsafe in any area of the school or with any group of students, tell an administrator or a member of the Foundations Team immediately so more adults can be deployed to the area to monitor the students. If you feel unsafe, vulnerable students probably feel unsafe, too.

INTERACT POSITIVELY

• Greet students and staff members in a welcoming and positive manner. Smile and use their names in your greetings. Remember that your words and actions contribute greatly to setting the tone and climate of the school.

• Intentionally seek out any student you have corrected for misbehavior in the past. Positively connect with the student by smiling, making a positive comment, or initiating a brief conversation about something that interests the student. This connection demonstrates that you see the student as a person—you don't just see the misbehavior that you previously corrected.

• Provide specific, descriptive praise that is age appropriate. Thank students for following the rules.

• Your positive interactions (greetings, talking with students, and positive feedback) should be at least three times more frequent than corrective interactions (correcting misbehavior). Remember the 3:1 positive ratio.

CORRECT BRIEFLY, CONSISTENTLY, RESPECTFULLY, AND CALMLY

• Know all the general rules and enforce all the rules and policies consistently.

• Step in whenever you see a potential problem. If low-level misbehavior is not corrected, the lack of oversight affects the overall climate of the school and increases the probability of more severe misbehavior.

• Correct student misbehavior consistently, both from student to student and from day to day. Remember that you are often more likely to be inconsistent on your good days—you might let students get away with behavior that you do not let them get away with on your bad days. Inconsistent correction encourages students to test the limits.

• Use brief one-liner corrections whenever possible. For example, say, "Please honor [school name]'s policy about appropriate language." "Please honor [school name]'s policy about public displays of affection." "Remember, 'catch and release!'"

• If a one-liner correction is not sufficient and you need to speak with a student, position the student so that you can continue to effectively supervise while you are speaking to him or her—that is, the student's back faces most of the other students (so the student is not on display) and you can see most of the other students in the area.

• Respond to student misbehavior as unemotionally as possible.

• Avoid publicly humiliating students when you correct their behavior. Use humor sparingly, respectfully, and ONLY with students you have a positive and respectful relationship with.

These samples can be printed from the Module B CD.

Supervisor Job Expectations for the Playground

- Always be on the playground before the students arrive.

- Know the area you are assigned to supervise and know all general rules and specific rules for games and equipment. Enforce all of the rules consistently.

- Intentionally meet students in a welcoming and positive manner as they enter the playground. Be positive, smile, and call students by name.

- Scan (look around) at all students in the area; don't just look at one area or in one direction. Look occasionally into other supervisors' areas to see if assistance is needed.

- Circulate through your assigned area and avoid talking with other adults on the playground. Students need your full attention. Move intentionally and somewhat unpredictably so that students cannot detect a pattern.

- Leave the area you are supervising only to deal with an emergency (such as taking a student into the building because of an injury). If you must leave, always tell another supervisor so she or he can supervise your area while you are away. Consider directing a responsible student to get help instead of leaving the area yourself.

- When interacting with a student (correcting misbehavior, for example), position the student so that you can continue to effectively supervise—that is, so that the student's back is to the group and you are facing the group.

- Within the first 5 minutes, intentionally seek out students who have had difficulty in the past. Positively connect with each of these students by smiling, making a positive comment, and/or briefly talking about something that interests the student.

- Move close to students who are beginning to have difficulties and stay longer in problem areas so students are aware that you are monitoring.

- Step in at the onset of any potential problem. If you let low-level misbehavior [...] lack of oversight affects the overall climate of the playground and increases th[...] severe misbehavior.

- Make a point of being more positive than corrective when interacting with st[...] particularly with students who have difficulty in the area. Praise and greet mo[...] correct misbehavior.

- Give students specific, descriptive praise that is age appropriate. Thank stude[...] rules.

- Correct student misbehavior consistently from student to student and from d[...]

- Respond to student misbehavior as unemotionally as possible. Never use an u[...] with students and always use a supportive stance (that is, off to one side, not [...] talking to individual students.

- Avoid publicly humiliating the student when you correct misbehavior.

- Use an instructional approach when you correct misbehavior—that is, state t[...] then have the student tell you the rule or ask the student to demonstrate the [...]

Playground

This information is designed to help staff increase consistency while supervising common areas and to provide teachers with a basis for teaching and re-teaching responsible behavior.

Goal: Students will play safely in all games and on all equipment on the playground, with everyone interacting with one another with courtesy and respect.

Responsible Playground Behavior

Students should not be asked to memorize or verbalize these expectations. Items marked with ** indicate expectations that students must understand fully and immediately.

1. Keep hands and feet to self. **
2. Rough play is not allowed on the playground. [Rough play includes, but is not limited to, pushing, shoving, grabbing, kicking, and tackling.] **
3. At the teacher's signal, students are to stop what they are doing and line up safely, quickly, and in an appropriate manner. **
4. Students will settle differences peacefully. **
5. Students will leave rocks, sticks, and gravel on the ground. **
6. Students will play within view of supervising staff and away from trees, puddles, and mud. **
7. Students will keep the building and grounds free of trash and litter.
8. Students should report any broken or dangerous item to supervising staff.
9. Students should stay away from all stray animals on school premises.
10. Students will take turns and use all equipment safely.
11. Students will not leave the playground area for any reason without permission.

Consequences for Infractions

When a student makes unsafe choices, the supervisor will calmly and consistently implement the mildest consequence that might be appropriate.

1. Verbal reminder
2. Positive practice
3. Have the student stand for 5 minutes for a first infraction.
4. For a second infraction, the teacher may select consequences from the alternative consequences list.
5. Office referral

Encouragement Procedures

1. Friendly interactions and verbal praise from playground supervisor will be used to encourage preferred behaviors.
2. Verbal praise from classroom teachers for appropriate and specific behaviors will be used to further emphasize appropriate behaviors.
3. Playground behaviors may be nominated in the Right Choice Awards program.
4. Particularly good playground experiences will be reported to the principal, who will make occasional classroom visits to compliment the students.

5. Have one or two people turn the list of expectations into a formal job description. Be sure the administrator reviews all draft documents. Invite staff feedback.

6. Arrange for all common area supervisors to meet and review the new job description (if any supervisors were not involved in the development), and arrange any necessary training.

7. Ensure that the job description is included in the Foundations Archive.

Develop a plan for training common areas supervisors.

Conduct an inservice for supervisors annually to ensure that they receive adequate training, and plan to conduct training for new supervisors when they are hired. For experienced supervisors, training might include just going over the job descriptions and reviewing effective supervisory techniques. For new or inexperienced playground or cafeteria supervisors, also model and role-play how to supervise, and provide positive and corrective feedback on the supervisors' performances.

For areas that involve the entire staff, such as hallway supervision, ensure that the entire staff is trained on the behavioral rules for students, how to assign appropriate consequences, and effective techniques for supervising the area. Review the description of supervisory responsibilities for the area. The training should include summaries of the essential supervisory elements—the team should view or read Presentations 4 and 5 on effective supervision and design some brief inservices on how the techniques apply to your common area settings and situations (hallways, morning arrival, dismissal, and so on).

Administrators: After supervisors have been trained, make an effort to be in common areas as frequently as possible to assist them. Your presence demonstrates that you value their efforts, you are assisting them in every way possible, and you notice their conscientiousness in being present and in their assigned areas. In the hallways of secondary schools and during arrival and dismissal in elementary schools, your presence also demonstrates to your teaching staff that you notice and appreciate their efforts in keeping the school environment safe and well supervised.

Elementary principals: A problem on many playgrounds is that supervisors huddle together and talk with each other, leaving no one to watch the students. Make sure your supervisors understand that the playground is potentially a very risky setting. Tell them that student safety demands active supervisors; therefore, you fully expect them to stay in their assigned zones (as tempting as it is to be with other supervisors and have a nice conversation with people over the age of nine). Be clear that the only time they should be out of their zones and interacting with other supervisors is when there is an emergency. Let them know that you will go out to the playground frequently, and when you cannot, you will look out at the playground frequently. If you see two supervisors in the same zone, you will know there is an emergency and you will drop everything to come out to assist. Most people want to demonstrate their best performances when they know they are being observed. This holds true for the students the supervisors observe as well as the supervisors you observe! Be sure to frequently acknowledge how much you notice and appreciate the supervisors' efforts to stay in their zones, circulate and scan, and interact positively with students.

Develop a plan for training all staff on their roles in the enforcement of schoolwide policies.

For each schoolwide policy, identify where the policy needs to be enforced and by whom. Consider dress code, for example: Who enforces dress code violations in the hallway first thing in the morning or between classes—just administrators and security, or will the policy also be enforced by teaching staff, maintenance staff, and paraprofessionals?

The school's training plan for the enforcement of policies should communicate as much detail as possible to ensure consistent and easy implementation by all staff members. Think through all the details of enforcing the policy—for example:

- A teacher sees a student with a dress code violation, but the student is not coming to the teacher's classroom. Should the teacher stop and correct the student? If the teacher does correct, will she then have difficulty starting her class? If so, there must be some provision for the teacher to transfer the student to an administrator or security person who will follow through with the correction.

- How will teachers correct dress code violations in their own classrooms? What consequences should they assign, and what procedures should they follow?

- Think through difficult situations such as male teachers correcting dress code violations with female students. Many schools have a "teacher colleague" system in place—in this case, the male teacher would ask his female teacher colleague to correct the female student and enforce the dress code.

Conduct this training annually, perhaps at the beginning of the school year, and be sure to provide the training to all who join the staff during the school year, including substitute teachers.

Module B, Presentation 6 covers supervision of common areas and schoolwide policies for all staff (rather than strictly supervisory staff).

Figure 2p shows some slides adapted from a PowerPoint presentation developed by an elementary school in Washington for their supervisor training inservice. The complete presentation is available on the Module B CD.

Figure 2p Sample slides from supervisor training inservice presentation (B-15); thanks to Puesta del Sol Elementary School in Bellevue, Washington

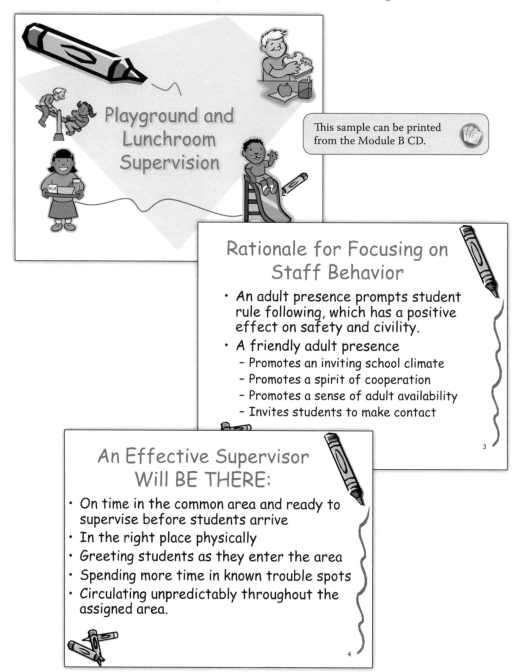

Module B: Managing Behavior in Common Areas and With Schoolwide Policies

Task 3 Action Steps & Evidence of Implementation

Action Steps	Evidence of Implementation
1. Evaluate the current supervision arrangements for each common area improvement priority. Consider: • Number of supervisors • Supervision schedule • Placement of supervisors throughout the setting or situation • Circulation of supervisors throughout the setting or situation. • Emergency communication procedures • Training for supervisors on emergency communication procedures 2. Brainstorm suggestions for any aspects of the supervision arrangements that need improving. Think beyond existing regularities! 3. Develop job descriptions for supervisors of particularly complex settings, such as playgrounds and cafeterias. When you have finished the **Revise** step, go on to the **Adopt** step. After your improvement proposal has been adopted: 4. Develop a plan for training common area supervisors each year and any time a new supervisor is hired. 5. Develop a plan for training all staff in their roles in the enforcement of schoolwide policies. 6. Document all the final decisions and procedures and place them in the Foundations Archive and Staff Handbook.	Foundations Process: Meeting Minutes, Current Priorities Foundations Archive: Job Descriptions for Common Area Supervisors Staff Handbook: Staff Roles and Responsibilities

Teaching Expectations to Students

CONTENTS

Introduction

Task 1: Organize to Ensure Expectations Are Taught

For the Foundations Team or task force working on a prioritized common area or schoolwide policy

---

Task 2: Teach and Launch Expectations for Multiple Common Areas and Schoolwide Policies

For the Foundations Team or task force working on common area or schoolwide policy

---

DOCUMENTS*

- How to Respond to Verbal Reminders PowerPoint (B-25)
- Expectations Posters for Common Areas, Elementary (B-22)
- Mutual Respect Poster (B-26)
- Lesson Templates (B-46, B-47, B-48, B-49, B-50)

* All documents listed are available on the CD. Other documents that are not shown in this presentation are also available on the CD (see Appendix C for a complete list).

INTRODUCTION

Is it worthwhile spending time teaching students behavioral expectations for common areas? The answer is a definite yes—your efforts will improve not only common areas, but classrooms and the overall school climate as well.

Common areas are very complex settings and situations. Students can't be expected to intuitively know how to behave—they need to be taught how to function in those specific settings and situations. Without guidance, many students might have to learn by trial and error what is acceptable behavior and what is not, and that method of learning is hard on both students and staff.

The following common area settings and situations are especially prone to problematic behaviors.

Hallways and locker areas in secondary schools. Without clear expectations, students move chaotically and gather in groups, clogging up the passageways. Minor conflicts arise, creating tension and sometimes building into major problems. If students understand how and why to keep hallways clear, the potential for problematic behavior is reduced.

Playground transitions to classrooms. Students need to be taught procedures that will help them calm down when playtime is over. They might learn, for example, to freeze in place when instructed, wait for the OK to walk off the playground, walk slowly to the pickup point, and then walk in lines to their classrooms. This procedure gives students several minutes of slow movement so they are more ready to be calm in class, and teachers don't have to spend the first 10 or 15 minutes of class dealing with playground energy.

Problematic student behavior in common areas tends to negatively affect classroom behavior. This is true of the playground (as in the example above) as well as other common areas in both elementary and secondary schools.

Is it worthwhile spending time teaching students the expectations of schoolwide policies, such as dress code and electronics? The answer again is a definite yes. When students clearly understand all policies, they perceive the enforcement of those policies as fair and, when the policies are implemented consistently, predictable.

Schoolwide policies can be very complex. They tend to be idiosyncratic and unique to each school. Students entering a new school—sixth graders entering middle school, for example—need to be not just informed about but also directly taught all schoolwide policies that they are expected to follow.

Schoolwide policy transgressions often account for a high percentage of disciplinary interactions with administrators and result in in-school suspensions, detentions, and so on.

This presentation focuses on the *T* in STOIC— Teach expectations with clarity. As you develop your plan to teach expectations to students, keep the following general considerations in mind.

> STOIC represents a framework for ensuring that common areas and schoolwide policies are addressed in comprehensive and cohesive ways. STOIC stands for:
>
> **S**tructure for success.
> **T**each expectations with clarity.
> **O**bserve and supervise.
> **I**nteract positively.
> **C**orrect fluently.

- Ensure that supervision is consistent with the lessons on behavioral expectations. Both the corrective consequences and the positive feedback that common area supervisors and all school staff provide should be in line with what students expect throughout the school.

- Arrange for the re-teaching of lessons to students with chronic problems, as needed.

- Ensure that comprehensive lessons are taught in instructional settings to all students. Lessons should cover rules, procedures, climate, and civility.

- Include expectations for responding to adults. Many supervisors report that when they ask students to stop, the students just keep on moving and do not respond. Teach the expectation that when an adult in authority speaks to a student, the student needs to stop and pay attention to the adult.

- Include expectations for specific skills that you emphasize in your school— conflict resolution and bullying prevention strategies, for example.

This presentation focuses on the steps for teaching the rules and procedures for common areas and schoolwide policies that are targeted as improvement priorities. Ideally, you should teach the rules and procedures for as many of your common areas and schoolwide policies (not just the prioritized ones) as you can at the beginning of the year. You can use the information in this presentation to accomplish that task as well.

Task 1: Organize to Ensure That Expectations Are Taught gives ideas for lessons and activities to cover all the information students need to be successful in any given common area.

Task 2: Teach and Launch Expectations for Multiple Common Areas and School-wide Policies describes how to create a coordinated plan for teaching the lessons, implementing the new procedures, and re-teaching the expectations when advisable.

TASK 1

Organize to ensure that expectations are taught

Once you've designed clear expectations for student behavior, a task discussed in Module B, Presentation 2, the next step is to design the lessons that staff will use to teach the expectations to students. These lessons should be well structured and include all necessary information in age-appropriate terms.

Identify who will be responsible for designing lessons for an area or a policy.

This entity might be the task force leading the improvement efforts, members of the Foundations Team, a group of teachers, or a combination of staff members from those groups. One group may design lessons for all common areas and schoolwide policies, or you might assign a separate group to each common area and schoolwide policy.

Consider student ages and the complexity of the settings when designing lessons.

Lessons should be age appropriate. Lessons for kindergartners should, of course, use simpler language than lessons for high school students. Include an adequate and appropriate amount of detail. Younger students need more detail. Students who are new to the school also need detailed lessons. For example, ninth graders need more detailed lessons on cafeteria behavior than the upper classes that have a year or more of cafeteria experience.

For complex common areas such as the cafeteria and playground, expect to teach multiple lessons. Distribute prioritized content across several days of short lessons. Cover the most important expectations on the first day, then go into more detail on subsequent days. Students might be overwhelmed if you present all the information in one long session on the first day. Also include cumulative reviews—that is, on Day 2, review Day 1 material; on Day 3, review material from Days 1 and 2, and so on. For example, prioritized cafeteria lesson topics might be scheduled as follows:

Topic	Day 1	Day 2	Day 3
Entering	X		
Waiting in line	X	X	
Noise level	X	X	
Making menu choices		X	
Treating adults with respect		X	X
Clean up	X	X	X
Recycling		X	X

Identify all information students need to be successful and responsible in the setting.

We suggest that you follow a basic structure similar to the one that follows. See the sample lessons on the Module B CD for some good examples of well-structured lessons.

Sample lesson templates and lesson plans for a variety of common areas and schoolwide policies are available on the Module B CD.

1. Goal of the common area—the purpose of the setting or situation and how students should behave in it. For example:

   - The lunch area will be a safe and clean environment where all people interact with courtesy and respect.
   - Washington Elementary students will demonstrate respectful behavior during assemblies by listening, participating, and following directions.

2. Written rules (if any), with details. For example:

   - Keep hands, feet, and objects to yourself.
   - Travel only on the right.
   - Come to school no earlier than 8:20 a.m. and leave school grounds by 3 p.m.

3. Procedures used in the common area. For example (front office behavior):

   - Enter office quietly.
   - Report to the counter or Student Services Window.
   - Wait your turn patiently.
   - Be courteous.
   - Follow directions of office staff.

4. Civility expectations. For example (assembly behavior):

   - Cooperate: Ignore distractions and follow directions.
   - Be responsible: Pay attention to the speaker.
   - Be empathetic: Listen to adult instructions.
   - Use self-control: Respond appropriately when pushed or hit.

5. How students should respond to adults in authority. For example (primary compliance instructions):

   - When an adult speaks to you, look at the person.
   - Listen to the person's words.
   - Nod your head or say, "OK."
   - Do what the person asks right away.

Use an effective lesson design for conducting the lessons.

A good basic organization plan for conducting lessons is the Model-Lead-Test format.

Model: Give direct information about what students are expected to do and how they are expected to behave by performing the procedures in detail for them.

Lead: Have students perform the procedures and provide constructive feedback.

Test: Ask questions to make sure students understand the procedures. If they are not proficient, go through the Model and Lead steps again.

Figure 3c at the end of this task presents a few templates that use variations of the Model-Lead-Test format. The templates can be printed from the Module B CD. You can also use posters to assist with the Modeling step. See "Post It" on the next page.

Figure 3a shows a few slides from a wonderful PowerPoint presentation that Fulton Elementary School in San Diego, California, uses to teach students how to respond appropriately to verbal reminders and reprimands. Adding a visual component to lessons can help grab students' attention and increase the likelihood that they will remember the main points. The example features pictures of the school's staff and students displaying the correct and incorrect responses, making the lesson even more memorable. You can see the entire lesson, which consists of 15 slides, on the Module B CD.

Figure 3a *Excerpts from the "How to Respond to Reminders" PowerPoint (B-25); thanks to Fulton K–8 and San Diego Unified School District in California*

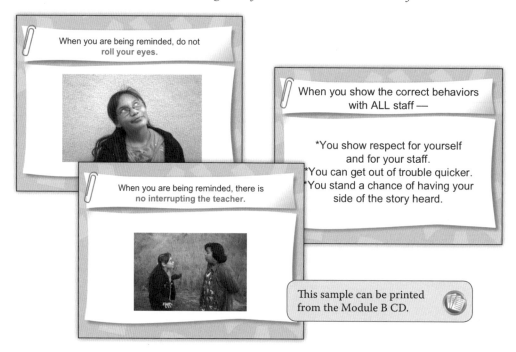

Module B: Managing Behavior in Common Areas and With Schoolwide Policies

Post It

You can also use posters to help with modeling. Prairie Heights Elementary School in Cedar Rapids, Iowa, created big posters (B-22 on the CD) of expectations and procedures that they display in the hallways, lunch room, restrooms, and on the playground. Each teacher also gets an 8.5" × 11" color copy of each poster to use for teaching behavioral lessons.

Hallway

What to do:

Stay on the right side of the hall.

No talking in the hallway while classes are in session. Use a soft voice before and after school.

Face forward and watch where you are going.

Keep hands and feet to yourself.

Walk at all times.

Lunch Room

What to do:

Use inside voices and kind language.

Form a single line. Stop to say your name clearly.

Clean your area.

Sit and stay seated with hands and feet to yourself.

Form a single line. Do not budge.

ALWAYS WALK

Playground

What to do:

Show respect to adults and other students. Stop-think-get help.

Leave gum and candy at home. Leave rocks, sticks, snow/ice and other dangerous items alone. Questions/problems, ask an adult.

Use polite language at all times. (No put downs.)

Dress appropriately for the weather.
• snow boots/pants are required to play in the snow
• jackets are required when below 60° F

When the whistle blows, stop playing and walk immediately to the door and form a single line.

Rest Rooms

What to do:

Go

Flush

Wash

Leave

 These samples can be printed from the Module B CD.

Figure 3b shows a poster adapted from a middle school in Texas that is used to teach and reinforce expectations for civility across different settings.

Figure 3b *Mutual Respect poster (B-26)*

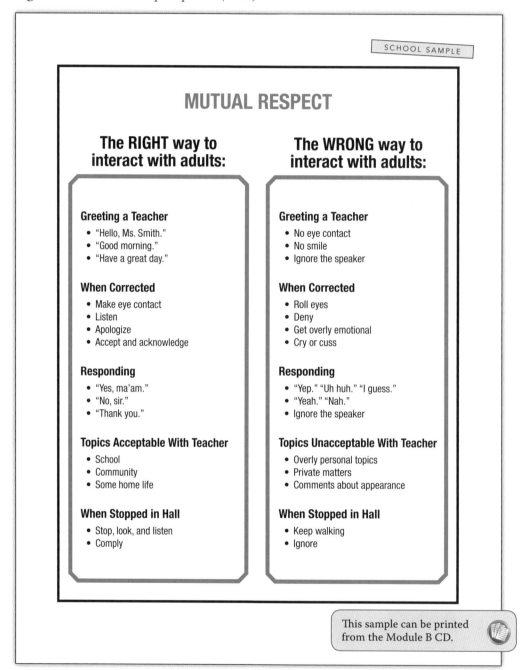

Module B: Managing Behavior in Common Areas and With Schoolwide Policies

Vary the lesson activities.

Try to engage students and make the lessons compelling so students want to pay attention. Here are some ideas that can liven up behavioral lessons:

- **Skits**

  Teachers performing examples (and non-examples) of expectations can be very powerful—and entertaining!

- **Whole group practice**

  This is a good technique for elementary students. "Class, let's practice. Everyone, stand up. Push your chairs in. Line up at the door." For some common areas, such as the playground, grade-level groups can get together and practice procedures.

- **Role-play**

  Have students perform the expectations with each other or with teachers.

- **Walking tours**

  Take students to the cafeteria (for example) and show them where to line up, how to ask for food, how to pay, where to sit, how to empty their trays, and so on. Students who are new to the school—ninth graders, for example—will especially benefit from tours.

- **T-charts**

  Include students in lesson instruction by having them fill out T-charts on the board.

- **Videos**

  Have staff or students prepare lessons on video.

Figure 3c   *Examples of lesson plan templates (B-46), p. 1 of 2*

Foundations Lesson Plan

Objective: Students will demonstrate an understanding of the student behaviors expected in the common area.	**Teacher Input:** Introduce and explain the student expectations, encouragement procedures, and consequences for infractions by using:	**Student Input:** Students will practice the expected behaviors through:	**Reflection:** Teacher and students reflect on, review, and summarize the expected behaviors with:
Share Goal for Common Area: **Highlight** the student behaviors that need to be exhibited in the common area.			

 This sample can be printed from the Module B CD.

FOUNDATIONS SAMPLE

Foundations Lesson Plan
Teaching Responsible Behavior in Common Areas
Locker Logic

Objective: Students will demonstrate an understanding of the lesson.	Teacher Input: Introduce, explain, and teach.	Student Input: Students will practice (work with) desired behavior related to the goal.	Reflection: Teacher and students reflect on, review, and summarize.
Demonstrate understanding of Locker Logic. Expectation #9 from agenda/map book.	Review the list of Locker Logic and discuss rationale. • Close door quietly with your hand. • Set your books down quietly in front of your locker. • Respect the locker area of your neighbor. • Organize the stacking of books and notebooks in your locker. • Keep your combination to yourself. • Make sure your locker is always locked. • Respect others' lockers.	✓ Ask for additional suggestions related to Locker Logic. ✓ Have students practice closing their lockers quietly and placing their books in front of their locker.	Develop posters for Locker Logic to be posted in hallway above the lockers.

 This sample can be printed from the Module B CD.

Common Area Skills Lesson Format

Introduction

Identify a specific area.

Specify a learning objective for this area—modify the goal statement developed for the staff manual.

Tell Phase

Identify five to eight critical behaviors—use behavioral expectations outlined in the staff manual.

Have students anticipate potential problems that arise in this common area and brainstorm appropriate ways to respond.

Show Phase

Use a T-chart to define what behavior should look and sound like within this setting.

Model the three to five critical behaviors (depending on the age and skill level of your students, consider discretely modeling each of the major steps for enacting these behaviors).

Do Phase

Go to the targeted common area.

Provide students with simulated practice:
1. Define the behavior(s).
2. Provide a rationale for using the behavior.
3. List the critical steps for enacting the behavior:
    a.
    b.
    c.
4. Model the behavior. (Steps 1–4 are a quick review.)
5. Set up situations that could potentially create problems for students and have students demonstrate appropriate responses (use Tell Phase B).

Feedback and praise:
1. Give students honest and specific feedback and praise.
2. Have the students give each other honest and specific feedback and praise.

Assign additional practice:
1. Have the students generate other settings in which these skills would apply.
2. Periodically have students report back about the use of these skills.

Conclusion—summarize the lesson!

This sample can be printed from the Module B CD.

SCHOOL SAMPLE

Guilford County Schools Responsible Discipline Process
Lesson Plan Template

Objective:	Teacher Input:	Student Input:	Reflection:
Students will demonstrate an understanding of the goal of the lesson.	Introduce/explain/teach	Students will "practice" (work with) desired behavior related to the goal.	Teacher and students reflect on/review/summarize.
Share Goal: **Highlight** Review the specific skills that are to be used in reaching the goal. A. B. C.	• T-charts (looks like/sounds like; appropriate/inappropriate) • Brainstorming/give examples • Discussion • Teacher demonstrations • Pictures/videos • Audio recordings • Selected readings (short stories, poems, current events, etc.) • Define/discuss key words • Guest speakers	• Discussion/give examples/brainstorming • Role-plays/skits/charades • Making a video/taking pictures • Developing an advertisement • Illustrations/cartoons/posters • Collages/cutout pictures to illustrate • Develop and teach a lesson • Write and perform songs/raps • Develop and play games • Puppet show • Writing activity • Classification activities (develop and present scenarios to fit each letter)	• Classification activities • Writing/sharing activities, 3-2-1, start/stop, crumple and toss • Self-assessment activities—Do I do these now? • Share what students developed with another class • Display finished project • Verbal feedback/praise/reinforcement from teacher • Discussion

This sample can be printed from the Module B CD.

SOCIAL SKILLS
Lesson Plan Form

SOCIAL SKILLS LESSON

INTRODUCTION
(1)   Define the skill: Demonstration of respect—the positive attitude towards others.

(2)   Provide a learning objective: Students will be able to exhibit the attitude—respect the rights of others.

TELL PHASE
(1)   Introduce the skill via questions.
      (a)   How do we know someone has a positive attitude?
      (b)   What does the person do and say?
      (c)   What happens to a person who exhibits a positive attitude?

SHOW PHASE
(1)   Model the behavior.
      (a)   Model positive behavior.
           Teacher skits—Sandra and Matt—Proper attitude
      (b)   Model negative behavior. Trish and Ollie—Bad attitude

(2)   Model discretely each of the major steps for enacting the behavior.
      (a)   Come into class quietly—talking in low voice.
      (b)   Go directly to seat, sit down, open notebook, and take out pen or pencil.
      (c)   When the teacher asks for your attention, stop talking.
      (d)   When the teacher asks for your attention, stop moving around.
      (e)   Listen carefully to instructions and try to follow directions at start of lesson.

(3)   With a student helper, direct a role-play of a typical situation in which this behavior is displayed.

(4)   Lead a discussion of alternative behaviors to accomplish the same goal.

DO PHASE
(1)   Define the behavior: Students will exhibit respect for classmates and the teacher.
(2)   Provide a rationale for using the behavior. Students brainstorm ideas.
(3)   List critical steps for enacting the behavior.
      (a)   Students list behaviors
      (b)   Show by instruction—use a T-chart—looks like/sounds like
      (c)   as above (see Show Phase [2])
(4)   Model the behavior. Student role-play
(5)   Have the students use the behavior in role-plays.
(6)   Have students give each other feedback about the role-play.
(7)   Have the teacher provide the students with feedback about the role-play.
(8)   Assign the students to use the skill in another setting.
(9)   Have the students report back about their homework assignment.

This sample can be printed from the Module B CD.

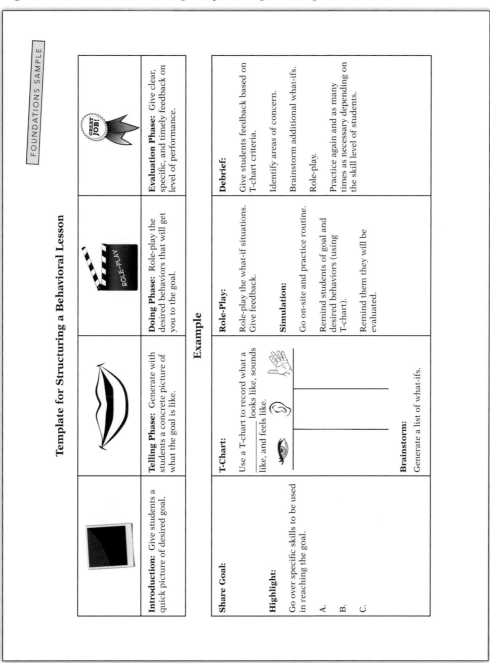

Template for Structuring a Behavioral Lesson

FOUNDATIONS SAMPLE

Introduction: Give students a quick picture of desired goal.

Telling Phase: Generate with students a concrete picture of what the goal is like.

Doing Phase: Role-play the desired behaviors that will get you to the goal.

Evaluation Phase: Give clear, specific, and timely feedback on level of performance.

Example

Share Goal:

Highlight:

Go over specific skills to be used in reaching the goal.

A.

B.

C.

T-Chart:

Use a T-chart to record what a ___ looks like, sounds like, and feels like.

Brainstorm:

Generate a list of what-ifs.

Role-Play:

Role-play the what-if situations. Give feedback.

Simulation:

Go on-site and practice routine.

Remind students of goal and desired behaviors (using T-chart).

Remind them they will be evaluated.

Debrief:

Give students feedback based on T-chart criteria.

Identify areas of concern.

Brainstorm additional what-ifs.

Role-play.

Practice again and as many times as necessary depending on the skill level of students.

This sample can be printed from the Module B CD.

Task 1 Action Steps & Evidence of Implementation

Action Steps	Evidence of Implementation
1. Identify who will be responsible for designing lessons for each common area or schoolwide policy improvement priority. This task may include evaluating and modifying current lessons and/or developing new lessons.	Foundations Process: Current Priorities, Planning Calendar
2. Before they begin designing lessons, the responsible staff members should view or read (or both) Task 1 of this presentation and review the sample lessons available on the Module B CD.	
3. Each responsible group should create and execute a plan for the process of designing lessons. The plan should include tasks, timelines, and specific people responsible.	
4. Archive the lessons in the Foundations Archive.	Foundations Archive: Lesson Plans for Teaching Common Area and Schoolwide Policy Expectations

TASK 2

Teach and launch expectations for multiple common areas and schoolwide policies

Once you've designed lessons for teaching responsible behavior in common areas and schoolwide policies, the next—and equally important—step is to develop a coordinated plan for teaching the lessons to students. A good plan addresses the following topics:

- Determine who will teach the lessons.
- Organize lesson instruction.
- Launch the new expectations for one or more common areas.
- Plan for re-teaching the lessons.

Determine who will teach the lessons.

Classroom teachers are often the logical choice to teach the lessons. They have a captive audience, and they can work the lessons into their daily schedules at their convenience.

Live feeds can be very effective. We know of some elementary schools that have fifth graders design and "act" in lessons that are filmed and broadcast live to the lower grades. The students demonstrate the proper way to line up in the bus loading area, clean up in the cafeteria, and wait turns on the playground, for example.

Older students can teach younger students. This is a very powerful lesson design. As in the live feed idea above, older students design lessons on the most universal expectations and present them (as roving presenters—see below) to classes of younger students, or they videotape lessons that teachers can show to their classes.

Roving presenters travel from classroom to classroom teaching the lessons. A great example of this technique comes from an elementary school situated on a very busy street. The principal and the crossing guard go to each classroom on the first day of school and teach about the importance of crossing the street safely. The principal's presence empowers the crossing guard with a high level of authority, which helps get the message about safety across to the students.

Assemblies. Teachers can also present schoolwide lessons during assemblies. We don't recommend holding assemblies on the first day of school because you probably won't be able to teach the expectations for assembly behavior before the assembly and those expectations are not the most critical information that students need to learn on the first day. If you have held assemblies on the first day in the past and they have worked well, feel free to continue that tradition. If you have not, we recommend that you delay assemblies until later in the week when the school year is off to a good start and you have had time to preteach assembly behavior. Then, during the assembly, you might teach expectations that are not essential on the first day, such as proper behavior with substitutes.

Organize lesson instruction.

For secondary schools, consider organizing the lessons by class period so that every teacher is involved. Each teacher spends only about 3 to 5 minutes per class period on the expectations. Figure 3d below shows a sample schedule.

Figure 3d   Sample schedule for teaching expectations for first 5 days of school

	1ST PERIOD	2ND PERIOD	3RD PERIOD	4TH PERIOD	5TH PERIOD	6TH PERIOD
	Teachers of freshmen allocate at least ten minutes per lesson; for other grade levels use professional judgment.					
MONDAY	**SECTION 1** START on Time! Basic Hallway/ Restroom Expectations	**SECTION 2** START on Time! Tardy Policy/ Sweep Procedures	**SECTION 3** Cafeteria Procedures: Teachers of 9th Graders—Tour	**SECTION 4** START on Time! Locker Logic	**SECTION 5** START on Time! Civility in the Halls and All School Settings	**SECTION 6** Dismissal, Bus Loading, Expectations to and From School & Arrival
TUESDAY	**SECTION 7** START on Time! Safety in Halls, Restrooms, and Courtyards	**SECTION 8** Safety Lesson 1: Threats Will Be Taken Seriously (in Foundations)	**SECTION 9** Fire Drill, Earthquake, Safety, and Lockdown (or "Women and Children First")	**SECTION 10** START on Time! Civil Interactions with Staff and School Pride	**SECTION 11** Safety Lesson 2: Right to Be Safe & Responsibility to Contribute to Safety (in Foundations)	**SECTION 12** Campus Environment (or "Loiterers Will Be Prosecuted")
WEDNESDAY	**SECTION 13** Safety Lesson 3: What Is Harassment? (in Foundations)	**SECTION 14** Dress Code: Video Broadcast During Last Ten Minutes of Class	**SECTION 15** Safety Lesson 4: Everyone Belongs in This School/ This School Belongs to Everyone (in Foundations)	**SECTION 16** Grading, Cheating, and Plagiarism (or "Advice from a Sixth-Year Senior")	**SECTION 17** Clubs and Service Opportunities at This School	**SECTION 18** Safety Lesson 5: Personal Power and Control, Part 1 (in Foundations)
THURSDAY	**SECTION 19** Graduation Requirements— How to Monitor Your Progress	**SECTION 20** Safety Lesson 6: Personal Power and Control, Part 2 (in Foundations)	**SECTION 21** Athletic Opportunities and Eligibility Requirements	**SECTION 22** Maturity (or "Why 'Yo Mama' Is NOT an Appropriate Response")	**SECTION 23** Safety Lesson 7: Teasing and Destructive Humor Can Be an Abuse of Power (in Foundations)	**SECTION 24** Personal Conduct/Social Expectations (or "Hey, Don't Say or Touch That!")
FRIDAY	**SECTION 25** Safety Lesson 8: When You Are on the Receiving End of an Abuse of Power (in Foundations)	**SECTION 26** Locker Maintenance and Academic Organization	**SECTION 27** Safety Lesson 9: Everyone Shares Responsibility to Stop Threats, Bullying, Harassment, and Other Abuses (in Foundations)	**SECTION 28** Dress Code Redux (or "We've Seen It All Before")	**SECTION 29** Student Success Is the Goal: Academic Help Is Available	**SECTION 30** Safety Lesson 10: Help is Available If You Need It (in Foundations)

At the elementary level, classroom teachers can set their own schedules. For school-wide lessons, create a schedule and inform the classroom teachers in advance. For example, tell them that there will be a live feed about playground procedures at 1:15

p.m. or that the principal will be visiting the classroom around 11 a.m. to talk about assembly behavior.

It's also important to create opportunities for students to demonstrate their knowledge of the procedures they've been taught. In some elementary schools, teachers hold a game-show-like competition with neighboring classrooms at the end of the first week of school. Teachers build up excitement for the game during the week, motivating students to want to learn and know the expectations.

Another aspect of organization is teaching expectations to as many students as efficiently and effectively as possible. For example, let's say you've developed the rules and procedures shown in "Proper Use of Playground Equipment" (see next page). To teach the lessons for equipment use, one teacher and a large group of students could move from the swings to the slide to the jungle gym and so on, until all the equipment is covered. However, a more efficient and probably more effective technique (students tend to pay attention better in smaller groups) is to enlist the help of other staff, break the large group of students into smaller groups, and rotate the students' lesson times at each piece of equipment. Depending on how many staff members are available, you might be able to assign stations—one person teaches swings and slides, another the jungle gym and horizontal ladder, and so on, while the students move from location to location.

This approach can also work in different common areas, such as the cafeteria, and on a larger scale. At the beginning of the school year, you might organize a rotating schedule for teaching lessons for all common areas and schoolwide policies. Assign staff members to stations—the auditorium for assembly expectations, the cafeteria, commons area, office area, and so on. During a dedicated period, students can move from station to station for lessons on the rules and procedures for each location. Actually being present in the area as they learn the expectations will help students remember the lessons. However, don't expect students to remember everything from this experience—they will still need plenty of review afterwards.

Launch new rules and procedures for one or more common areas.

Ensure that supervision will be consistent with the expectations that students were taught. All supervisors should know the expectations as well as or better than the students, and they should know how and when to assign consequences from a hierarchical list—consistently from staff member to staff member and from student to student.

If you are launching new procedures during the school year, begin lessons about a week before the procedures are to go into effect. A week's worth of brief lessons gives students time to absorb and practice the material, so by the time launch day arrives, they should be able to follow the expectations smoothly.

Double the usual number of supervisors in the settings during the first week. More supervisors equal more positive feedback to students, more direct supervision, and faster corrective feedback.

Proper Use of Playground Equipment

(These rules and procedures are excerpts from an example in Module B, Presentation 2. See B-27 on the Module B CD for the complete text.)

Swings

- Take turns using swings.
- Remain seated (no seat drops).
- Next student in line counts to 50 (1 equals back and up).
- Alternate the person you count for, whenever possible.
- Always swing straight.
- Do not hold on to other swings.
- Do not throw swings over bar to shorten chains.
- If swings have been thrown over, ask an adult to return them to the appropriate position.
- Do not jump out of swings.

Slide

- Sit in the center of the slide and come down feet first with bottom on slide.
- Use only the ladder to reach the top of the slide.
- Only one person on the ladder at a time.
- Do not put rocks on the slide.

Jungle Gym

- Use this equipment for climbing.
- Do not jump off the jungle gym.

Horizontal Ladder

- Begin on the end farthest from the building.
- If you let go of the ladder, go back to the end of the line.
- After reaching the opposite side, climb down and return to the end of the line.

Horizontal Bars

- Stand in lines taking turns using the bars for sitting, hanging, spinning, and practicing pull-ups.
- No Cherry Drops (twirling by the knees, then dismounting without the use of hands) allowed.

Arrange for at least two follow-up observations in each setting. Foundations Team or task force members who worked on the common area can conduct the observations, then discuss what is working well and what is not. The task force can analyze any problems and determine whether the new procedures need a few tweaks or a revision, or whether the expectations need to be re-taught. If all is going well—celebrate!

Provide positive feedback to staff and students whenever possible. If the observations show that the cafeteria is much better than it used to be, let staff and students know through the school newsletter, website, announcements, written memos, and the like. Think about including parents as well. Most schools would benefit from more public relations to let families and surrounding communities know about their successes.

Plan for re-teaching the lessons.

A few situations will arise during the school year when you'll need to re-teach the lessons to individuals or the whole student body: when new students transfer into the school, before and after holidays, and when individual students demonstrate chronic misbehavior related to the expectations.

Newcomers. It is critical to teach common area expectations to students who are new to the school. An efficient way to ensure they get appropriate instruction is to use videos. You might have students create video lessons for all the common areas. The videos can be available in the office or another appropriate place where new students can view them. Another idea is to assign a peer mentor to each new student. The mentor can explain the common area expectations (and other aspects of the school) to the new student during his or her first two or three days at the school. This job is a good example of Meaningful Work (Wise, Marcum, Haykin, Sprick, & Sprick, 2011)—students can apply for or be assigned to the job of New Student Mentor.

All students. The entire student body should review the expectations at the following times:

- *After major vacations.* Students tend to "forget" school expectations after a significant amount of time away.

- *Before major vacations.* Students also tend to forget expectations in the excitement of anticipating vacation time.

- *Before special days.* Elementary students are often overly excited in the days leading up to Halloween, for example.

- *Before, during, and after major schoolwide testing and sports competitions* (secondary schools).

- *Any time behavior appears to be breaking down.* (If hallway incidents are increasing, for example, it's time to re-teach hallway expectations.)

Individual students. For students who demonstrate chronic misbehavior related to the expectations, your first intervention should be to re-teach the schoolwide expectations. This is another instance when prerecorded videos of the lessons can be efficient, effective teaching tools. For elementary students, you can also consider remedial recess or remedial cafeteria time. The student goes to recess or lunch accompanied by a counselor or paraprofessional who re-teaches the expectations and has the student practice appropriate procedures.

Task 2 Action Steps & Evidence of Implementation

Action Steps	Evidence of Implementation

Develop a coordinated plan for introducing lessons on common area and schoolwide policy expectations.
 	
a. Identify who will teach the lessons.
b. Create a schedule for teaching the lessons.
c. Identify procedures for launching new rules and procedures.
 	
   • Ensure consistency between supervision and expectations.
   • Lead up to the start date by teaching brief daily lessons for a week.
   • Double the usual number of supervisors for the first week of implementation.
   • Identify when follow-up observations will be conducted.
 	
d. Identify when and how lessons will be re-taught.
	Foundations Process: Planning Calendar, Meeting Minutes
	
	Foundations Archive: Lesson Plans for Teaching Common Area and Schoolwide Policy Expectations

Effective Supervision, Part 1: Protect, Expect, and Connect

DOCUMENTS*

- Supervisory Skills Checklist (B-08)

* All documents listed are available on the CD.

> Presentations 4 and 5 are designed for paraprofessionals who supervise common areas. Presentation 6 is similar to 4 and 5, but it is designed for the professional staff and focuses on supervising settings such as hallways. With any staff group, use either Presentations 4 and 5 *or* Presentation 6, but not all three.

INTRODUCTION

This presentation and the next focus on the essential skills and knowledge you need for supervising the common areas of your school.

The presence of adults in common areas prompts students to follow the rules. Think about your own behavior when you are driving on a highway. Most of us follow the speed limit when we're supervised—when state troopers are visible or we know that they could appear at any time. When authority figures are not visible, most of us push the limits. It's no different with students. And just as following the speed limit increases safety and civility for everyone on the road, student rule following increases safety and civility in school.

Another dynamic—beyond policing—is at work here as well. Kids with whom you've built relationships typically want to demonstrate their best behavior to you. This idea is analogous to adults taking special care to clean their houses before company arrives—they clean not because they fear consequences assigned by authorities if they don't have a clean house, but because they want to put their best foot forward for people they respect and have a relationship with.

The presence of friendly, confident adults in a school environment also promotes:

- An inviting school climate
- A spirit of cooperation and camaraderie
- A sense of adult availability

The Foundations Team in your school will ensure that a couple of prerequisites have been addressed so that you can supervise effectively. The team should make arrangements for adequate supervision—the correct number of supervisors, for example. And the team should ensure that students are taught how they are expected to behave.

Students need to know that the expectations they are taught apply consistently to the whole school, not just to an individual supervisor. Every supervisor should be able to confidently say to a student, "I know you had a lesson on . . ." or "I know your teacher talked to you about this . . ." That level of confidence increases the assumption of compliance that we discussed in earlier presentations.

In this presentation we discuss preventive supervisory practices—how to **protect**, **expect**, and **connect**.

Task 1: Protect Students explains how effective supervisors need to *be there* and *be aware* to keep students safe.

Task 2: Expect Responsible Student Behavior describes the importance of understanding and communicating expectations and intervening early with any misbehavior.

Task 3: Connect With Students describes methods for providing noncontingent attention, positive feedback, and at least three times more positive than corrective attention to every student.

Module B, Presentation 5 covers **correct** and **reflect**—what supervisors should do in response to student misbehavior and how they can self-assess and work to continually improve their skills.

Use the Supervisory Skills Checklist, Figure 4a on pp. 98–101 (Form B-08 on the Module B CD), to self-assess your strengths and areas that need improvement as a common area supervisor. All supervisors working through Presentations 4 and 5 should have a copy of the checklist and complete each section as they read the corresponding section in the presentation (Protect, Expect, Connect, Correct, Reflect). You do not have to turn the checklist in to anyone—it is purely an exercise in reflecting on your own skills. However, the supervisors as a group might want to discuss their answers and share at least one of the skills that need improvement. In addition, we encourage you to share your goals with your supervisor and ask for feedback on the skills he or she would most like you to improve.

> The numbered items within each task correspond to items on the Supervisory Skills Checklist (shown in Figure 4a).

Note: When we refer to *your supervisor*, we mean the person you report to. This person would probably be the principal in a small- or medium-size school; in a large school, it might be an assistant principal or another staff member.

Supervisory Skills Checklist (p. 1 of 4)

Setting: _____

Directions: Rate the items using the 3-point scale at right. Use your ratings to fill out the Strengths and Goals sections at the end of the checklist. (This checklist is for your own self-reflection and goal setting. You do not need to share it or turn it in.)

3 = Always
2 = Most of the time
1 = Need to improve

Protect

____   1. I am always on time for my supervisory responsibility.

____   2. I know which zones or areas I am responsible for supervising, and I know the layouts, problem areas, and purposes of the zones or areas.

____   3. I am prepared to handle emergencies, and I know how to work with and support other supervisors. I leave the area I am supervising only to deal with an emergency and only after I have told another adult. If I am the only adult on duty, I know the backup systems for getting assistance.

____   4. As much as possible, I continuously move throughout the area I supervise. I move intentionally and monitor my movements so that students cannot detect a pattern. I move through all sections of my assigned area, regardless of the surface (mud, bark mulch, gravel, etc.).

____   5. I visually scan the area continuously, and I listen for unusual sounds and changes in noise level. I purposefully observe all students in the entire area; I don't observe only a portion of the area or look in only one direction.

____   6. When interacting with a student (when correcting misbehavior, for example), I am careful to position the student so that I can continue to effectively supervise—that is, so that the student's back is to the group and I am facing the group.

____   7. I never allow other adults to usurp my time when I am on my way to my assignment or while I am supervising.

Expect

____   8. I know the rules, procedures, and basic civilities students are expected to use when entering the setting, while in the setting, and when leaving the setting.

____   9. I am prepared to enforce all of the behavioral expectations for students in the setting.

____   10. Within the first 5 minutes, I intentionally seek out students who have difficulty in the setting. I positively connect with each of these students by smiling, making a positive comment, and/or briefly talking about something that interests the student.

____   11. I move close to students who are beginning to have difficulties, and I stay longer in problem areas so that students are aware that I am monitoring.

 This form can be printed from the Module B CD.

Supervisory Skills Checklist (p. 2 of 4)

_____ 12. I step in at the onset of any potential problem. I do not hesitate to correct or precorrect low-level misbehavior because I know that frequent low-level misbehavior negatively affects the overall climate of the setting and increases the probability of more severe misbehavior.

Connect

_____ 13. I always intentionally meet students in a welcoming and positive manner as they enter the setting—I am positive, I smile, and I call students by name.

_____ 14. I seek out students who might be isolated, interact with them, and gently encourage them to get involved with other students.

_____ 15. I give students specific, descriptive praise that is age appropriate, and students can tell that I am sincere.

_____ 16. I strive for a ratio of at least 3:1 positive to corrective interactions with every student I supervise. In general, I make a point of being more positive than corrective when interacting with students, particularly with students who have difficulty in the area.

Correct

_____ 17. I use an instructional approach when I correct misbehavior; I state the rule for the student, then, if appropriate, I have the student tell me the rule or demonstrate the correct behavior.

_____ 18. I correct student misbehavior consistently from student to student and from day to day.

_____ 19. I always respond to student misbehavior as unemotionally as possible.

_____ 20. I correct misbehavior in a way that avoids publicly humiliating students.

_____ 21. I am aware of and use a variety of productive corrections for different instances of student misbehavior.

_____ 22. I always use a professional tone with students, and I always use a supportive stance (off to one side, not directly in front) when I talk to individual students.

_____ 23. I try to prevent student noncompliance by providing clear and effective directions.

_____ 24. I respond thoughtfully when students fail to follow directions. I choose corrections and responses based on the circumstances, and I use the mildest correction or response that reasonably fits the misbehavior.

Supervisory Skills Checklist (p. 3 of 4)

Reflect

_____ 25. I understand the concept of continuous improvement, and at least once per month I reflect on things I am doing well and things I could improve in my role as supervisor.

_____ 26. I am reflective about my stylistic tendencies, and I strive to build on strengths and modify weaknesses.

Reflect on Your Personality Style (most people's personalities are a mix of styles):

- **Assertive**

Strength: An assertive person tends to be very direct—which is good, because students need clear information about what is acceptable and not acceptable.

Possible Weakness: Assertive people might come on too strong or intimidate some of the shyer students. They might engage in power struggles with students or even display borderline aggressive behavior.

- **Businesslike**

Strength: Businesslike people tend to initiate interactions confidently and are likely to be very direct, clear, consistent, and calm with students.

Possible Weakness: People with a businesslike style might be perceived as too aloof with young children. Some students may mistake a businesslike manner to mean that the adult does not care or is not interested in them.

- **Quiet**

Strength: Quiet people are likely to be unemotional in their response to misbehavior. Students are not likely to be able to press their buttons or escalate their emotions.

Possible Weakness: Quiet people might not appear assertive enough for students to take seriously. They might even need to raise their voices slightly when correcting misbehavior. Some students might mistake a quiet manner to mean that the person doesn't care or isn't interested in them.

- **Nurturing**

Strength: A nurturing person is likely to build relationships naturally with students, making them feel valued and cared for, and is likely to be very tolerant of individual differences and supportive of students others do not like.

Possible Weakness: Nurturing people might be so protective of some students that they avoid being firm, enforcing the rules, and providing consistent consequences. These people need to use a slightly different tone of voice when correcting misbehavior so students know they are serious about problem behavior.

_____ 27. At lease twice per year, I make an appointment with my supervisor and ask for feedback on things I can do to be more effective as a supervisor. (*Note:* If your job automatically structures regular performance reviews, you might not need to ask for an appointment.)

 This form can be printed from the Module B CD.

Supervisory Skills Checklist (p. 4 of 4)

STRENGTHS (effective practices I want to applaud):

GOALS (supervisory techniques I want to improve):

TASK 1

Protect students

The responsibilities of common area supervisors include protecting students (and staff) from safety concerns. Two staff behaviors that will ensure effective supervision are *be there* and *be aware*.

1. I am always on time for my supervisory responsibility (Form B-08, p. 1).

   Be on time. If you are assigned to supervise, be in the common area ready to work before students arrive. If you have a scheduling conflict, be sure to resolve it well before your supervisory assignment begins. If you are late or miss the assignment entirely, other supervisors will have to cover for you and the overall supervision of the area will be compromised. You might also create a safety liability for the school.

2. I know which zones or areas I am responsible for supervising, and I know the layouts, problem areas, and purposes of the zones or areas (Form B-08, p. 1).

   Be in the right place physically. Coordinate assignments with other supervisors. For example, in the cafeteria, supervisors might be assigned to specific jobs, such as greeting students as they enter, monitoring the lines, and circulating among certain groups of tables. Know your assigned station.

   Spend more time in known trouble spots. If fights tend to occur near a soccer field, for example, be sure to circulate through that area often. See "In the Zone."

   Be in the right place mentally. Look and act alert and interact with students. Create a *presence*. If you are supervising the hallway, but at the same time you are

---

In the Zone

For playgrounds, high school courtyards, and other large, complex settings, we recommend that you and your supervisors develop maps of the settings that denote supervisory zones and known trouble spots. The areas do not need to be the same size; known trouble zones may be smaller in physical size, for example. Distribute the maps to all appropriate supervisors so they have the same detailed information and can operate on the same wavelength. (See Module B, Presentation 2 for more information.)

grading papers with your head down instead of observing and interacting with students—well, you are *not* a presence. Engage the students. Exude confidence and friendliness.

3. I am prepared to handle emergencies, and I know how to work with and support other supervisors. I leave the area I am supervising only to deal with an emergency and only after I have told another adult. If I am the only adult on duty, I know the backup systems for getting assistance (Form B-08, p. 1).

   Be supportive of other supervisors. If you see another supervisor in a potentially troublesome situation, move toward that area. You don't necessarily have to interfere, but your presence will tell students that staff are a united front in managing misbehavior. You can also serve as a witness to any incident that might occur.

   Be willing to investigate or ask for help with any safety or emergency situations. For example, as a supervisor you are obligated to do something about a stranger on the playground. If you don't feel comfortable approaching the person, call the office or another supervisor so that the situation is investigated appropriately.

   Be knowledgeable about the procedures (main and backup systems) for requesting help.

*E*xample From the Field

I was visiting an elementary school and wearing a visitor's badge that I received at the office. As I walked down the hallway, I was carrying some papers that obscured the badge. A teacher who was escorting her students saw me. As she came closer, she veered toward me, peeked over the papers to see my badge, and said, "Oh, I just wanted to check that you have a visitor's badge. It's great to have you in our school. We just always want to make sure that visitors have checked into the office. Hope you have a really great day!" Then she proceeded down the hallway with her students. I was so impressed with this interaction. It told me that this staff knew how to be friendly, respectful, and inviting while at the same time totally committed to the safety of their students.   —R.S.

4. As much as possible, I continuously move throughout the area I supervise. I move intentionally and monitor my movements so that students cannot detect a pattern. I move through all sections of my assigned area, regardless of the surface in that area (mud, bark mulch, gravel, etc.) (Form B-08, p. 1).

Circulate unpredictably throughout your assigned area. Restrooms in particular should be checked at random times.

One elementary school we worked with had a problem with the boys' restrooms—the students splashed water, threw paper towels, wrote on the walls, and so on. The staff were mostly female, so they were reluctant to enter the boys' restrooms unannounced. Finally they established a procedure where a staff member stood outside the restroom and listened. If she heard giggling or noises that suggested the boys were making a mess, she would announce, "On three, I'm coming in. One . . . two . . . three." This simple procedure created enough supervision that the problem was largely solved.

On playgrounds, supervisors are sometimes reluctant to circulate because of the uneven terrain or wet conditions. In the wet Pacific Northwest, for example, students are often on the playground even in mist or light rain, and an all-too-common sight is supervisors huddled together talking under a covered area instead of circulating through their respective zones. Prepare for all conditions with appropriate footwear and outerwear.

5. I visually scan the area continuously, and I listen for unusual sounds and changes in noise level. I purposefully observe all students in the entire area; I don't observe only a portion of the area or look in only one direction (Form B-08, p. 1).

Visual scanning. Your eyes are continually sweeping the setting—primarily your assigned area, but occasionally other supervisors' areas as well. No other situation should gain your undivided attention. If someone wants to talk to you, scan your area first, then briefly engage with the person, with the "eyes in the back of your head" still on duty.

Scan known trouble spots often, and pay attention to unusual crowds of students. Be alert for subtle signs that trouble is brewing—a student's furtive glance from a group might mean that the students are in possession of something they shouldn't have or are planning something they shouldn't do. Walk over to the group and say, "How are you doing today, gentlemen? It's good to see you." Your presence alone can reduce the probability that any improper activities will continue.

Work the line. Waiting in lines is boring and provides students with ample opportunities for misbehavior. But if an adult interacts positively with the students, is alert for line cutting and other potential conflicts, and generally creates a diversion for the students, misbehavior can be kept to a minimum.

Listen. Be sensitive to unusual sounds in the setting or situation. If students are suddenly too quiet, too noisy, or gradually become more noisy, investigate the cause of the change.

6. When interacting with a student (when correcting misbehavior, for example), I am careful to position the student so that I can continue to effectively supervise—that is, so that the student's back is to the group and I am facing the group (Form B-08, p. 1).

   This positioning also keeps the misbehaving student from making eye contact with other students. Stand slightly sideways (not face to face) to the student and try to be relaxed and positive instead of tense and negative.

7. I never allow other adults to usurp my time when I am on my way to my assignment or while I am supervising (Form B-08, p. 1).

   If another adult stops to talk with you and you don't have any spare time, just explain that you need to get to your assignment on time or continue supervising.

*E*xample From the Field

At a school where I had spent quite a bit of time training the supervisors in *Foundations*, I visited the playground and began to chat with the supervisor on duty. After a couple of minutes, the supervisor said, "Please excuse me, Dr. Sprick, I don't mean to be rude, but I can't stand here and talk with you. You taught me better—I've got to circulate!"   —R.S.

Task 1 Action Steps

Reflect on the strengths and skills you can improve in the **Protect** category. Rate each item from 1 through 7 on the Supervisory Skills Checklist (Form B-08) as follows:

- 3 means you consistently do it without even thinking about it.
- 2 means you do it most of the time, but there is room for improvement.
- 1 means you need to be more conscientious about implementing it.

TASK 2

Expect responsible student behavior

In this task, we describe the importance of understanding and communicating the expectations and intervening early with misbehavior.

8. I know the rules, procedures, and basic civilities students are expected to use when entering the setting, while in the setting, and when leaving the setting (Form B-08, p. 1).

Effective supervisors understand in detail the behavioral expectations for students in any given setting (see "What's the Difference Between Rules, Procedures, and Expectations?" on the next page). If you are supervising the cafeteria, for example, you need to know how students are expected to enter the area, stand in line, get their food, interact with the cashier, find a seat, and interact with their tablemates. You also need to know the broader expectations for how students are to treat other students and staff (how to respond to corrections, for example), the school dress code, and so on. You need to know all these expectations so you know what behaviors to correct.

In some high schools, supervisors have given up asking students whether they have hall passes because many teachers don't bother to use them. Those schools would benefit greatly from clarifying the hall pass procedure with every staff member and getting everyone's commitment to follow the same procedure. All adults would then present a united front to students, the supervisors could confidently take the appropriate actions with students who don't have hall passes, and only those students with legitimate reasons would be in the hallways.

Dress code is another example of an expectation that needs consistent understanding and enforcement across supervisors. All staff should periodically discuss, as a group, how the dress code is currently being interpreted. If students begin coming to school with green hair, staff need to know whether that is a violation. If one staff member does nothing and another sends students to the office, the dress code expectations are not clear enough. This concept holds true for ID badges, cell phones, and other schoolwide policies.

Another category of behavior that can be particularly difficult at the secondary level is intimacy between students. Staff may feel uncomfortable discussing the issue, but you have to clarify these expectations. What are appropriate displays of affection? What are inappropriate displays? Again, the supervisors need to be able to represent a united front about what is and is not acceptable behavior in your school.

What's the Difference Between Rules, Procedures, and Expectations?

We sometimes use these terms interchangeably, but to be precise, *rule* refers to general statements such as "No food in the auditorium," "Walk, don't run, in the hallways," and "Sit and stay in your assigned seat on the bus." *Procedure* refers to instructional statements such as "Pick up a single tray, one fork and one spoon, and go through the serving line in single file" and "When the bell rings, wait for your table to be dismissed, then walk to the exit." We use the term *expectations* to encompass both rules and procedures and to imply that students need to be taught and should understand that they are *expected* to follow all the rules and procedures.

To use a driving metaphor, the Guidelines for Success are like the big-picture rules of the road, such as "Drive safely" and "Be aware of traffic around you." Driving *rules* include "Make a full stop at stop signs," "Wear your seat belt," and "Don't pass when climbing a hill." *Procedure* means the actions the driver must take to accomplish her task, such as turning the key to start the car, shifting gears as the car picks up speed, and moving at an appropriate speed when in heavy traffic. The expectations include all the guidelines, rules, and procedures, and the driver must know and follow all the expectations to reach her destination safely.

In general, avoid assigning harsh consequences for students' procedural errors, especially if they are unintentional, because it may jeopardize your relationships with the students. Instead, provide gentle reminders of the proper procedures, particularly at the beginning of the year when students are still learning what they are expected to do in many different settings.

9. I am prepared to enforce all of the behavioral expectations for students in the setting (Form B-08, p. 1).

Your role as supervisor is vital to the school's efforts to establish and enforce consistency. So for every expectation, you need to be ready to provide positive feedback to students when they are doing well and to step in to correct when they make errors. Even if you don't care about a particular rule or procedure, you must enforce it because the students need consistency. If you don't, you might be setting up students and your fellow supervisors for a problem—"Mrs. Jorgensen doesn't make us do that!"

You should also know the language others in the school use to correct expectations. For example, one *Foundations* school has staff uniformly use the phrase "Please follow Fletcher's policy of . . ." In secondary schools, you might need to correct public displays of affection. Ask your supervisor if the school has common language for such difficult situations. When students hear a correction they've learned to respect, it will mean more to them. A secondary school principal who is an avid fisherman came up with a great line that his staff can use to break up public displays of affection—"catch and release!"

The skill of enforcing expectations includes actively communicating high expectations for student behavior throughout the time you are supervising common areas. In every interaction with students, your actions and your tone of voice should say, "I know you're a responsible person and I know we're going to get along."

10. I intentionally seek out students who have difficulty in the setting within the first 5 minutes. I positively connect with each of these students by smiling, making a positive comment, and/or briefly talking about something that interests the student (Form B-08, p. 1).

Effective supervisors intervene early to address low-level misbehavior. We emphasize being positive with students, but that does not mean you should ignore behaviors such as disrespect. Don't let students get away with low-level misbehaviors—always *do something*.

Interact positively with potential (known) troublemakers early in the recess or lunch period. Approaching a student and offering a friendly greeting accomplishes two things: First, it demonstrates to the student that adults are present and they see him. Second, it communicates to him that he does not need to misbehave to be noticed and valued—he is valued just because he is an important part of the school. This strategy is especially valuable with a student that you have previously corrected, because it shows that you do not hold a grudge and that you notice his positive behavior, not just the misbehavior you corrected the day before.

The interaction must be positive and communicate high expectations, however. For example, say: "Hi, Michael. It's good to see you. How did the soccer game go? Have a great day. Let me know if you need anything."

Don't say: "Michael, I don't want any trouble from you today, do you understand? We had problems yesterday and I am not going to put up with any more shenanigans today."

The second example communicates low expectations and invites defiance. The first example offers support and tells the student that no matter what problems you two have had in the past, the student deserves a fresh start each day.

11. I move close to students who are beginning to have difficulties, and I stay longer in problem areas so that students are aware that I am monitoring (Form B-08, p. 1).

   Continually listen, scan, and circulate through the area so you can spot problems that are just beginning. Proximity management (moving closer to the problem students) is very effective for nipping misbehavior in the bud. If a particular section of your zone tends to be problematic, spend more time there—you might even circle back around after starting toward another section.

12. I step in at the onset of any potential problem. I do not hesitate to correct or precorrect low-level misbehavior because I know that frequent low-level misbehavior negatively affects the overall climate of the setting and increases the probability of more severe misbehavior (Form B-08, p. 2).

   Foundations emphasizes being positive with students, but that does not mean that you should ignore misbehaviors such as disrespect. Don't let students get away with low-level misbehaviors—always DO SOMETHING. Responding *in some way* is more important than *how* you respond.

Task 2 Action Steps & Evidence of Implementation

Action Steps	Evidence of Implementation
Reflect on the strengths and skills you can improve in relation to the **Expect** category of skills. Rate Supervisory Skills Checklist Items 8–12 (Form B-08) as follows: • 3 means you consistently do it without even thinking about it. • 2 means you do it most of the time, but there is room for improvement. • 1 means you need to be more conscientious about implementing it.	Interviews with staff

TASK 3

Connect with students

School climate is not set by the color of the walls, the number of windows, or the size of the gymnasium—it is created by the actions and personalities of the adults and how they interact and connect with the students. The staff who work the common areas are a big part of setting a positive tone. Are they warm, friendly, and inviting, or are they cold and hostile? Chances are the overall schoolwide climate is, at least in part, a reflection of the demeanor of the supervisory staff.

In Task 3, we explain three variables that work together to create a positive school climate: noncontingent attention, positive feedback, and the 3:1 ratio of interactions.

13. I always intentionally meet students in a welcoming and positive manner as they enter the setting—I am positive, I smile, and I call students by name (Form B-08, p. 2).

Effective supervisors provide all students with noncontingent acknowledgment; that is, they interact with students not just because the students are behaving well, but because they are fellow human beings who deserve to be treated with respect. You can provide noncontingent attention with:

* Nonverbal greetings, such as eye contact and smiles.
* Verbal greetings. Address students by their names and show an interest in them (without being too nosy or personal), but avoid being overly friendly or hyping things up.

*E*xample From the Field

A teacher who was attending one of my workshops thoughtfully recalled one of her own high school experiences that relates to noncontingent attention. She went to a large high school with 3,200 11th and 12th graders. She was very surprised when, during the first week of her first year at the school, the campus police officer greeted her by name. She learned that over the summer this officer studied the yearbook from the feeder school and learned all the incoming juniors' names and faces. By the second week of school, he knew every student and greeted everyone by name. The teacher said that the actions of this very significant staff member made her feel recognized and important at a huge school where it was so easy to feel lost. At graduation, the teacher's class presented a special award to the police officer who had affected each student so positively.   —R.S.

People feel more connected to places where their names are known. As much as possible, learn students' names and use their names when you are talking with them. This technique is very powerful for getting people on your side (as any salesperson will tell you). If you have trouble pronouncing or remembering names from languages you do not speak, keep trying. Students appreciate the effort.

Example From the Field

Martha was a beloved cafeteria supervisor at my kids' school years ago. I learned the line, "You were absent yesterday, and I missed you," from her. My son, who was in first grade, came home from school after being absent the previous day. When I asked about his day, he said, "It was good. Martha said something interesting to me. She said, 'Matt, you were absent yesterday, and I missed you. It's good to have you back.'" I thought that was a really nice gesture from a staff member to a little first grader, and I filed it away in my memory as a one-time occurrence. Matt wasn't absent again during the next few years.

Three years later, my daughter (a first grader) came home from school after being absent the previous day. I asked about her day, and she said, "Martha said to me, 'Jessica, you were absent yesterday, and the school was not as good a place without you. It's good to have you back.'"

Well, it hit me that Martha was on to something. Kids remembered her words. She made them feel important and valued. The next time I saw Martha, I thanked her and asked how she kept track of the absences. (The school had about 550 students at the time.) She explained that she also worked in the office, so at the end of the day she copied the absentee list and put it on the clipboard she carried in the cafeteria and on the playground. She knew many of the students by name, and if a name on the list wasn't familiar to her, she tried to learn who the child was. Then she looked for the children during recess or lunch and told them: "I missed you. The school was not as good a place without you. It's good to have you back."
                                                                            —R.S.

Think about using this technique. Sometimes you may have to lie, but it is a very reasonable lie. A few simple—and perhaps unexpected—words can make a student feel like an important part of the school.

You will probably encounter some students who are unresponsive to your attention—they remain silent and offer no eye contact for weeks or months. Persist with these students. Remember that you are the adult, and it's your responsibility to provide and model friendly, respectful behavior for every student.

14. I seek out students who might be isolated, interact with them, and gently encourage them to get involved with other students (Form B-08, p. 2).

    Greet and chat with students who seem to have no social peers and gently encourage them to get involved in activities around them. Don't let them become clingy, however. If a student's isolation concerns you, tell your supervisor or school counselor.

15. I give students specific, descriptive praise that is age appropriate, and students can tell that I am sincere (Form B-08, p. 2).

    Effective supervisors provide positive feedback to students when they are meeting expectations. "Good job putting the dodgeballs away." "Thanks for turning in your homework on time every day this week." "You are setting a good example for other students by waiting in line quietly."

    Effective positive feedback is:

    - **Quick.** A compliment that goes on too long can be embarrassing.

    - **Specific.** Tell students exactly what they've done right.

    - **Contingent.** Don't make a big deal out of an ordinary action or behavior. Kids, especially secondary students, will see right through a compliment for, say, walking down the hallway. (Although if walking down the hallway is a vast improvement over the student's usual hallway behavior, the compliment means something.)

    - **Age appropriate.** You might praise a first grader for asking to go to the restroom, but such praise would be inappropriate and highly embarrassing to a secondary student.

    - **Reasonably private.** Students might be embarrassed by public praise and your efforts might backfire.

16. I strive for a ratio of at least 3:1 positive to corrective interactions with every student I supervise. In general, I make a point of being more positive than corrective when interacting with students, particularly with students who have difficulty in the area (Form B-08, p. 2).

    Effective supervisors also strive for a 3:1 ratio of positive interactions with every student. For every corrective interaction (response to misbehavior), they provide at least three positive interactions (noncontingent attention or positive feedback for appropriate behavior).

The Criticism Trap. In 1971, Dr. Wes Becker wrote about studies he had conducted with teachers who were reprimanding and reminding students about out-of-seat behavior during work periods. He encouraged the teachers to reprimand students more immediately and more consistently. The teachers assumed this would decrease the behavior. In fact, the number of students getting out of their seats at the wrong times actually increased.

Dr. Becker called this phenomenon the *Criticism Trap.* Although the teachers thought they were doing something effective, the students, who were starved for attention, were getting out of their seats at least in part to get their teachers to look at them and talk to them. The students' need for attention was satisfied when their teachers told them to get back in their seats—and typically they did sit down, at least initially. When students took their seats, the teachers were reinforced for reprimanding. But soon the students realized, consciously or unconsciously, that they were not getting attention when they did what the teachers wanted, so they left their seats again. The teachers reprimanded again, giving the desired attention, and the students were again reinforced for getting out of their seats.

In this scenario, all parties involved get what they want in the short run. However, if this destructive pattern is allowed to continue, no one gets what he or she wants in the long run. Over time, students behave less and less responsibly, and the teacher gets more frustrated and more negative. The only real way out of the Criticism Trap is to have more interactions with students when they are behaving responsibly than when they are misbehaving.

In Presentation 5, we discuss correcting misbehavior. No matter how well you protect, expect, and connect, there will be misbehavior. However, effective protect, expect, and connect skills can reduce the amount of correction that you have to do and will make your job more pleasant and satisfying.

Task 3 Action Steps

1. Complete the **Connect** section of the Supervisory Skills Checklist (Form B-08) by rating Items 13–16 as follows:
   - 3 means you consistently do it without even thinking about it.
   - 2 means you do it most of the time, but there is room for improvement.
   - 1 means you need to be more conscientious about implementing it.

2. Before going on to the next presentation, set some goals for improving your protect, expect, and connect skills. Privately, ask you supervisor for feedback.

Effective Supervision, Part 2: Correct and Reflect

Presentations 4 and 5 are designed for paraprofessionals who supervise common areas. Presentation 6 is similar to 4 and 5, but it is designed for the professional staff and focuses on supervising settings such as hallways. With any staff group, use either Presentations 4 and 5 *or* Presentation 6, but not all three.

INTRODUCTION

In the previous presentation, you learned about three elements of effective supervision practices—**protect, expect**, and **connect**. This presentation is about the fourth and fifth elements—**correct** and **reflect**.

Even when proactive strategies are implemented well, inevitably some students still misbehave. It's human nature to break rules and test limits. Adults are susceptible, too. If a police officer isn't immediately visible, most of us drive faster than the speed limit even though we know what the expectation is and can see the posted rules about speed. Students will make errors, but if you know how to handle those errors, your job will be less stressful. With proper correction strategies, you can help to change student behavior, which in turn leads to less misbehavior to correct.

The focus of the first three tasks in this presentation is the essential supervision skill **correct**—how to respond effectively to student misbehavior. The last task is about **reflecting** on how you can continually improve your skills.

Task 1: Correct Misbehavior Fluently—Briefly, Consistently, Calmly, and Respectfully explains how and why to use the four essential qualities of effective correction.

Task 2: Use Productive Corrections describes a range of responses you can use when students misbehave and then discusses how to choose one.

Task 3: Prevent Noncompliance provides techniques for giving directions that convey an assumption of compliance. It also suggests steps to take when students do not comply.

Task 4: Reflect on Your Strengths and Potential Weaknesses encourages you to look at your supervisory style and continue to strive to model appropriate behavior for—and inspire—all students.

Each supervisor working through this presentation should have a copy of the Supervisory Skills Checklist, Figure 5a on the next page (Form B-08), and complete each section as he or she works through the corresponding section in the presentation. You do not have to turn the checklist in to anyone—it is purely an exercise in reflecting on your own skills.

> The numbered items within each task correspond to items on the Supervisory Skills Checklist.

Figure 5a   *Supervisory Skills Checklist (Form B-08)*

Supervisory Skills Checklist (p. 1 of 4)

Setting: _____

Directions: Rate the items using the 3-point scale at right. Use your ratings to fill out the Strengths and Goals sections at the end of the checklist. (This checklist is for your own self-reflection and goal setting. You do not need to share it or turn it in.)

| 3 = Always |
| 2 = Most of the time |
| 1 = Need to improve |

Protect

____ 1. I am always on time for my supervisory responsibility.

____ 2. I know which zones or areas I am responsible for supervising, and I know the layouts, problem areas, and purposes of the zones or areas.

____ 3. I am prepared to handle emergencies, and I know how to work with and support other supervisors. I leave the area I am supervising only to deal with an emergency and only after I have told another adult. If I am the only adult on duty, I know the backup systems for getting assistance.

____ 4. As much as possible, I continuously move throughout the area I supervise. I move intentionally and monitor my movements so that students cannot detect a pattern. I move through all sections of my assigned area, regardless of the surface (mud, bark mulch, gravel, etc.).

____ 5. I visually scan the area continuously, and I listen for unusual sounds and changes in noise level. I purposefully observe all students in the entire area; I don't observe only a portion of the area or look in only one direction.

____ 6. When interacting with a student (when correcting misbehavior, for example), I am careful to position the student so that I can continue to effectively supervise—that is, so that the student's back is to the group and I am facing the group.

____ 7. I never allow other adults to usurp my time when I am on my way to my assignment or while I am supervising.

Expect

____ 8. I know the rules, procedures, and basic civilities students are expected to use when entering the setting, while in the setting, and when leaving the setting.

____ 9. I am prepared to enforce all of the behavioral expectations for students in the setting.

____ 10. Within the first 5 minutes, I intentionally seek out students who have difficulty in the setting. I positively connect with each of these students by smiling, making a positive comment, and/or briefly talking about something that interests the student.

____ 11. I move close to students who are beginning to have difficulties, and I stay longer in problem areas so that students are aware that I am monitoring.

Supervisory Skills Checklist (p. 2 of 4)

____ 12. I step in at the onset of any potential problem. I do not hesitate to correct or precorrect low-level misbehavior because I know that frequent low-level misbehavior negatively affects the overall climate of the setting and increases the probability of more severe misbehavior.

Connect

____ 13. I always intentionally meet students in a welcoming and positive manner as they enter the setting—I am positive, I smile, and I call students by name.

____ 14. I seek out students who might be isolated, interact with them, and gently encourage them to get involved with other students.

____ 15. I give students specific, descriptive praise that is age appropriate, and students can tell that I am sincere.

____ 16. I strive for a ratio of at least 3:1 positive to corrective interactions with every student I supervise. In general, I make a point of being more positive than corrective when interacting with students, particularly with students who have difficulty in the area.

Correct

____ 17. I use an instructional approach when I correct misbehavior; I state the rule for the student, then, if appropriate, I have the student tell me the rule or demonstrate the correct behavior.

____ 18. I correct student misbehavior consistently from student to student and from day to day.

____ 19. I always respond to student misbehavior as unemotionally as possible.

____ 20. I correct misbehavior in a way that avoids publicly humiliating students.

____ 21. I am aware of and use a variety of productive corrections for different instances of student misbehavior.

____ 22. I always use a professional tone with students, and I always use a supportive stance (off to one side, not directly in front) when I talk to individual students.

____ 23. I try to prevent student noncompliance by providing clear and effective directions.

____ 24. I respond thoughtfully when students fail to follow directions. I choose corrections and responses based on the circumstances, and I use the mildest correction or response that reasonably fits the misbehavior.

Supervisory Skills Checklist (p. 3 of 4)

Reflect

____ 25. I understand the concept of continuous improvement, and at least once per month I reflect on things I am doing well and things I could improve in my role as supervisor.

____ 26. I am reflective about my stylistic tendencies, and I strive to build on strengths and modify weaknesses.

Reflect on Your Personality Style (most people's personalities are a mix of styles):

- **Assertive**

    Strength: An assertive person tends to be very direct—which is good, because students need clear information about what is acceptable and not acceptable.

    Possible Weakness: Assertive people might come on too strong or intimidate some of the shyer students. They might engage in power struggles with students or even display borderline aggressive behavior.

- **Businesslike**

    Strength: Businesslike people tend to initiate interactions confidently and are likely to be very direct, clear, consistent, and calm with students.

    Possible Weakness: People with a businesslike style might be perceived as too aloof with young children. Some students may mistake a businesslike manner to mean that the adult does not care or is not interested in them.

- **Quiet**

    Strength: Quiet people are likely to be unemotional in their response to misbehavior. Students are not likely to be able to press their buttons or escalate their emotions.

    Possible Weakness: Quiet people might not appear assertive enough for students to take seriously. They might even need to raise their voices slightly when correcting misbehavior. Some students might mistake a quiet manner to mean that the person doesn't care or isn't interested in them.

- **Nurturing**

    Strength: A nurturing person is likely to build relationships naturally with students, making them feel valued and cared for, and is likely to be very tolerant of individual differences and supportive of students others do not like.

    Possible Weakness: Nurturing people might be so protective of some students that they avoid being firm, enforcing the rules, and providing consistent consequences. These people need to use a slightly different tone of voice when correcting misbehavior so students know they are serious about problem behavior.

____ 27. At lease twice per year, I make an appointment with my supervisor and ask for feedback on things I can do to be more effective as a supervisor. (*Note:* If your job automatically structures regular performance reviews, you might not need to ask for an appointment.)

Supervisory Skills Checklist (p. 4 of 4)

STRENGTHS (effective practices I want to applaud):

GOALS (supervisory techniques I want to improve):

 This form can be printed from the Module B CD.

TASK 1

Correct misbehavior fluently: briefly, consistently, calmly, and respectfully

Task 1 explains how and why to use the four essential qualities of effective, fluent correction. *Briefly* is the first and, of course, means "don't talk too much." Students should have been taught the expectations, so just refer to what they've been taught. We give you advice on how to be brief, yet effective, in Task 2.

17. I use an instructional approach when I correct misbehavior: I state the rule for the student, then, if appropriate, I have the student tell me the rule or demonstrate the correct behavior (Form B-08, p. 2).

    Just telling the student what she is doing wrong won't be nearly as effective as reminding her what she *should* be doing. For example, if you see a student swiveling around in her chair in the cafeteria and you say, "Stop that," the student might comply by stopping the swiveling but then begin another misbehavior. If you instead say, "Sasha, the rule is you must sit facing the opposite side of the table, with your legs and feet under the table," you are giving a specific positive reminder of the behavior expected for the circumstances. The student might have genuinely forgotten the expectation, especially if it is early in the school year or the student is young. Then, if you say, "Please show me you understand the expectation," you give the student a chance to demonstrate the expectation and—importantly—earn positive feedback from you. "Nice cafeteria behavior, Sasha."

18. I correct student misbehavior consistently from student to student and from day to day (Form B-08, p. 2).

    Effective supervisors correct misbehavior consistently. This means that they ensure that *every* observed misbehavior receives a response and that responses to similar misbehaviors are the same. Supervisors sometimes vary their responses from student to student or from day to day, and sometimes responses for similar misbehaviors vary from supervisor to supervisor. Unfortunately, these inconsistencies can creep into our repertoire of corrections.

    Student-to-student inconsistency. When you allow one student to run in the hallway without consequences and intervene with another student who exhibits the same behavior, you're almost guaranteed to hear the second student cry, "That's not fair!" When you are inconsistent in applying the rules from student to student, it's easy for students to assume you are discriminating unfairly, and the result can be hurt feelings, resentment toward you, escalating emotions, and so on.

Day-to-day inconsistency. Everyone has good days and bad days. Most people think that they are more impatient and inconsistent on their bad days, but it's worthwhile to examine your supervisory practices on good days, too. When you're relaxed, calm, and refreshed, a student running down the hallway might not bother you at all, and so you ignore it. But the degree to which a behavior bothers you is not the proper criterion for deciding whether to correct the student—if the student is breaking the rules, you need to intervene.

Supervisor-to-supervisor inconsistency. Imagine a bus loading area packed with waiting students. A supervisor is present, but she is busy grading papers and allows students to mill around chaotically. Only when a few students begin to push and shove one another does she interact with the students, telling them to stop their behavior. Fast-forward to the next week: A different supervisor is on duty, and this person is operating with the understanding that students are supposed to wait in lines. Students resist his efforts to follow procedures. Because the previous supervisor did not enforce any rules about waiting in lines, the students view the second supervisor as mean, uptight, angry, and maybe even incompetent as he attempts to enforce the expectations. The actions of the first supervisor put the second supervisor in an untenable position.

Why is correcting misbehavior consistently important?

- When you don't respond to misbehavior, you send a message that the expectation is not important.

- Engaging in misbehavior without getting caught is potentially very reinforcing to students.

- Inconsistent responses give students intermittent reinforcement—the most powerful kind of reinforcement. For some students, the reinforcement of getting away with misbehavior once vastly outweighs several instances when they are caught and corrected.

- Inconsistent responses can result in fairness issues.

So our tip for supervisors on how to correct consistently is: DO SOMETHING! Responding *in some way* is more important than *how* you respond. Ted Kulongoski (former governor of Oregon) said, "It is not the severity of the consequence that will change behavior, it is the certainty." We need to create that certainty with consistent correction practices.

19. I always respond to student misbehavior as unemotionally as possible (Form B-08, p. 2).

Effective supervisors correct misbehavior calmly, without emotion.

Why is correcting misbehavior calmly important?

- Emotional adult responses are inappropriate models for students. Harsh behavior modeled by an adult will often result in the same harsh behavior from the student.

- Emotional adult responses might escalate the emotional intensity of a misbehaving student. Adults usually know when and how to stop their own emotional escalations, but children and adolescents might not. In response to adults' emotions, students might escalate into behavior that calls for severe discipline, such as suspension.

- Emotional adult responses increase the likelihood of adult-student power struggles.

- Emotional adult responses are very reinforcing for some students.

The following tips can help supervisors correct calmly.

- Remind yourself, "I am the adult in this situation." Some students enjoy purposely angering adults. Avoid falling into their traps.

- Don't take the misbehavior or a student's response to your correction personally. Don't let students push your buttons.

- Take a few seconds to think before you respond.

- Consider the misbehavior a teaching opportunity. The student can learn that the misbehavior is not going to serve him well—it will be easier to just follow the expectations.

*E*xample From the Field

A veteran teacher who attended one of my training sessions told me this story. "I learned very early in my career about staying calm in both common areas and the classroom. My mother was also a teacher. Thirty-five years ago, I was getting on a bus to go to my first teaching job, and my mother told me, 'They can't get your goat if they don't know where it's tied.' I followed that advice with great success. The calmer you stay, the less information you give to kids about things you might take personally." —R.S.

20. I correct misbehavior in a way that avoids publicly humiliating students (Form B-08, p. 2).

Effective supervisors correct misbehavior respectfully. This means that you should respond in ways that afford students dignity and respect. Use respectful words, tone of voice, and body language. Never belittle or condescend to students. Phrases such as "What's wrong with you?" "Were you raised in a barn?" and "Use your head!" are hurtful to children, especially those who are insecure about their intelligence or family backgrounds. Avoid hurtful, disrespectful words by simply stating the rule or procedure the student should be following instead of making judgmental or critical statements.

Keep your responses as private as possible to avoid having an audience while you correct. Get the student's attention and quietly say, "I need to speak to you, please." When other students are around, go to the misbehaving student and explain that you need to speak to him or her. "Step over here with me, please."

Why is correcting misbehavior respectfully important?

Respectful adult responses model appropriate behavior for students, contribute to a positive school climate, and foster student cooperation and compliance. In addition, they allow students to save face in front of peers. Students might feel they need to react and act tough when they've been shamed or embarrassed in front of an audience.

 Treat people as if they were what they ought to be, and you help them to become what they are capable of being."

JOHANN WOLFGANG VON GOETHE (1749–1832), German author, scientist, and statesman

Task 1 Action Steps

Reflect on strengths and skills you can improve in the **Correct** category of skills. Rate Supervisory Skills Checklist Items 17–20 (Form B-08) as follows:

- 3 means you consistently do it without even thinking about it.
- 2 means you do it most of the time but have room for improvement.
- 1 means you need to be more conscientious about implementing it.

TASK 2

Use productive corrections

This task describes a range of responses you can use when students misbehave and discusses how to choose a response. Plan to discuss this menu with your supervisor or your representative on the Foundations Team.

21. I am aware of and use a variety of productive corrections for different instances of student misbehavior (Form B-08, p. 2).

    We've advised you to always *do something* to correct misbehavior—briefly, calmly, consistently, and respectfully. So what are your choices of actions to take?

    a) Effective supervisors have a menu of productive responses to student misbehavior that are appropriate for a variety of situations. The consequences listed on pages 123–128 are effective in common areas. They appear in order (more or less) from mild to severe.

    b) Effective supervisors choose corrections and responses based on the circumstances. Some tips include:

       Use the mildest correction or response that reasonably fits the misbehavior. The milder the response, the more likely you'll follow through with it. If you find yourself saying, "Stop that! I don't want to have to . . . ," you are being inconsistent.

       Gradually increase the severity level of the correction or response when a student misbehaves repeatedly. See "Increasing the Severity Level" below.

    Remember: DO SOMETHING! *What* you do is less important than just *doing something*. Students should always expect consistent responses to their misbehavior from school staff.

Increasing the Severity Level

Here's an example of how to gradually increase the severity of reprimands (see "Gentle verbal reminders and reprimands" on the next page).

Let's say I'm a hall supervisor. I'm standing in the middle of the hallway during a passing period, greeting and interacting with students. I see Tim running. Firmly and calmly, I give him a one-liner:

Tim, wait a minute. You need to walk in this school. Thanks.

Increasing the Severity Level (continued)

A few days later, I see Tim running in the hallway again. This time I deliver an instructional reprimand, remaining calm and respectful:

Tim, come here for a moment, please. I spoke to you a couple of days ago about running the hall. Now I want to give you information about why I—and any other adult in this school—will stop you if we see you running. Running in the hallways is not safe. There are lots of people in the halls and someone might get hurt. An adult will always stop you because we care about safety. OK. See you later.

A few days later, Tim is running in the hallways again. I change tack and use a bit of humor combined with a brief delay, but I'm still calm, consistent, and respectful:

Tim, I've told you before that you must walk in the hallways in this school. You'll actually get places faster if you walk! If you had been walking instead of running, you'd be way down to the cafeteria by now. But instead, you're stuck here talking to me. Any time you run, you're going to get stuck talking to an adult because we care about making the hallways safe for everyone.

Menu of Consequences and When and How to Use Them

☑ **Proximity management**
Use when time is short, the problem is minor, or you are unsure what else to do.

- Move near the student as you circulate.
- Don't make eye contact until after the student stops the misbehavior.
- Don't talk to the student or invade the student's personal space.

☑ **Gentle verbal reminders and reprimands**

- When you are physically close to the student (within about three or four feet), deliver the reminder calmly and slowly.
- Lower your voice and say the student's name.
- State the desired behavior.
- Keep the message brief.

- Don't ask the student if he was misbehaving. He'll probably say "no" and you'll begin to argue.
- Don't invade the student's personal space.
- Move away from the student a second or two before you finish the instruction. Pausing may invite an argumentative response.

Following are different types of reprimands along with suggestions about when to use them:

- **Quick reprimands,** or **one-liners,** are brief statements of the positive expectations. Use when time is short, the problem is minor, or you are not sure what else to do. (See "One-Liners: Staff Can Correct Consistently With Common Responses" on the next two pages.)

- **Instructional reprimands** are explanatory statements (may be longer than one-liners). Use when a student needs more information about or the rationale for an expectation.

- **Humorous reprimands** are disarming responses that avoid direct confrontation. Use when humor is a natural part of your interactions with students. Be sure you don't confuse humor with humiliation or ridicule, however. Never belittle, humiliate, or ridicule students.

- **Relationship reprimands** are brief responses based on established relationships between adults and students. Use when a student wants to do the right thing for *you*—the student thinks, "I need to behave because I don't want to disappoint Martha."

☑ Brief delay
Use when a student is en route somewhere.

- Tell the student, "Stay where you are and think about [the particular expectation]."
- Have the student stand and wait for no more than 10 to 20 seconds.

☑ Positive practice
Use when the misbehavior has a physical component.

- Have the student demonstrate the expected behavior. For example:

  "Go back and walk around the game."
  "Open your locker and close it the correct way, please."
  "Come back down and walk, don't run, up the stairs."

- Make sure the student's corrected behavior matches the expectations.

One-Liners: Staff Can Correct Consistently With Common Responses

One-liners are quick, practiced responses you can use to correct students, and they provide a great way to develop staff unity and a common language for correcting misbehavior. One-liners can keep you from becoming sidetracked or emotional. You can say a one-liner quickly as you walk past, for example, a student using bad language in the hallway and you don't have time to stop and discuss the behavior.

General one-liners:

- That's not OK. The expectation is to . . .
- Hands, feet, and objects to yourself.
- Voice levels are too loud. Bring them down, please.
- Take a timeout. When I come back, be ready to tell me what you need to do.
- Stand here next to me for 20 seconds.
- That behavior wouldn't be acceptable on the job. Please tone it down. (for inappropriate display of affection)
- That language is not acceptable here at school. (for swearing)

Hallway one-liners:

- Keep moving, please.
- Remember to walk in the hallways.
- It's time to go to class.
- Walk and talk.
- Class begins in 30 seconds.

Cafeteria one-liners:

- Pick up your tray and walk with me.
- Stand (or sit) here. I'll talk to you as soon as I can.
- Say "please" when you ask someone to pass something to you.
- Your food choices for today are . . . Please decide now.
- Clean your tray.
- Put your waste in the trash can.

One-Liners: Staff Can Correct Consistently With Common Responses (continued)

Recess one-liners:

- Tell (or show) me the right way to . . .
- This game is off limits for the remainder of recess.
- Take a timeout. When I get back, be ready to tell me what you need to do.
- Either play responsibly or move to another game.
- It looks like you're having fun, but you need to find something else to do.
- I'm glad you know the rules. I will monitor the situation. (for tattling)
- Stay away from him and stay closer to me so that I can monitor the situation. (for teasing)

Fletcher High School in Jacksonville, Florida, developed an effective one-liner that all staff use consistently. When staff see low-level misbehavior, they say to students, "Please honor Fletcher's policy of . . . " and insert the behavior—walking in the hallways, caps off inside the building, voice level 2 in the cafeteria, and so on.

A secondary school principal who is an avid fisherman came up with a great line that his staff can use to break up public displays of affection—"catch and release!"

☑ Restitution

Use when the student has done some obvious damage to property or another person's feelings.

- Identify an action the student can take that will "make it right."
- Have the student repair damage that he or she is responsible for—for example, pick up litter that he dropped or apologize to someone she harmed.
- Don't focus on assigning fault or blame.

Note: A student who must clean up a mess should use only soap and water—no chemicals.

☑ Notifying the student's teacher

Use when the behavior concerns you—it is very disrespectful, for example, or is chronic and growing worse.

- Notify the student's classroom or homeroom teacher so the teacher can use the situation as an opportunity to instruct the student in more appropriate ways to behave. (This can also demonstrate to the student that all staff are on the same page when it comes to expectations and consequences.)
- Don't notify the teacher for the purpose of having the teacher punish the student.

☑ Change in location

Use when the student's current location on the playground, cafeteria, or similar area might be a contributing factor to the misbehavior.

- Have the student move to a different location or operate within a restricted space. For example, move the student to a different table in the cafeteria or restrict the student to a limited area of the playground.
- The change in location sets the student up for more appropriate behavior that you should then positively reinforce.

☑ Stay with supervisor

Use when misbehavior occurs on the playground, cafeteria, bus loading area, and similar areas.

Students like independence. When a student exhibits repeated misbehavior, requiring the student to stay with you will likely be appropriately aversive to the student.

☑ Demerits

Use when mild, accumulative consequences will allow you to set up a more consistent policy. If you were to use harsher consequences, you might hesitate to assign them for every misbehavior.

- Assign one demerit for each instance of misbehavior. Demerits function as warnings.
- Tell the student that the demerits will accumulate, and after a certain number—three or four, for example—you will plan to notify the principal (in some schools this is referred to as a Level 2 Notification).

☑ Timeout at a set location

Use when the goal is to restrict the student's social interactions for a brief period. On the playground, for example, you might use a bench placed away from the play equipment; in the cafeteria, an empty table.

- Have the student go to an area of the setting that is separate from the main activity (but visible to supervisors). The goal is to restrict the student's social interactions for a brief period—1 or 2 minutes.
- Don't send several students at one time to the area—that just provides them with more social time.

☑ **Timeout at the place the infraction occurred**

Use when there are limited options for set timeout areas or if you have more than one or two students who need timeout.

Tell the students to stand where they are for a minute or two.

☑ **Behavior Improvement Form**

Use when a student is in timeout. This activity gives students a chance to reflect on their behavior, and it interrupts and distracts them from their misbehavior.

Have the student fill out one of these short forms. Figures 5b and 5c on pp. 129 and 130 show two versions of the Behavior Improvement Form.

☑ **Referral to a more intensive consequence**

- Write a Level 2 (moderate) notification* so the student is assigned detention or goes to the school's problem-solving room (for example).
- For dangerous, illegal, or out-of-control behavior, write a Level 3 (severe) referral* on the student so the student has to go to the principal's office.

Note: As part of the *Foundations* process, the Foundations Team and your administrator have defined the behaviors that warrant Level 2 and Level 3 consequences.

Task 2 Action Steps

Reflect on the strengths and skills you can improve in relation to the **Correct** category of skills. Rate Supervisory Skills Checklist Item 21 (Form B-08) as follows:

- 3 means you consistently do it without even thinking about it.
- 2 means you do it most of the time but have room for improvement.
- 1 means you need to be more conscientious about implementing it.

Figure 5b Behavior Improvement Form, Version 1 (B-09)

Behavior Improvement Form (Version 1)

Name: _Amar_   Date: _3/22_

Teacher: _Mrs. Delphia_   Period: _4_   Class: _Eng._

1. Describe the incident.

   Javier and I were fooling around and I poked him with my pencil and hurt him.

2. Describe your behavior during the incident.

   I was poking Javier because he was poking me when we were supposed to be reading.

3. How would the teacher describe your behavior during the incident?

   She would say I should ignore Javier and do my reading.

4. How could you have behaved in a different way?

   I could have kept on reading and not poked Javier when he poked me.

5. If this happens again, how do you plan to behave or respond?

   I will continue to read and ignore anyone who bothers me. If that doesn't work, I will move.

6. Are you willing to commit to making this effort?

   Yes

7. How can we help you be successful?

 This form can be printed from the Module B CD.

Behavior Improvement Form (Version 2)

Name: __LaRennah__   Grade/Class: __2__

Teacher: __Mr. Montoya__   Period/Time: __9:45__

1. What was your behavior?

    On the way to recess, I pushed Adam out of the way.

2. What could you do differently?

    I could let him go first.
    I could walk and not run to get to the playground.

3. Will you be able to do that?

    Yes, I can walk and not try to cut in front of people.

 This form can be printed from the Module B CD.

TASK 3

Prevent noncompliance

Task 3 provides techniques for giving directions that convey an assumption of compliance and suggests steps to take when students do not comply.

22. I always use a professional tone with students, and I always use a supportive stance (off to one side, not directly in front) when I talk to individual students (Form B-08, p. 2).

With body language and tone of voice, effective supervisors convey that they assume that students will follow directions.

- Have the student face out of the area so that you are watching the common area as you speak and can continue to supervise other students. This positioning also keeps the misbehaving student from making eye contact with other students.

- When speaking to the student, stand slightly sideways (not face to face) and try to be relaxed and positive instead of tense and negative.

- Go to the student—that is, don't give directions from a distance. Directions given from a distance are more likely to be ignored or challenged.

- Avoid having an audience. Give the student as much privacy as possible.

- Use body language that conveys calm and confidence. Keep your hands at your sides, in your pockets, or behind your back rather than on your hips or folded across your chest. Stand tall and move purposefully.

23. I try to prevent student noncompliance by providing clear and effective directions (Form B-08, p. 2).

Effective supervisors are careful to provide clear, specific directions to students. Following are some recommendations for giving directions.

- First, get the student's attention.

- Use clear and simple language.

  ◦ State the direction positively. Use *do* statements instead of *don't* statements. ("Walk in the hall," not "Don't run in the hall.")
  ◦ Don't frame the direction as a question. Saying, "Wouldn't you like to . . . ," invites the student to answer, "No."
  ◦ Be as brief as possible.

- Give only one or two directions at a time. Giving too many directions at once is more likely to lead to noncompliance.

- Give the student reasonable time to respond.

- Avoid staring down the student.

24. I respond thoughtfully when students fail to follow directions. I choose corrections and responses based on the circumstances, and I use the mildest correction or response that reasonably fits the misbehavior (Form B-08, p. 2).

Effective supervisors respond thoughtfully when students don't follow directions the first time. Try the following strategies:

- Use humor—but be careful to avoid sarcasm and ridicule. See "Hints for Using Humor" on the next page.

- Appeal to cooperation.

- Use the broken-record technique. Just keep repeating your direction in response to the student's objections or complaints.

- Offer the student a reasonable choice, when possible. Our colleague Mickey Garrison recounted a good example of offering a reasonable choice. As she escorted some students to the library, one of them insisted on bringing a cookie, but no food was allowed in the library. So Mickey told the student he had three choices. She said, "You can eat the cookie immediately, you can take it to your locker and leave it there, or you can give the cookie to me. But I have difficulty showing restraint with cookies—if you give it to me, I may eat it!"

- Let the student know what will happen if he or she does not follow the direction.

Following are some suggestions for what *not* to do:

- Don't argue with the student.

- Don't escalate the emotional intensity of the situation.

- Don't let the student get away with it.

- Don't physically try to make the student comply.

- Don't threaten the student with consequences, especially when you don't know whether you can follow through with them.

Hints for Using Humor

Humor can be a powerful and effective way to respond to misbehavior, especially with older students. Let's say a student makes a smart-aleck comment as the teacher is presenting a lesson. If the teacher is quick-witted enough, she might be able to respond to the student's comment in a way that makes the student laugh, and a tense moment will be diffused. The sensitive use of humor brings people closer together. Sarcasm or ridicule makes a student feel hostile and angry that you made a joke at his expense.

If you do use humor in response to a misbehavior, plan on talking to the student later to make sure he understands that his behavior was not acceptable and that he knows you expect him to behave more responsibly in the future. In addition, you can check to see that you did not embarrass the student with your humorous comment.

If students continue to ignore directions or walk away when directions are given, use the Jot It Down strategy. Recount aloud what happened as you write it down on a piece of paper. For example:

> *"Marika, this situation is very serious. I want to make sure I understand so I'm going to write everything down."*

> *Then relate the incident as you write. Because you are writing, your words will necessarily be measured. "I said, 'line up at the door,' and Marika said, 'I don't have to.'"*

The power of this strategy is that by taking the time to write down the incident, you break eye contact with the student and you give the student a moment to think. As you are writing, the student will probably comply with your direction.

If the student is still noncompliant, take the following steps.

- **Inform** the student that you will follow up on the matter, and make sure you do follow up.

- **Record** in detail what happened, in objective language.

- **Complete a referral form.** If you don't know the student's name, describe him or her. If the student has been in trouble before, the administrator in charge of discipline will probably know who he or she is from the description.

If the administrator doesn't know who the student is, the incident might be a one-time occurrence from a usually well-behaved child. Make sure you record and report any subsequent incidents in case a pattern of misbehavior is developing.

If the incident represents or becomes a pattern of misbehavior, discuss the situation (and share your records) with your immediate supervisor or Foundations Team representative (or both).

Task 3 Action Steps

Reflect on the strengths and skills you can improve in relation to the **Correct** category of skills. Rate Supervisory Skills Checklist Items 22–24 (Form B-08) as follows:

- 3 means you consistently do it without even thinking about it.
- 2 means you do it most of the time but have room for improvement.
- 1 means you need to be more conscientious about implementing it.

TASK 4

Reflect on your strengths and potential weaknesses

Task 4 encourages you to look at your supervisory style and continue to strive to model appropriate behavior for—and inspire—all students.

25. I understand the concept of continuous improvement, and at least once per month I reflect on things I am doing well and things I could improve in my role as supervisor (Form B-08, p. 3).

    Your role in the school is important. Teachers, administrators, and students depend on you to keep common areas safe and to set a positive climate for the school. You owe it to them to be good at your job this year and even better next year. The 1s and 2s on your Supervisory Skills Checklist will provide you with valuable information about the goals you can set for improvement.

26. I am reflective about my stylistic tendencies, and I strive to build on strengths and modify weaknesses (Form B-08, p. 3).

    For the purpose of self-reflection, we can define four basic personality styles: assertive, businesslike, quiet, and nurturing. Of course, most people's personalities are a mix of styles, and people are able to display different styles in different situations. Each style has its strengths and weaknesses when it comes to interacting with students. Think about your own style as you read through the following descriptions, and consider your strengths and potential weaknesses as you set your goals for continuous improvement.

Assertive

Strength: An assertive person tends to be very direct—which is good, because students need clear information about what is acceptable and not acceptable.

Possible Weakness: Assertive people might come on too strong or intimidate some of the shyer students. They might try so hard to get their point across that they engage in power struggles with students, leading some students to realize the entertainment value in pushing the assertive person's buttons. It's fine to be assertive, but this personality type should take care to avoid displaying aggressive behavior.

Businesslike

Strength: Businesslike people tend to initiate interactions confidently and are likely to be very direct, clear, consistent, and calm with students.

Possible Weakness: People with a businesslike style might be perceived as too aloof with young children. Some students may mistake a businesslike manner to mean that the adults do not care or are not interested in them. A businesslike person can ensure that every student feels valued by providing noncontingent attention such as greeting students by name and asking about their activities.

Quiet

Strength: Quiet people are likely to be unemotional in their response to misbehavior. Students probably cannot press their buttons or escalate their emotions.

Possible Weakness: Quiet people might not appear assertive enough for students to take seriously. They might even need to raise their voices slightly when correcting misbehavior. Some students might mistake a quiet manner to mean that the person doesn't care about or isn't interested in them. These personality types shouldn't let their quiet manner keep them from interacting with students. They can make every student feel valued by greeting students and using students' names.

Nurturing

Strength: A nurturing person is likely to build relationships naturally with students, making them feel valued and cared for, and is likely to be very tolerant of individual differences and supportive of students others do not like.

Possible Weakness: Nurturing people might be so protective of some students that they avoid being firm, enforcing the rules, and providing consistent consequences. These people need to use a slightly different tone of voice when correcting misbehavior so students know they are serious about problem behavior. The nurturing personality needs to remember that the most caring thing you can do for students is enforce rules and procedures consistently.

27. At lease twice per year, I make an appointment with my supervisor and ask for feedback on things I can do to be more effective as a supervisor (Form B-08, p. 3).

    Note: If your job automatically schedules regular performance reviews, you might not need to ask for an appointment.

    Ensure that your process of continuous improvement includes seeking recommendations and opinions from others on how to become an even better supervisor.

The Supervisory Skills Checklist ends with two areas where you can summarize your strengths—skills you do well—and your goals for improvement. Consider sharing these ideas with your supervisor.

Task 4 Action Steps

1. Reflect on the strengths and skills you can improve in relation to the **Correct** category of skills. Rate Supervisory Skills Checklist Items 25–27 (Form B-08):

   - 3 means you consistently do it without even thinking about it.
   - 2 means you do it most of the time but have room for improvement.
   - 1 means you need to be more conscientious about implementing it.

2. Set some goals for improvement and, if possible, discuss and share those goals with other supervisors.

3. Plan to complete the Supervisory Skills Checklist at least once per year. Plan to review *Foundations* Module B, Presentations 4 and 5 (either print or video) every year or every other year.

Supervising Common Areas and Schoolwide Policies—for All Staff

DOCUMENTS*

- Foundations Continuum of Behavior Support (B-14)
- The Art of Supervising Secondary School Hallways (B-31)

* All documents listed are available on the CD.

Presentations 4 and 5 are designed for paraprofessionals who supervise common areas. Presentation 6 is similar to 4 and 5, but it is designed for the professional staff and focuses on supervising settings such as hallways. With any staff group, use either Presentations 4 and 5 *or* Presentation 6, but not all three.

INTRODUCTION

This presentation is geared toward helping all staff members understand their roles and responsibilities in supervising common area settings and situations, such as hallways and arrival period, as well as enforcing schoolwide policies such as dress code and electronics use. The overall goal is staff unity, with everyone on the same page.

As a teacher, you play a vital role in establishing the culture and climate of the school both in your classroom and in the common areas. Teachers' responsibilities don't begin and end at the classroom door. The confidence, authority, and respect that you display in class should be with you as you walk the halls, work the dismissal period, oversee bus loading, and pass through the commons area. During any of these activities, you might be called on to enforce dress code policy, confiscate a smartphone, or intervene in a fight, as well as provide positive feedback or give a reward ticket to a student who is behaving responsibly.

Figure 6a shows a graphic representation of the continuum of positive behavior support available through *Safe & Civil Schools*. At the base of the triangle, supporting everything above it, are the processes of team leadership, the improvement cycle, and data collection and analyses—processes that unify the staff in continuous improvement. On the next layer up are common areas and schoolwide policies—the goal here is staff unity in managing and supervising those aspects of the school. This staff unity is essential for creating a positive school *culture*.

The culture of a school comprises the beliefs, values, and practices that staff communicate to students and families. Therefore, it is essential that *all* staff consistently communicate the *same* beliefs, values, and practices. The goal of this presentation is to assist staff in doing just that with all schoolwide policies and in all common area settings. Inconsistent implementation of any schoolwide policy or practice gives students very bad information about what is expected of them and about what the school believes to be important. For example, if only seven out of ten staff members enforce a dress code policy, the school would be better off having no dress code at all than to continually give mixed messages to students about the importance of following school policy. So school culture and climate is set by the daily collective behavior of the school staff.

The Foundations Team in your school has probably already completed the S and T portions of STOIC (Structure and Teach expectations). *Foundations* Module B, Presentation 2 provides information about structuring common areas and schoolwide policies for success. Module B, Presentation 3 provides information on designing and implementing lessons to teach students to be successful. All students need to be taught the expectations explicitly and to know that the expectations apply consistently to the whole school and every staff member. You should be able to say to any student, "I know you had a lesson on . . ."

Figure 6a *The Foundations continuum of behavior support (B-14)*

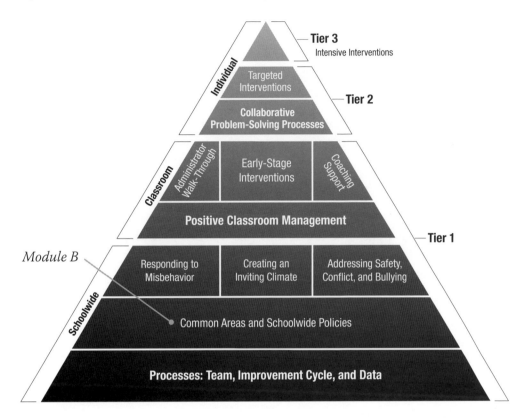

This presentation expands on the important supervisory skills represented by the O (Observe and supervise), I (Interact positively), and C (Correct fluently) in the STOIC acronym.

Why are excellent supervisory skills important?

The presence of adults in common areas prompts students to follow the rules. Think about your own behavior when you drive on a highway. Most of us follow the speed limit

> STOIC represents a framework for ensuring that common areas and schoolwide policies are addressed in comprehensive and cohesive ways. STOIC stands for:
>
> **S**tructure for success.
> **T**each expectations with clarity.
> **O**bserve and supervise.
> **I**nteract positively.
> **C**orrect fluently.

when we're supervised—when state troopers are visible or we know they could appear at any time. When authority figures are not visible, most of us push the limits. It's no different with students. And just as following the speed limit increases safety and civility for everyone on the road, student rule following increases safety and civility in school.

Another dynamic—beyond policing—is at work here as well. Kids with whom you've built relationships typically want to demonstrate their best behavior to you. This behavior is analogous to adults taking special care to clean their houses before company arrives. They clean not because they fear consequences assigned by authorities if they don't have a clean house, but because they want to put their best foot forward for people they respect and have a relationship with.

The presence of friendly, confident adults in a school environment also promotes an inviting school climate, a spirit of cooperation and camaraderie, and a sense of adult availability.

Over time, your administrator or Foundations Team will provide information about when, where, and how you are expected to assist with supervision and enforcement of each schoolwide policy and about your role in assisting with supervision of any common areas. Remember that staff unity and common language will create the daily climate, and the daily climate, over time, *is* the school culture.

What are common areas and schoolwide policies?

A *common area* is a school setting or situation in which students are supervised by a variety of different staff members or by one or more paraprofessionals. Examples of common area settings include:

- Hallways and restrooms
- Cafeterias
- Courtyards and commons (i.e., school locations where secondary-level students congregate during free periods)
- Playgrounds
- Buses (to and from school, loading and unloading areas)
- Outside entry areas before and after school
- Parking lots
- Classrooms that do not have dedicated supervisors—different teachers bring and supervise their own students. (e.g., computer labs)
- Front office

Common area *situations* are dependent on circumstances more than a particular location. A unified, consistent approach to supervision is still needed, however. Examples of common area situations include:

- Assemblies
- Behavior with substitute teachers
- Arrival
- Dismissal

Common area settings and situations that are under the direct and consistent supervision of a single certified staff member are *not* considered common areas:

- Classrooms
- Computer labs with certified computer lab teachers
- Library/media centers with certified library/media specialists

Note that although expectations within such classrooms should be under the control and supervision of the certified specialist, some limited schoolwide policies related to specialists can be beneficial. We address this topic in Module B, Presentation 2.

Schoolwide policies are not related to a particular area of the school; they include any policies or procedures that students are expected to follow in *all* school settings. Staff members need to enforce these policies consistently no matter where they are on the school campus. The following examples are schoolwide policies:

- Attendance
- Tardiness
- Cell phones and other electronics
- Dress code
- ID badges
- Appropriate language
- Bullying and harassment
- Elementary specialists (music, library, PE, art, and computer)

"The Art of Supervising Secondary School Hallways" (Figure 6b on the next page) brings together many of the concepts from this presentation and applies them to one common area every school has—hallways. You can use this document when training all staff who may be in the hallways with students—school resource officers, campus monitors, maintenance staff, paraprofessionals, and so on. This document is written for middle and high school hallways, but it can easily be adapted for elementary hallways. It can also be used as a guide for developing job descriptions for other common areas, such as the bus loading area. Copies of "The Art of Supervising Secondary School Hallways" (B-31) can be printed from the Module B CD.

The tasks in this presentation include:

Task 1: Observe (Supervise) Strategically describes the importance of knowing the expectations and being present, engaged, and aware.

Task 2: Interact Positively discusses how to establish a positive school climate by providing noncontingent attention and positive feedback, striving for a ratio of positive to corrective interactions of at least 3:1, and interacting positively with the most challenging students *before* they have a chance to misbehave.

Task 3: Correct Fluently explains the importance of correcting briefly, consistently, calmly, and respectfully, and provides a suggested menu of productive responses to misbehavior.

Figure 6b   *The Art of Supervising Secondary School Hallways (B-31)*

The Art of Supervising Secondary School Hallways

OBSERVE ACTIVELY

- Stand at your doorway for as much of the passing period as possible.
- If you have class following the passing period, stay close to your doorway so you can supervise both your classroom and the hallway outside your classroom.
- If you have preparation time following the passing period, circulate throughout your assigned area intentionally and somewhat unpredictably so that students cannot detect a pattern. Pay particular attention to blind corners and potential trouble spots.
- Listen and visually scan for unusual activity (for example, an increase or a decrease in noise level or a group of students looking around furtively). Move close to students who are beginning to have difficulties and stay longer in problem areas so students are aware that you are monitoring.
- If you ever feel unsafe in any area of the school or with any group of students, tell an administrator or a member of the Foundations Team immediately so more adults can be deployed to the area to monitor the students. If you feel unsafe, vulnerable students probably feel unsafe, too.

INTERACT POSITIVELY

- Greet students and staff members in a welcoming and positive manner. Smile and use their names in your greetings. Remember that your words and actions contribute greatly to setting the tone and climate of the school.
- Intentionally seek out any student you have corrected for misbehavior in the past. Positively connect with the student by smiling, making a positive comment, or initiating a brief conversation about something that interests the student. This connection demonstrates that you see the student as a person—you don't just see the misbehavior that you previously corrected.
- Provide specific, descriptive praise that is age appropriate. Thank students for following the rules.
- Your positive interactions (greetings, talking with students, and positive feedback) should be at least three times more frequent than corrective interactions (correcting misbehavior). Remember the 3:1 positive ratio.

CORRECT BRIEFLY, CONSISTENTLY, RESPECTFULLY, AND CALMLY

- Know all the general rules and enforce all the rules and policies consistently.
- Step in whenever you see a potential problem. If low-level misbehavior is not corrected, the lack of oversight affects the overall climate of the school and increases the probability of more severe misbehavior.
- Correct student misbehavior consistently, both from student to student and from day to day. Remember that you are often more likely to be inconsistent on your good days—you might let students get away with behavior that you do not let them get away with on your bad days. Inconsistent correction encourages students to test the limits.
- Use brief one-liner corrections whenever possible. For example, say, "Please honor [school name]'s policy about appropriate language." "Please honor [school name]'s policy about public displays of affection." "Remember, 'catch and release!'"
- If a one-liner correction is not sufficient and you need to speak with a student, position the student so that you can continue to effectively supervise while you are speaking to him or her—that is, the student's back faces most of the other students (so the student is not on display) and you can see most of the other students in the area.
- Respond to student misbehavior as unemotionally as possible.
- Avoid publicly humiliating students when you correct their behavior. Use humor sparingly, respectfully, and *only* with students you have a positive and respectful relationship with.

This sample can be printed from the Module B CD.

TASK 1

Observe (Supervise) strategically

Know the expectations.

Effective supervisors understand in detail the behavioral expectations for students in any given setting. If you are supervising morning arrival, for example, you need to know everything that is expected of students from the moment they step onto the campus or get off the bus until they arrive at their classrooms. You also need to know the broader expectations for how students are to treat other students and staff (how to respond to corrections, for example), the school dress code, and so on. You need to know all of these expectations so you know which behaviors to correct.

In some high schools, staff have given up asking students whether they have hall passes because many teachers don't bother to hand out passes. Those schools would benefit greatly by clarifying the hall pass procedure with every staff member and getting everyone's commitment to follow the same procedure. All adults would then present a united front to students, staff in the hallways could confidently take the appropriate actions with students who don't have hall passes, and only students with legitimate reasons would be in the hallways. The level of confidence that staff unity provides increases the assumption of compliance, and it conveys to students the idea that all the adults are thinking, "We know you know the way to . . ."

Dress code is another example of an expectation that needs consistent understanding and enforcement by all staff members. All staff should periodically discuss, as a group, how the dress code is currently being interpreted. If students begin coming to school with green hair, staff need to know whether that is a violation. If one staff member does nothing and another sends students to the office, the dress code expectations are not clear enough. This concept holds true for ID badges, cell phones, and other schoolwide policies.

Another category of behavior that can be particularly difficult at the secondary level is intimacy between students. Staff may feel uncomfortable discussing the issue, but you have to clarify the expectations. What are appropriate displays of affection? What are inappropriate displays? Again, supervisors need to present a united front about what is and is not acceptable behavior in your school.

A skill that goes hand in hand with knowing the expectations is communicating to students that you have high expectations for their behavior. Your body language and tone of voice should convey the assumption that students will be cooperative and compliant. Stand tall, move purposefully, and stay relaxed. You are also modeling confidence, quiet authority, and pride in being part of the school.

Staff should also develop unity around a consistent common language to use when correcting students. For example, one Foundations school has staff uniformly use the phrase "Please follow Fletcher's policy of . . ." When students hear a correction they've learned to respect, it will mean more to them.

Be present and engaged.

Being present and engaged when supervising common areas will help ensure everyone's safety and make you an effective supervisor.

Be on time. If you are assigned to supervise, be in the common area ready to work before students arrive. Resolve any scheduling conflicts well before your supervisory assignment begins. If you are late or miss the assignment entirely, other supervisors will have to cover for you and the overall supervision of the area will be compromised. You might also create a safety liability for the school.

Be in the right place physically. Coordinate assignments with other supervisors. In the cafeteria, for example, supervisors might be assigned to specific jobs such as greeting students as they enter, monitoring the lines, and circulating among certain groups of tables. Know your assigned station.

Spend more time in known trouble spots. If fights tend to occur near a soccer field, for example, be sure to circulate through that area often.

For playgrounds, high school courtyards, and other large, complex settings, we recommend that schools develop maps of each setting that denote supervisory zones and known trouble spots.

Figure 6c shows two maps from Juan Rodriguez Cabrillo High School in Long Beach, California. Map A shows the school's west campus (the school has west, east, and north campuses). During each passing period, 2,000 students circulate through the area shown on the map. At one time, only administrators and school resource officers supervised the passing periods, despite the vast area and many blind spots. Through the work of the school Foundations leadership team, the entire faculty committed to supervising two of three passing periods. That enabled about 60 adults to be present in the hallways and breezeways during passing periods rather than the six or seven present before. The black dots on Map B represent the new level of supervision. What a difference! It's almost like having a state trooper posted every two or three miles along the highway or knowing that company is coming to your home every evening.

Figure 6c   *Juan Rodriguez Cabrillo High School (Long Beach, California) school maps show (a) students (small dots) during a typical passing period, and (b) supervisory positions (large dots) after faculty committed to supervising the passing periods*

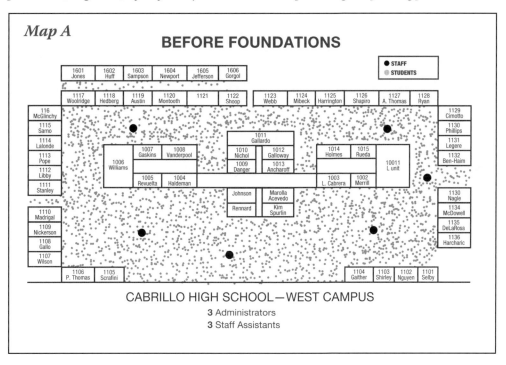

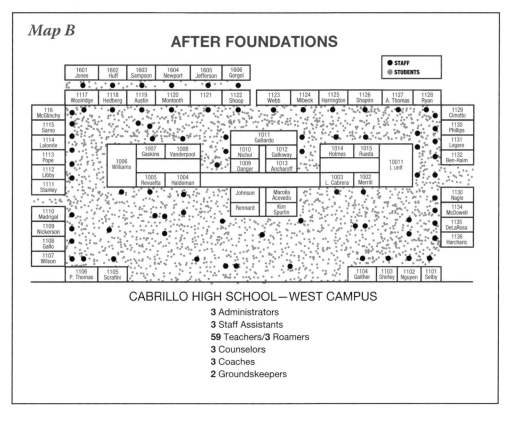

Circulate unpredictably throughout your assigned area. Restrooms in particular should be checked at random times. One elementary school we worked with had a problem with the boys' restrooms—the students splashed water, threw paper towels, wrote on the walls, and so on. The staff were mostly female, so they were reluctant to enter the boys' restrooms unannounced. Finally, they established a procedure where the staff member stood outside the restroom and listened. If she heard giggling or noises that suggested the boys were making a mess, she would announce, "On three, I'm coming in. One. Two. Three." This simple procedure created enough supervision that the problem was largely solved.

*E*xample From the Field

> At a school where I had spent quite a bit of time training the supervisors in *Foundations,* I visited the playground and began to chat with the supervisor on duty. After a couple minutes, the supervisor said, "Please excuse me, Dr. Sprick, I don't mean to be rude, but I can't stand here and talk with you. You taught me better—I've got to circulate!" —R.S.

Work the line when students are required to wait in lines. Waiting in lines is boring and provides ample opportunities for misbehavior. But if an adult interacts positively with the students, watches for line cutting and other potential conflicts, and generally creates a diversion for the students, misbehavior can be kept to a minimum.

Be in the right place mentally. Look and act alert and interact with students. Create a *presence.* If you are supervising the hallway but at the same time grading papers with your head down instead of observing and interacting with students—well, you are *not* a presence. Engage the students. Exude confidence and friendliness.

Be supportive of other supervisors. If you see another supervisor in a potentially troublesome situation, move toward that area. You don't necessarily have to interfere, but your presence will tell students that the staff are united in managing misbehavior. You can also serve as a witness to any incident that might occur.

Be willing to investigate or ask for help with any safety or emergency situations. For example, as a supervisor you are obligated to do something about a stranger on the playground. If you don't feel comfortable approaching the person, call the office or another supervisor so that the situation is investigated appropriately.

Be knowledgeable about the procedures (main and backup systems) for requesting help.

*E*xample From the Field

While visiting an elementary school, I wore a visitor's badge that I had received at the office. As I walked down the hallway, I was carrying papers that obscured the badge. A teacher who was escorting her students saw me. As she came closer, she veered toward me, peeked over the papers to see my badge, and said, "Oh, I just wanted to check that you have a visitor's badge. It's great to have you in our school. We just always want to make sure that visitors have checked into the office. Hope you have a really great day!" Then she proceeded down the hallway with her students. I was so impressed with this interaction. It told me that this staff knew how to be friendly, respectful, and inviting, while being totally committed to the safety of their students.   —R.S.

Be aware.

Awareness of your surroundings is essential for effective supervision of common areas.

Use visual scanning. Your eyes should continually sweep the setting—primarily your assigned area, but occasionally other supervisors' areas as well. No other situation should gain your undivided attention. If someone wants to talk to you, scan your area first, then briefly engage with the person, with the "eyes in the back of your head" on duty.

Scan known trouble spots often, and pay attention to unusual crowds of students. Be alert for subtle signs that trouble is brewing—a student's furtive glance from a group might mean that the students are in possession of something they shouldn't have or are planning something they shouldn't do. Walk over to the group and say, "How are you doing today, gentlemen? It's good to see you." Your presence alone can reduce the probability that any improper activities continue.

Listen. Be sensitive to unusual sounds in the setting or situation. If students are suddenly too quiet, there's a surge of noise, or there's a gradual low-level increase in noise, investigate the cause of the change.

Interact frequently with all students.

Tasks 2 and 3 that follow are all about when and how to interact with students. You obviously interact with students when you correct misbehavior, but it's even more important to interact in positive ways to create a positive and welcoming school climate.

Task 1 Action Steps

1. For all prioritized common areas and schoolwide policies, ensure that you know the exact expectations for student behavior.

2. Ensure that you know your role and responsibilities (including where and when) for assisting with common area and schoolwide policy supervision.

3. Use the first section of the document "The Art of Supervising Secondary School Hallways" (B-31), found on the Module B CD, as a guide for identifying your strengths and areas you can improve as a supervisor.

TASK 2

Interact positively

School climate is not set by the color of the walls, the number of windows, or the size of the gymnasium—it is created by the actions and personalities of the adults and how they interact with the students. The staff who work the common areas are a big part of setting that positive tone. Are they warm, friendly, and inviting, or are they cold and hostile? Chances are the overall schoolwide climate is, at least in part, a reflection of staff demeanor in the common areas.

Four variables work together to create a positive school climate: noncontingent attention, positive feedback, 3:1 ratio of interactions, and interacting positively with challenging students before they misbehave.

Provide noncontingent attention.

Effective supervisors provide all students with noncontingent acknowledgment; they interact with students not just because the students are behaving well, but because they are fellow human beings who deserve to be treated with dignity and respect.

You can provide noncontingent attention with:

- Nonverbal greetings, such as eye contact and smiles.
- Verbal greetings. Address students by name and show an interest in them (without being too nosy or personal), but avoid being overly friendly or hyping things up.

People feel more connected to places where their names are known. As much as possible, learn students' names and use their names when you are talking with them. This technique is very powerful for getting people on your side (as any salesperson will tell you). If you have trouble pronouncing or remembering names from languages you do not speak, keep trying. Students appreciate the effort.

You will probably encounter some students who do not respond to your attention—they remain silent and offer no eye contact for weeks or months. Persist with these students. Remember that you are the adult, and it's your responsibility to provide and model friendly, respectful behavior for every student.

Provide positive feedback.

Effective supervisors provide positive feedback to students when they are meeting expectations. For example:

"Good job putting the dodgeballs away."
"Thanks for turning in your homework on time every day this week."
"You are setting a good example for other students by waiting in line quietly."

Effective positive feedback is:

- **Quick.** A compliment that goes on too long can be embarrassing.

- **Specific.** Tell students exactly what they've done right.

- **Contingent.** Don't make a big deal out of an ordinary action or behavior. Kids, especially secondary students, will see right through a compliment for, say, walking down the hallway. (Although the compliment means something when walking down the hallway is a vast improvement over the student's usual hallway behavior.)

- **Age appropriate.** You might praise a first grader for asking to go to the restroom, but such praise would be inappropriate and highly embarrassing to a secondary student.

- **Reasonably private.** Students might be embarrassed with public praise and so your efforts might backfire.

Strive for at least a 3:1 ratio of interactions.

Effective supervisors also strive for a high ratio of positive to corrective interactions with *every* student; that is, for every corrective interaction (response to misbehavior), they provide at least three positive interactions (noncontingent attention or positive feedback for appropriate behavior).

Providing high ratios of positive feedback and noncontingent attention is especially important in common areas. Students who are starved for attention learn they don't have to misbehave to get noticed. With some tough students, you might have to strive toward a 15:1 positive to corrective ratio.

It can be easy to fall into a pattern of paying more attention to misbehavior than to providing positive feedback and noncontingent attention—but beware this Criticism Trap.

The Criticism Trap. In 1971, Dr. Wes Becker wrote about studies he conducted with teachers who were reprimanding and reminding students about out-of-seat behavior during work periods. He encouraged the teachers to reprimand students more immediately and more consistently. The teachers assumed this would decrease the behavior. In fact, the number of students getting out of their seats at the wrong times actually increased.

Dr. Becker called this phenomenon the *Criticism Trap*. Although the teachers thought they were doing something effective, the students, who were starved for attention, were getting out of their seats at least in part to get their teachers to look at them and talk to them. The students' need for attention was satisfied when their teachers told them to get back in their seats—and typically they did sit down, at least initially. When students took their seats, the teachers were reinforced for reprimanding. But soon the students realized, consciously or unconsciously, that they were not getting attention when they did what the teachers wanted, so they got out of their seats again. The teachers reprimanded again, giving the desired attention, and the students were again reinforced for getting out of their seats.

In this scenario, all parties involved get what they want in the short run. However, if this destructive pattern is allowed to continue, no one gets what he or she wants in the long run. Over time, students behave less and less responsibly, and the teacher gets more frustrated and negative. The only real way out of the Criticism Trap is to have more interactions with students when they are behaving responsibly than when they are misbehaving.

More information about ratios of interactions appears in Module C, Presentation 3.

Interact positively with the most challenging students *before* they have a chance to misbehave.

Approaching a student to offer a friendly greeting accomplishes two things. First, it demonstrates to the student that adults are present and they see him. Second, it communicates to him that he does not need to misbehave to be noticed and valued—he is valued just because he is an important part of the school. This strategy is especially valuable with a student you corrected previously because it shows that you do not hold a grudge and you notice his positive behavior, not just the misbehavior you corrected the day before. A simple "Good morning, Malik" is a powerful way to communicate that you are ready for a fresh start with a student you corrected earlier in the day.

In the next task, we discuss correcting misbehaviors. No matter how well you and other staff supervise and interact positively with students, some students will misbehave. However, if you continually strive to provide noncontingent attention and positive feedback, you can reduce the amount of correction you need to do, make your job more pleasant and satisfying, and contribute to a school climate that benefits all students and staff.

Task 2 Action Steps

1. Reflect on whether you capitalize on your supervisory time to interact positively with all students.

2. Use the second section of "The Art of Supervising Secondary School Hallways" (B-31) as a guide for identifying your strengths and areas you can improve as a supervisor.

TASK 3

Correct fluently

Even when proactive strategies are well implemented, inevitably some students still misbehave. It's human nature to break rules and test limits. Adults are susceptible, too. If a police officer isn't immediately visible, most of us drive faster than the speed limit even though we know the expectation and can see the posted rules about speed.

The focus of this presentation is the essential supervisory skill of correction—how to respond effectively to student misbehavior.

Correct misbehavior consistently.

Effective supervisors correct misbehavior consistently. This means that:

- *Every* observed misbehavior receives a response.
- Responses to similar misbehaviors are the same.

Supervisors sometimes vary their responses from student to student or from day to day, and sometimes responses for similar misbehaviors vary from supervisor to supervisor. Unfortunately, these inconsistencies can creep into our repertoire of corrections.

Student-to-student inconsistency. When you allow one student to run in the hallway without consequences and intervene with another student who exhibits the same behavior, you're almost guaranteed to hear the second student cry, "That's not fair!" When you are inconsistent in applying the rules from student to student, it's easy for students to assume you are discriminating unfairly, and the result can be hurt feelings, resentment toward you, escalating emotions, and so on.

Day-to-day inconsistency. Everyone has good days and bad days. Most people think that they are more impatient and inconsistent on their bad days, but it's worthwhile to examine your supervisory practices on good days, too. When you're relaxed, calm, and refreshed, a student running down the hallway might not bother you at all, and so you ignore it. But the degree to which a behavior bothers you is not the proper criterion for deciding whether to correct the student. If the student is breaking the rules, you need to intervene.

Supervisor-to-supervisor inconsistency. Imagine a bus loading area packed with waiting students. A supervisor is present, but she is busy grading papers and allows students to mill around chaotically. Only when a few students begin to push and shove one another does she interact with the students, telling them to stop their behavior. Fast forward to the next week: A different supervisor is on duty, and this person is operating with the understanding that students are supposed to wait in lines. Students resist his efforts to follow procedures. Because the previous supervisor did not enforce any rules about waiting in lines, the students view the second supervisor as mean, uptight, angry, and maybe even incompetent as he attempts to enforce the expectations. The actions of the first supervisor put the second supervisor in an untenable position.

Why is correcting misbehavior consistently important?

- When you don't respond to misbehavior, you send a message that the expectation is not important.

- Engaging in misbehavior without getting caught is potentially very reinforcing to students.

- Inconsistent responses give students *intermittent* reinforcement—the most powerful kind. For some students, the reinforcement of getting away with misbehavior once vastly outweighs several instances when they are caught and corrected.

- Inconsistent responses can result in fairness issues.

So our tip for supervisors on how to correct consistently is: DO SOMETHING! Responding *in some way* is more important than *how* you respond. Ted Kulongoski (former governor of Oregon) said, "It is not the severity of the consequence that will change behavior, it is the certainty." We need to create that certainty with consistent correction practices.

Correct misbehavior calmly.

Effective supervisors correct misbehavior calmly—that is, without emotion.

Why is correcting misbehavior calmly important?

- Emotional adult responses are inappropriate models for students. Harsh behavior modeled by an adult will often result in the same harsh behavior from the student.

- Emotional adult responses might escalate the emotional intensity of a misbehaving student. Adults usually know when and how to stop their own emotional escalations, but children and adolescents might not. In response to an adult's emotions, students might escalate into behavior that calls for severe discipline, such as suspension.

- Emotional adult responses increase the likelihood of power struggles between students and adults.

- Emotional adult responses are very reinforcing for some students.

To correct students calmly in common areas, keep the following tips in mind.

- Remind yourself, "I am the adult in this situation." Some students enjoy purposely angering adults. Avoid falling into their traps.

- Don't take the misbehavior or the response to your correction personally— don't let students push your buttons.

- Take a few seconds to think before you respond.

- Consider the misbehavior a teaching opportunity. The student can learn that the misbehavior is not going to serve him well, and it will be easier to just follow the expectations.

*E*xample From the Field

A veteran teacher who attended one of my training sessions told me the following story: "I learned very early in my career to stay calm in both common areas and the classroom. My mother was also a teacher. Thirty-five years ago, I was getting on a bus to go to my first teaching job, and my mother told me, 'They can't get your goat if they don't know where it's tied.' I followed that advice with great success. The calmer you stay, the less information you give to kids about things you might take personally." —R.S.

Correct misbehavior respectfully.

Effective supervisors correct misbehavior respectfully. This means responding in ways that afford students dignity and respect. Use respectful words, tone of voice, and body language. Avoid hurtful, disrespectful words by simply stating the rule or procedure the student should be following, rather than making judgmental or critical statements ("What's wrong with you?"). Keep your responses as private as possible; try to avoid having an audience while you correct a student.

Why is it important to correct misbehavior respectfully?

Respectful adult responses model appropriate behavior for students, contribute to a positive school climate, and foster student cooperation and compliance. In addition, they allow students to save face in front of their peers. Students might feel they need to react and act tough when they've been shamed or embarrassed in front of an audience.

Following are tips for correcting respectfully:

- Get the student's attention and quietly say, "I need to speak to you, please."

- When other students are around, go to the misbehaving student and explain that you need to speak to him or her. "Step over here with me, please."

- When correcting a student, position yourself in a nonconfrontational stance. Have the student face out of the area so that you are looking toward the common area as you speak and can continue to supervise other students. This positioning also keeps the misbehaving student from making eye contact with other students. Stand slightly sideways (not face to face) to the student and try to be relaxed and positive instead of tense and negative.

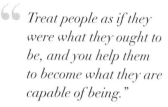

Treat people as if they were what they ought to be, and you help them to become what they are capable of being.

JOHANN WOLFGANG VON GOETHE (1749–1832), German author, scientist, and statesman

- Use body language that conveys that you are calm and confident. Keep your hands at your sides, in your pockets, or behind your back rather than on your hips or folded across your chest. Stand tall and move purposefully.

Avoid power struggles.

Avoid getting into a power struggle or engaging in interactions that escalate emotional reactions. Detailed information about dealing with noncompliance and avoiding emotional escalation is covered in Module D, Presentation 5.

Identify a menu of productive responses to misbehavior.

We've advised you to always *do something* to correct misbehavior—calmly, consistently, and respectfully. If 100% of the staff correct 100% of the misbehavior 100% of the time, most misbehavior will just go away. This tactic is analogous to posting state troopers every mile on the highway—drivers are very unlikely to speed, knowing that the chance of getting a ticket is so high. So what actions should you take?

a) Effective supervisors have a menu of productive responses to student misbehavior that are appropriate for a variety of situations. The consequences listed on pages 160–165 are effective in common areas. They appear in order (more or less) from mild to severe.

b) Effective supervisors choose corrections and responses based on the circumstances. Some tips include:

Use the mildest correction or response that reasonably fits the misbehavior. The milder the response, the more likely you'll follow through with it. If you find yourself saying, "Stop that! I don't want to have to . . . ," you are being inconsistent.

For example, use a verbal reminder for talking too loud, a brief delay for running, positive practice for slamming locker doors, proximity management when students are starting to get rowdy, and restitution (such as writing a formal apology) for disrespectful comments.

Gradually increase the severity level of the correction or response when a student misbehaves repeatedly. See "Increasing the Severity Level" below.

Remember: DO SOMETHING! *What* you do is less important than just *doing something*. Students should always expect consistent responses to their misbehavior from school staff. Staff unity with regard to common areas and schoolwide policies creates a safe, inviting, and vibrant school culture.

Increasing the Severity Level

Here's an example of how to gradually increase the severity of reprimands. Let's say I'm a hall supervisor. I'm standing in the middle of the hallway during a passing period, greeting and interacting with students. I see Tim running. Firmly and calmly, I give him a one-liner:

Tim, wait a minute. You need to walk in this school. Thanks.

A few days later, I see Tim running in the hallway again. This time I deliver an instructional reprimand, remaining calm and respectful:

Tim, come here for a moment, please. I spoke to you a couple of days ago about running in the hall. Now I want to give you information about why I—and any other adult in this school—will stop you if we see you running. Running in the hallways is not safe. There are lots of people in the halls and someone might get hurt. An adult will always stop you because we care about safety. OK. See you later.

A few days later, Tim is running in the hallway again. I change tack and use a bit of humor combined with a brief delay, but I'm still calm, consistent, and respectful:

Increasing the Severity Level (continued)

Tim, I've told you before that you must walk in the hallways in this school. You'll actually get places faster if you walk! If you had been walking instead of running, you'd be way down to the cafeteria by now. But instead, you're stuck here talking to me. Any time you run, you're going to get stuck talking to an adult because we care about making the hallways safe for everyone.

Menu of Consequences and When and How to Use Them

☑ **Proximity management**

Use when time is short, the problem is minor, or you are unsure what else to do.

- Move near the student as you circulate.
- Don't make eye contact until after the student stops the misbehavior.
- Don't talk to the student or invade the student's personal space.

☑ **Gentle verbal reminders and reprimands**

- When you are physically close to the student (within about three or four feet), deliver the reminder calmly and slowly.
- Lower your voice and say the student's name.
- State the desired behavior.
- Keep the message brief.
- Don't ask the student if she was misbehaving. She'll probably say "no" and you'll begin to argue.
- Don't invade the student's personal space.
- Move away from the student a second or two before you finish the instruction. Pausing may invite an argumentative response.

Following are different types of reprimands along with suggestions about when to use them:

- **Quick reprimands,** or **one-liners,** are brief statements of the positive expectations. Use when time is short, the problem is minor, or you are not sure what else to do. (See "One-Liners: Staff Can Correct Consistently With Common Responses" on the next two pages).

- **Instructional reprimands** are explanatory statements (may be longer than one-liners). Use when a student needs more information about or the rationale for the expectation.

- **Humorous reprimands** are disarming responses that avoid direct confrontation. Use when humor is a natural part of your interactions with students. Be sure you don't confuse humor with humiliation or ridicule, however. Never belittle, humiliate, or ridicule students.

- **Relationship reprimands** are brief responses based on established relationships between adults and students. Use when a student wants to do the right thing for *you*—the student thinks, "I need to behave because I don't want to disappoint Martha."

One-Liners: Staff Can Correct Consistently With Common Responses

One-liners are quick, practiced responses you can use to correct students, and they provide a great way to develop staff unity and a common language for correcting misbehavior. One-liners can keep you from becoming sidetracked or emotional. You can say a one-liner quickly as you walk past, for example, a student using bad language in the hallway and you don't have time to stop and discuss the behavior.

General one-liners:

- That's not OK. The expectation is to . . .
- Hands, feet, and objects to yourself.
- Voice levels are too loud. Bring them down, please.
- Take a timeout. When I come back, be ready to tell me what you need to do.
- Stand here next to me for 20 seconds.
- That behavior wouldn't be acceptable on the job. Please tone it down. (for inappropriate display of affection)
- That language is not acceptable here at school. (for swearing)

Hallway one-liners:

- Keep moving, please.
- Remember to walk in the hallways.
- It's time to go to class.
- Walk and talk.
- Class begins in 30 seconds.

One-Liners: Staff Can Correct Consistently With Common Responses (continued)

Cafeteria one-liners:

- Pick up your tray and walk with me.
- Stand (or sit) here. I'll talk to you as soon as I can.
- Say "please" when you ask someone to pass something to you.
- Your food choices for today are . . . Please decide now.
- Clean your tray.
- Put your waste in the trash can.

Recess one-liners:

- Tell (or show) me the right way to . . .
- This game is off limits for the remainder of recess.
- Take a timeout. When I get back, be ready to tell me what you need to do.
- Either play responsibly or move to another game.
- It looks like you're having fun, but you need to find something else to do.
- I'm glad you know the rules. I will monitor the situation. (for tattling)
- Stay away from him and stay closer to me so that I can monitor the situation. (for teasing)

Fletcher High School in Jacksonville, Florida, developed an effective one-liner that all staff use consistently. When staff see low-level misbehavior, they say to students, "Please honor Fletcher's policy of . . ." and insert the behavior—walking in the hallways, caps off inside the building, voice level 2 in the cafeteria, and so on.

A secondary school principal who is an avid fisherman came up with a great line for his staff to use to break up public displays of affection—"catch and release!"

✓ **Brief delay**

Use when a secondary student is en route somewhere.

- Tell the student, "Stay where you are and think about [the particular expectation]."
- Have the student stand and wait for no more than 10 to 20 seconds.

☑ **Positive practice**

Use when the misbehavior has a physical component.

- Have the student demonstrate the expected behavior. For example:

    "Go back and walk around the game."
    "Open your locker and close it the correct way, please."
    "Come back down and walk, don't run, up the stairs."

- Make sure the student's corrected behavior matches the expectations.

☑ **Restitution**

Use when the student has done some obvious damage to property or another person's feelings.

- Identify an action the student can take that will "make it right."
- Have the student repair damage that he or she is responsible for—for example, pick up litter that he dropped or apologize to someone she harmed.
- Don't focus on assigning fault or blame.

Note: A student who must clean up a mess should use only soap and water—no chemicals.

This consequence requires planning and analysis by both student and teacher for more complex incidents. Constructive restitution:

- Requires effort from the offender.
- Is seen as adequate compensation by the victim.
- Does not encourage further misbehavior.
- Is relevant to the misbehavior.
- Strengthens the offender.

☑ **Change in location**

Use when the student's current location on the playground, cafeteria, or similar area might be a contributing factor in the misbehavior.

- Have the student move to a different location or operate within a restricted space. For example, move the student to a different table in the cafeteria or restrict the student to a limited area of the playground.
- The change in location sets the student up for more appropriate behavior that you should then positively reinforce.

☑ **Stay with supervisor**

Use when misbehavior occurs on the playground, cafeteria, bus loading area, and similar areas.

Students like independence. When a student exhibits repeated misbehavior, requiring the student to stay with you will likely be appropriately aversive to the student.

☑ **Demerits**

Use when mild, accumulative consequences will allow you to set up a more consistent policy. If you were to use harsher consequences, you might hesitate to assign them for every misbehavior.

- Assign one demerit for each instance of misbehavior. Demerits function as warnings.
- Tell the student that the demerits will accumulate, and after a certain number—three or four, for example—you will plan to notify the principal (in some schools this is referred to as a Level 2 Notification).

☑ **Timeout at a set location**

Use when the goal is to restrict the student's social interactions for a brief period. On the playground, for example, you might use a bench placed away from the play equipment; in the cafeteria, an empty table.

- Have the student go to an area of the setting that is separate from the main activity (but visible to supervisors). The goal is to restrict the student's social interactions for a brief period—1 or 2 minutes.
- Don't send several students at one time to the area—that just provides them with more social time.

☑ **Timeout at the place the infraction occurred**

Use when there are limited options for set timeout areas or if you have more than one or two students who need timeout.

Tell the students to stand where they are for a minute or two.

☑ **Behavior Improvement Form**

Use when a student is in timeout. This activity gives students a chance to reflect on their behavior, and it interrupts and distracts students from their misbehavior.

Have the student fill out one of these short forms. Figures 5b and 5c in Presentation 5 (pages 129 and 130) show two versions of the Behavior Improvement Form.

☑ **Notifying the student's teacher**

Use when the behavior concerns you—it is very disrespectful, for example, or is chronic and growing worse.

- Notify the student's classroom or homeroom teacher so the teacher can use the situation as an opportunity to instruct the student in more appropriate ways to behave. (This can also demonstrate to the student that all staff are on the same page when it comes to expectations and consequences.)
- Don't notify the teacher for the purpose of having the teacher punish the student.

☑ **Referral to a more intensive consequence**

- Write a Level 2 (moderate) notification* on the student so he or she is assigned detention or goes to the school's problem-solving room (for example).
- For dangerous, illegal, or out-of-control behavior, write a Level 3 (severe) referral* on the student so the student has to go to the principal's office.

Note: Foundations recommendations on levels of referrals and when to use them are discussed in Module D.

Task 3 Action Steps

1. Use the third section of "The Art of Supervising Secondary School Hallways" (B-31) to reflect on the degree to which you correct fluently (briefly, calmly, consistently, and respectfully). Then integrate those ideas with your reflections from the previous two tasks about communicating high expectations and providing a lot of attention for positive behavior.

2. Provide feedback to your Foundations Team about ways to provide annual refresher sessions on common area and schoolwide policy supervision. Consider:
   - What time or times of year?
   - What kind of format?

Adopting, Implementing, and Monitoring Improvements to Common Areas and Schoolwide Policies

CONTENTS

INTRODUCTION

Once the Foundations Team or task force develops a proposal to revise and improve a schoolwide policy or a common area's policies and procedures, they need to guide the proposal through the adoption process and launch the new policies. After the team or task force determine that the new policies are effective, they need to actively monitor the common area or schoolwide policy to ensure that the new policies continue to be fully implemented. If revisions become necessary in the future, the Foundations Team will be responsible for managing that task.

No matter how comprehensive a policy is, it will be effective only if the initial implementation is monitored and revised when needed. This monitoring process, part of the **Implement** step of the Improvement Cycle, is the beginning of another trip around the cycle. To ensure that new schoolwide policies and common area procedures remain effective, you will need to collect and review data regularly, revise the policies and procedures when appropriate, obtain staff approval, teach the revisions to staff and students, and implement the revisions. The Improvement Cycle never ends (it's a circle, not a dead-end line!), and it's the key to a successful *Foundations* implementation.

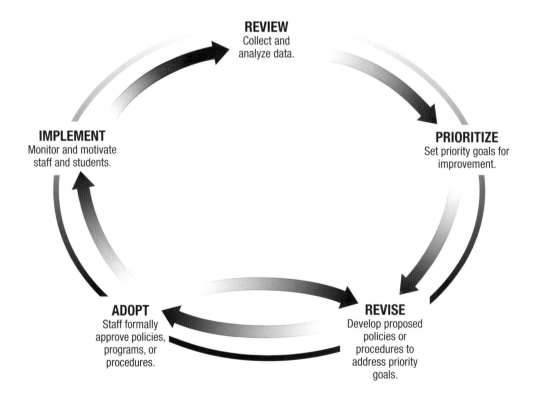

So who is this presentation for? If the Foundations Team worked on the common area or schoolwide policy, all the tasks in this presentation apply to the team. If a special task force worked on the area or policy, that task force stays in place though the **Adopt**, **Implement**, and **Review** steps of the Improvement Cycle. Once there is general agreement that the new procedures are working well, the task force can disband. The Foundations Team will lead the long-term implementation and review of data for the area or policy.

Task 1: Adopt and Implement the Proposed Improvements describes how the team can guide revised policies through the steps of informing the staff and conducting a vote, getting suggestions for revision (if necessary), formally adopting the improvement proposal, and implementing the new procedures or policy. (This task is an abbreviated version of the **Adopt** step discussed in Module A, Presentation 3, "The Improvement Cycle.")

Task 2: Collect and Analyze Data on the Implemented Procedures explains how to conduct observations, seek feedback from staff and students, and review incident referral data to monitor newly implemented schoolwide or common area policies.

Task 3: Decide Whether to Revise or Re-Teach describes the steps to take and decisions that must be made after you've reviewed monitoring data.

Task 4: Integrate Multiple Common Areas and Schoolwide Policies Into a Continuous Improvement Cycle describes how newly implemented policies and procedures can be integrated into an ongoing process of annual review to monitor implementation and efficacy.

TASK 1

Adopt and implement the proposed improvements

The team will inform the staff, conduct a vote on the revised policies, and gather suggestions for revision, if necessary. Once the improvement proposal is formally adopted, the team will guide implementation.

Note: This task is an abbreviated version of the **Adopt** step discussed in Module A, Presentation 3, "The Improvement Cycle." Before you start, print a copy of the Adoption and Implementation Checklist for Common Areas and Schoolwide Policies to help track your progress (see Figure 7a on p. 173).

Conduct a staff vote on the proposal.

You've analyzed the structure and organization of your target common area or schoolwide policy and written an improvement proposal. The next step is to present the proposal to the entire staff for adoption or rejection.

a. Confirm the date when the proposed policy will be presented at a staff decision meeting.

b. Share the proposed policy with the staff before the faculty meeting by email or by putting print copies into mailboxes. Determine who will be responsible for this and when it will be done.

c. Decide which team members will prepare a 5-minute presentation about the proposal and coordinate the voting. If a special task force guided the development of the proposal, the Foundations Team or the task force could oversee the voting process.

d. Staff members discuss the proposal. (Important: Limit discussion to 10 minutes.)

e. Confirm the selected voting procedure and criteria necessary for staff adoption of the policy (see Module A, Presentation 3, Task 3 for more information about voting procedures. Voting rubrics are available on the Module B CD). Make copies of ballots, if necessary.

f. Staff vote to adopt or reject the proposal.

If the proposal is rejected, develop an alternative proposal that addresses staff concerns and present it to the staff for adoption or rejection. This process may repeat twice, for a total of three voting cycles. If staff have still not reached consensus, the issue goes to the principal for a final decision. (See Module A, Presentation 3, Task 3 for more information.)

Implement the new policies or procedures.

When a proposal has been adopted, develop and execute an implementation plan. Your plan should cover the following information.

Identify specific changes to the common area's structural variables and/or supervision arrangements.

Establish how the procedures will be taught to students. Be sure to address:

- How will effective lessons be written and provided to teachers?
- How and when will the lessons be presented?
- How and when will re-teaching occur for new students and students who have continuing problems?

Module B, Presentation 3 provides more information about teaching procedures and expectations to students.

Determine how initial and ongoing training will be provided to existing and new supervisors for:

- Emergency procedures
- Behavioral expectations for students
- Effective supervision

See Module B, Presentation 2, Task 3 for more information about teaching supervisory techniques and expectations to staff.

Identify procedures for assisting staff members and students during the initial stages of implementation. At least two team members should be available in the common area (or at strategic locations for a new schoolwide policy) during the first few days of implementation to answer questions and work out any pressing problems. Ask staff for suggestions about specific support strategies that might be useful, and ask them to think about special assistance that students with disabilities might need to adapt to the new policies and procedures. For example, students with autism spectrum disorders might find change difficult, so the team and the special education staff should discuss a plan to prepare the students, perhaps by preparing additional, more detailed lessons and teaching those lessons for several days before the change is implemented.

> ## ஐ FOUNDATIONS RECOMMENDATION ര
>
> *At least two team members should be available in the common area for the first few days of implementation to answer questions and work out any pressing problems.*

Use the Adoption and Implementation Checklist to track progress on your implementation.

Form B-11, The Adoption and Implementation Checklist for Common Areas and Schoolwide Policies, is provided on the Module B CD (see Figure 7a on the next page).

Task 1 Action Steps & Evidence of Implementation

Action Steps	Evidence of Implementation
1. The Foundations Team or task force charged with revising the schoolwide policy or common area procedures should: • Present the proposal to staff for adoption. • Plan implementation of the new policies and procedures, including teaching procedures to students and staff.	Foundations Process: Current Priorities
2. Use the Adoption and Implementation Checklist (Form B-11) for each identified common area or schoolwide policy improvement priority. • Identify tasks that have been completed. • Identify tasks that need to be done. • Develop and execute a plan for completing the remaining tasks for each identified common area priority.	Foundations Process: Current Priorities

Figure 7a *Adoption and Implementation Checklist for Common Areas and Schoolwide Policies (B-11)*

Adoption and Implementation Checklist for Common Areas and Schoolwide Policies

✔		TASK	IMPLEMENTATION SUGGESTIONS & NOTES
☐	1	The improvement proposal was presented to the entire staff for adoption or rejection. If rejected, it was revised as necessary.	
☐	2	The proposal has been adopted.	
☐	3	Lessons have been developed for teaching the procedures to students.	See Module B, Presentation 3, Task 1 for information about designing lessons and teaching students.
☐	4	A plan for how and when lessons will be taught to students has been designed.	
☐	5	A plan for training staff members on the procedures and on supervisory expectations has been developed.	See Module B, Presentation 2, Task 3 for information about training staff.
☐	6	A date when the new procedures or policy goes into effect has been established.	
☐	7	Additional supervision has been arranged for the first 2 weeks of implementation.	
☐	8	Students have been taught the procedures.	
☐	9	Staff have been trained on the procedures or policy and on supervisory expectations.	

© 2014 Pacific Northwest Publishing

 This form can be printed from the Module B CD.

TASK 2

Collect and analyze data on the implemented procedures

Once the improved common area procedures or schoolwide policies have been implemented, you need to collect data to objectively judge whether the behavioral improvements that you envisioned have actually been accomplished and to ensure that behavior does not deteriorate over time. This task explains how to monitor newly implemented policies and procedures by conducting observations, seeking feedback from staff and students, and reviewing incident referral data.

Conduct observations of the common area or schoolwide policy.

See Module A, Presentation 4, Task 3 for more detailed information about conducting observations of common areas.

Observation data are a crucial part of the monitoring process for common areas. Schedule formal observations 4 to 6 weeks after the launch of the new policies and procedures. Use the same observation form and compilation and interpretation procedures used for previous observations of the common area so that you can compare before-and-after results directly.

If you can enlist the same staff members who conducted the previous observations, the data will be even more directly comparable. Include members of the Foundations Team or task force that formulated the policy because they will know the policies, procedures, and supervision requirements best. Also consider including a staff member who wasn't directly involved previously to bring a fresh perspective to the observation and to enhance faculty buy-in to the *Foundations* process. Schedule at least three observers.

Be sure to schedule the observations in advance and make arrangements for the observers' duties to be covered during the observation period. As we recommend for the **Review** step, conduct two or three observations of the common area on different days of the week—Tuesday, Wednesday, and Friday, for example. Schedule observations for typical days, not for days with special events. Avoid days right before a holiday or major testing, or when assemblies are planned.

If you can assemble two or three teams of two observers, you can stagger the days and time, but be sure to assign observers to all known problem areas and times. Each observer should complete a separate form. Afterward, all the observers can get together to complete a single consensus observation form.

Consider taking videos of the common area during critical times and in key areas. Use of video will depend on your district and school policies.

In addition to formal observations, members of the Foundations Team and the administrator should conduct daily informal observations to evaluate how well the policy is being implemented. These informal observations can be valuable in combination with the formal observations to identify strengths and weaknesses of the policy implementation.

Note: We mostly refer to common areas in this task, but you can also conduct observations of schoolwide policies. To observe a policy such as dress code, first identify a context, such as morning arrival. The observers then take note of how many students are violating the policy as they enter the school, how staff intercept and interact with those students, whether staff assign appropriate consequences, and, if the offending students are sent to the office, whether proper procedures are followed and the students return to class as soon as possible.

Seek feedback from staff, students, and, if applicable, parents.

Staff. Asking staff for their feedback provides a reality check about the policy and also promotes the idea to staff that they are stakeholders in the process of implementing and revising the policy. Wait 4 to 6 weeks after implementation before you seek feedback to allow any kinks to get ironed out. As part of regular monitoring efforts, seek additional feedback once per semester. Methods for soliciting feedback include:

- Break into groups during a faculty meeting for 10-minute discussions about policy implementation.

- Have assigned faculty groups (e.g., grade-level, departments, vertical planning teams) meet for 10–15 minutes to respond to a set of prepared questions about the policy implementation.

- Email or distribute draft copies of the policy with a short survey.

- Have Foundations Team members seek input from the staff members they represent.

Consider these options for questions and feedback from staff:

- Ask for three or four strengths *and* weaknesses of the policy. Inquire how student behavior now compares with what it was like before the policy was implemented.

- Use the Common Area Observation Form (Form B-03) to select questions and ratings for the staff feedback. For example, ask the staff to complete the 3-point ratings of the expected student behaviors in the common area.

- Ask the staff to respond to the appropriate common area questions from the survey that was given in the fall.

- Ask the staff to identify possible changes in the policy related to student expectations, staff supervision expectations, and encouragement and correction procedures.

Students. Feedback from students can provide an interesting perspective on how the policy is affecting both student and staff behavior. Wait 4 to 6 weeks after implementation before you seek feedback so any kinks get ironed out.

- *Survey.* Teachers can ask students three or four questions about their perceptions of the policy. Each student can respond in writing on a simple ballot (question number plus answer options of yes/no, 1–5 ratings, or smiling/frowning faces, for example). The Foundations Team or task force should write questions that will identify positive outcomes of the policy and suggestions for improvement.

- *Class discussion.* Teachers can lead a 5- to 10-minute class discussion about the policy. With older students (fourth grade and above), a student can record the major comments and feedback offered by the class.

- *Focus groups.* Two staff members can lead two or three student focus groups. One staff member leads the discussion while the other takes notes and observes. Each group should comprise no more than four to six students who are representative of the specific target group (a grade level or all male students, for example). Develop a script that includes an introduction and prepared questions.

  With the focus groups, stress that you are asking students to help the team and school address issues about the common area. Also emphasize that the students' names will not be tied to specific comments.

Parents. If policies or procedures affect parents, seek their opinions and suggestions about the improvements. For example, parents are involved in arrival and dismissal policies because many of them drop off and pick up their children during those times. You might opportunistically ask parents directly (How is the new drop-off procedure working?), send a brief survey home with students, or hold an after-school meeting ("Coffee with the Principal") to discuss the new procedures.

Review incident referral data.

See Module A, Presentation 4, Task 4 for more detailed information about using incident referral data.

Incident referral data can yield meaningful insight into the effectiveness of the newly implemented policies and procedures. For monitoring purposes, it is most useful to have data about incident referrals from before the policies or procedures were implemented. About 4 to 6 weeks after the initial implementation, compare the before and after data. Has the number of incident referrals from the common area gone up or down since the implementation? Also identify any meaningful trends—are there more referrals from specific grade levels or classrooms, during a particular time of day or day of the week, in certain locations in the school, or for specific types of misbehavior?

If preimplementation data aren't available, a review of office referral data can still be useful. You can establish a baseline data set of incident referrals for the common area to serve as comparison data in the future. Identify any meaningful trends regarding grade levels, classrooms, and so on.

Identify who will be responsible for collecting and analyzing incident referral data as part of the common area monitoring process. Also note how often this review will take place. Typically, either the Foundations Team's Data/Evaluations Coordinator or the principal is responsible, and the review may take place once per semester or perhaps every nine weeks.

Task 2 Action Steps & Evidence of Implementation

Action Steps	Evidence of Implementation
1. Set up a schedule of postimplementation monitoring activities for the common area. For example, 4–6 weeks after implementation: • Conduct observations. • Seek feedback from staff and students. • Review incident referral data. • Revise or re-teach the policy, if appropriate. (See Task 3 of this presentation for more information.) If the policy was developed by a special task force and is found to be functioning well, the task force can disband because its mission is complete.	Foundations Process: Current Priorities
2. Finalize documentation of the policy or procedures and place it in the Foundations Archive and Staff Handbook. 3. Thereafter, the Foundations Team should collect data on the policy as part of their scheduled data collection—for example, during twice-yearly observations of all common areas, quarterly reviews of incident data, and annual surveys of staff, students, and parents. (See Module A, Presentation 4 for detailed information about data collection.)	Foundations Archive: Schoolwide Policies, Common Area Policies and Procedures Staff Handbook: Policies and Procedures in Place

TASK 3

Decide whether to revise or re-teach

In this task, we describe steps to take and decisions that must be made after you review the monitoring data.

Note: Before you start, print a copy of the Monitoring Checklist for Common Areas and Schoolwide Policies (Form B-12) to track your progress (see Figure 7c on p. 183).

Decide if you need to revise or re-teach.

At a Foundations Team meeting, have the team or staff members responsible for the data analysis report the results. If the adopted policies or procedures are working well—congratulations! Celebrate your success. Chances are, however, you'll need to tweak the plan to some extent. The team needs to decide whether the adopted policies or procedures should be revised or just re-taught to students or staff (or both). (Information about using data to make decisions appears in Module A, Presentation 4, "Data-Driven Processes.")

Figure 7b on the next page summarizes the decision-making process. Following are decisions you might make as you work through the evaluation flowchart.

Decision: The new policies or procedures have had a positive effect. The adopted policies or procedures do not need to be revised.

If data suggest that the policies or procedures are effective and should continue to be implemented as originally planned, inform staff and students of the positive outcome. Celebrate! Let staff and students know that their efforts and cooperation were responsible for the success of the improvement initiative. (If the policy was developed by a special task force, the task force can now disband.)

Decision: The new policies and procedures have had no impact or a negative impact on student behavior.

The policies or procedures are not working! Determine whether staff are implementing the policies and procedures as designed.

If they are, reconvene the team or task force and develop a new proposal that addresses the shortcomings of the recently adopted policies or procedures.

If they are *not*, you cannot know whether the policies and procedures are effective. Provide staff members with encouragement, motivation, and additional training.

Figure 7b *Evaluation flowchart (B-13)*

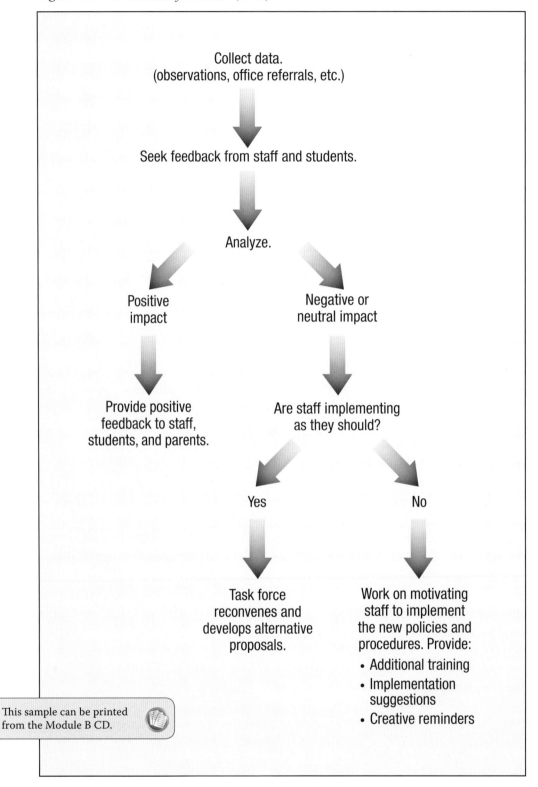

Collect data.
(observations, office referrals, etc.)

Seek feedback from staff and students.

Analyze.

Positive impact

Negative or neutral impact

Provide positive feedback to staff, students, and parents.

Are staff implementing as they should?

Yes

No

Task force reconvenes and develops alternative proposals.

Work on motivating staff to implement the new policies and procedures. Provide:

- Additional training
- Implementation suggestions
- Creative reminders

This sample can be printed from the Module B CD.

Decision: The policies or procedures do not need to be revised, but they do need to be re-taught to students or staff (or both).

Students. Decide whether new lesson plans are needed or whether the existing lesson plans can be reused. You may be able to use shorter lessons plans for re-teaching. You'll also need to plan when and how to re-teach, and share the plan (dates, times, methods, and so on) with the faculty. (Teaching expectations to students is covered in more detail in Module B, Presentation 3.)

Staff. Plan how and when staff will review the policies and procedures or certain supervision skills. We recommend short 10- to 20-minute sessions. (Training staff about policies and procedures and supervision techniques is covered in Module B, Presentations 2, 4, 5, and 6.)

If staff members are not implementing the policies and procedures as designed, they may need encouragement and motivation along with (or even instead of) additional training.

Decision: The policies or procedures need to be revised by the team.

If there is time during the Foundations Team meeting, write the revisions. If not, schedule another team meeting for the near future for the purpose of writing the revisions.

Present the completed revisions to the staff. Follow the **Revise** and **Adopt** steps of the Improvement Cycle: Seek staff feedback about the draft revisions, share copies of the final revised policy before conducting a staff vote, hold a 10-minute discussion and vote, and use the same approval criteria used for the initial adoption.

If the revisions affect only the staff, decide when and how to review the changes with the staff and when to begin implementation. Establish the expectations that absent staff members will review on another day.

If any of the student expectations have changed, decide when and how to teach the revised expectations and policies to students.

Document the final new policies and procedures in writing.

Prepare detailed descriptions of all policies and procedures for the Foundations Archive.

Prepare summaries of essential information to include in the Staff Handbook.

Samples of written documentation for hallway, playground, cafeteria, and assembly policies are available on the Module B CD (see Appendix C).

Review policies and procedures with students periodically.

Keep in mind that all policies and procedures should be reviewed with the entire student body periodically throughout the school year. Consider scheduling reviews for the following times:

- After major vacations—students tend to forget school expectations after a significant amount of time away.

- Before major vacations—students also tend to forget expectations in the excitement of anticipating vacation time.

- Before special days—elementary students are often overly excited in the days leading up to Halloween, for example.

- Before, during, and after major schoolwide testing and, in secondary schools, sports competitions

- Any time behavior appears to be breaking down (if hallway incidents are increasing, then it's time to re-teach hallway expectations).

Use the Monitoring Checklist to track progress on your implementation.

Form B-12, Monitoring Checklist for Common Areas and Schoolwide Policies, is provided on the Module B CD (see Figure 7c on the next page).

Figure 7c Monitoring Checklist for Common Areas and Schoolwide Policies (B-12)

Monitoring Checklist for Common Areas and Schoolwide Policies

✓		TASK	IMPLEMENTATION SUGGESTIONS & NOTES
☐	1	Observation of the common area were conducted 4 to 6 weeks after implementation.	See Module A, Presentation 4, Task 3 for detailed information about conducting common area observations.
☐	2	Staff were asked for feedback 4 to 6 weeks after implementation.	
☐	3	Students were asked for feedback 4 to 6 weeks after implementation.	
☐	4	Incident referral data relating to the common area or schoolwide policy were reviewed 4 to 6 weeks after implementation.	See Module A, Presentation 4, Task 4 for detailed information about analyzing and interpreting incident referral data.
☐	5	Results of the monitoring were reported to staff.	
☐	6	The positive effect of the new policy or procedures was celebrated.	
☐	7	Students were re-taught the procedures or policy, when needed.	
☐	8	Staff were retrained in supervisory expectations, when needed.	
☐	9	The policy or procedures were revised in response to the data analysis, when needed.	
☐	10	A schedule for ongoing monitoring has been developed, and a person responsible for organizing the monitoring has been identified.	
☐	11	The new policy or procedures have been documented in writing and archived.	
☐	12	Plans are in place to review the policy or procedures at critical times during the year.	

© 2014 Pacific Northwest Publishing

 This form can be printed from the Module B CD.

Task 3 Action Steps & Evidence of Implementation

Action Steps	Evidence of Implementation
1. Hold a Foundations Team meeting to present the results of the data review. As a team, make the following decisions about the adopted policies and procedures: • Are they working well and require no revision? If so, celebrate with staff and students. • Do they need to be re-taught to students or staff (or both) but not revised? If so, plan for re-teaching students and reviewing with staff. • Do they need to be revised? If so, follow the **Revise**, **Adopt**, and **Implement** steps of the Improvement Cycle as you draft the revisions. Plan to re-teach the expectations to students and review the policies and procedures with staff.	Foundations Process: Meeting Minutes, Data Summaries, Current Priorities
2. Document the final new policy or procedures in writing and archive.	Foundations Archive: Policies and Procedures in Place
3. Plan to review the policy and procedures with students at critical times during the year.	Foundations Process: Planning Calendar
4. Begin using the Monitoring Checklist (Form B-12) for each identified common area or schoolwide policy improvement priority. • Identify tasks that have been completed. • Identify tasks that need to be done. • Develop and execute a plan for completing tasks that remain for each identified common area priority.	Foundations Process: Current Priorities

TASK 4

Integrate multiple common areas and schoolwide policies into a continuous improvement cycle

Task 4 describes how newly implemented policies and procedures can be integrated into an ongoing process of annual review to monitor implementation and efficacy. Reevaluate the implemented policies and procedures.

Reevaluate the implemented policies and procedures.

During next year's first quarterly review, reevaluate the new policies and procedures. Use data—surveys, observations, and disciplinary referrals—to determine whether the targeted common area should continue to be an improvement priority or whether it has improved and is no longer a priority. For example, if you worked on the cafeteria during the current school year, you should reevaluate the cafeteria data next fall when the new school year begins. If all is well, the cafeteria will no longer be a priority. Unless subsequent data indicate otherwise, the Foundations Team doesn't need to devote any more time and attention to cafeteria policies and procedures.

Maintain your success over years.

Once you've addressed the major concerns about common areas and schoolwide policies by successfully implementing improvements, plan a maintenance schedule.

Keep in mind that if 3 or more years have passed since data for a common area or schoolwide policy were collected and analyzed, you should reassess the area or policy and gather input from staff about the efficacy of the policies and procedures.

Policy and practice should always align. Over several years (or sometimes just a year), practice sometimes evolves to be better than the policy. When this happens, the policy should be updated. Sometimes practice diverges from policy in a negative way. In that case, staff should be trained to implement the policy as it stands. Whether the change is good or bad, you should know about it and take any steps necessary to ensure that the environment is safe, respectful, and positive.

We recommend that, after all aspects of *Foundations* have been developed (usually a 2- to 4-year process), you review the policies and procedures on a rotating basis every 3 years. As we've explained previously, if the data review shows that the policies and procedures are still working well, no changes are necessary. If student misbehavior has increased or if any safety issues have arisen, revise the policies and procedures.

Use the Foundations Implementation Rubric and the Module B Implementation Checklist.

We provide two tools to help you evaluate the status of your implementation.

- The Foundations Implementation Rubric and Summary (Form B-01) provides a relatively quick overview of the status of each module and prioritized common area and schoolwide policy. It's available on the Module B CD and in Appendix A of this book.

- The Module B Implementation Checklist (Form B-02) is a detailed list of the module's processes and objectives. It's on the Module B CD and in Appendix B of this book.

Instructions and suggestions for when and how to use these tools are included. Note that each *Foundations* module includes its own Implementation Checklist in an appendix and on the CD. Additional information about Implementation Checklists apears in Module F, Presentation 7, Task 1.

The schedule below provides a sample long-term plan for data review that includes how and when you might use the Foundations Implementation Rubric and the Implementation Checklists. Of course, these monitoring tools can be used at any time, as needed. (The schedule also gives you a good idea of the continuous nature of the *Foundations* Improvement Cycle.) This sample schedule doesn't include situations that will undoubtedly arise in real life—you might need to revise hallways more than once or conduct more frequent and detailed analyses of arrival and dismissal procedures. Your monitoring schedule will reflect your specific needs.

Sample Long-Term Schedule: Improvement Priorities, Data Review & Monitoring

Year 1	Work on:

- Modules A and B (Continuous Improvement Process, Common Areas and Schoolwide Policies)
- Cafeteria
- Guidelines for Success

In late spring, work through the Foundations Implementation Rubric for Modules A, B (cafeteria), and C2 (Guidelines for Success).

Use the Modules A and B Implementation Checklists to assess status as you near completion of those modules.

Year 2	Work on:

- Module C (Inviting Climate)
- Hallways

In the fall, evaluate cafeteria data.

In late spring, work through the Foundations Implementation Rubric for Modules A, B (cafeteria and hallways), and C.

Use the Module C Implementation Checklist to assess status as you near completion of Module C.

Year 3	Work on:

- Module D (Responding to Misbehavior)
- Playground

In the fall, evaluate hallway data.

In late spring, work through the Foundations Implementation Rubric for Modules A, B (cafeteria, hallways, playground), C, and D.

Use the Module D Implementation Checklist to assess status as you near completion of Module D.

Year 4	Work on:

- Module E (Safety, Conflict, Bullying)
- Arrival and dismissal

In the fall, evaluate playground data.

In late spring, work through the Foundations Implementation Rubric for Modules A, B (cafeteria, hallways, arrival, and dismissal), C, D, and E.

Use the Module E Implementation Checklist to assess status as you near completion of Module E.

Monitor Year 1 priorities:

- Module A Implementation Checklist
- Module B Implementation Checklist for cafeteria
- Module C Implementation Checklist for Guidelines for Success (C2 only)

Year 5	Work on:

- Module F (Classroom Management and Sustaining Foundations)
- Assemblies
- Guest teachers

In the fall, evaluate arrival and dismissal data.

In late spring, work through the Foundations Implementation Rubric for Modules A, B (playground, arrival and dismissal, assemblies, guest teachers), C, D, E, and F.

Use the Module F Implementation Checklist to assess status as you near completion of Module F.

Monitor Year 2 priorities:

- Module B Implementation Checklist for hallways
- Module C Implementation Checklist

Year 6	In the fall, evaluate assemblies and guest teacher data.
	Work through the Foundations Implementation Rubric for all modules.
	Monitor Year 3 priorities:
	• Module B Implementation Checklist for playground • Module D Implementation Checklist
Year 7	In the fall, work through the Foundations Implementation Rubric for all modules and all common areas and schoolwide policies.
	Monitor Year 4 priorities:
	• Module A Implementation Checklist • Module B Implementation Checklist for arrival, dismissal, and cafeteria • Module C Implementation Checklist for Guidelines for Success (C2 only) • Module E Implementation Checklist
Year 8	In the fall, work through the Foundations Implementation Rubric for all modules and all common areas and schoolwide policies.
	Monitor Year 5 priorities:
	• Module B Implementation Checklist for assemblies, guest teachers, and hallways • Module B Implementation Checklist for hallways • Module C Implementation Checklist • Module F Implementation Checklist
Year 9	In the fall, work through the Foundations Implementation Rubric for all modules and all common areas and schoolwide policies.
	Monitor Year 6 priorities:
	• Module B Implementation Checklist for playground • Module D Implementation Checklist

A plan such as the one shown above provides ongoing prompts so that you never go more than 3 years without carefully analyzing any area or policy. However, if at any time data indicate a concern with any area or policy, move that area or policy up on your calendar plan. For example, let's say your first quarterly data review in Year 2 reveals a safety concern with morning arrival. Don't wait until Year 4 to address that problem! Any time data show that an area is problematic, move that area up to become one of the current year's priorities.

It's sometimes difficult to keep track of events scheduled to occur over the long term, such as every 3 years, so ensure that the plan is well documented and stored in the Foundations Archive. The Foundations Team Data/Evaluation Coordinator should be sure that his or her successor on the team knows about this long-term maintenance plan and where to find it in the archives.

Task 4 Action Steps & Evidence of Implementation

Action Steps	Evidence of Implementation
1. Reevaluate the policy or procedures during the next school year's first quarterly review.	Foundations Process: Data Summaries
2. Establish a long-term maintenance schedule of data reviews.	Foundations Process: Planning Calendar
3. If data show that the policy or procedures have had a positive impact—celebrate! 4. If data show that the policy or procedures have had a negative or neutral impact, decide whether to revise, re-teach, or help staff implement them better.	Foundations Process: Current Priorities
5. Use the Foundations Implementation Rubric and Summary (Form B-01) and Module B Implementation Checklist (Form B-02) to monitor long-term progress.	Foundations Process: Foundations Implementation Rubric and Implementation Checklists

BIBLIOGRAPHY

Adams, C. (2011). Recess makes kids smarter. *Instructor, 120*(5), 55–59. Retrieved from http://www.scholastic.com/teachers/article/recess-makes-kids-smarter

Allensworth, E. M., & Easton, J. Q. (2007). *What matters for staying on track and graduating in Chicago public schools: A close look at course grades, failures, and attendance in the freshman year.* Retrieved from http://ccsr.uchicago.edu/sites/default/files/publications/07%20What%20Matters%20Final.pdf

American Lung Association, Epidemiology and Statistics Unit, Research and Health Education Division (2012). *Trends in asthma morbidity and mortality.* Retrieved from http://www.lung.org/finding-cures/our-research/trend-reports/asthma-trend-report.pdf

Applied Survey Research and Attendance Works (2011). *Attendance in early elementary grades: Associations with student characteristics, school readiness and third grade outcomes* (mini-report). Retrieved from http://www.attendanceworks.org/wordpress/wp-content/uploads/2010/04/ASR-Mini-Report-Attendance-Readiness-and-Third-Grade-Outcomes-7-8-11.pdf

Archer, A., & Gleason, M. (1990). *Skills for school success.* North Billerica, MA: Curriculum Associates.

Baker, M. L., Sigmon, N., & Nugent, M. E. (2001). *Truancy reduction: Keeping students in school* (Juvenile Justice Bulletin). Retrieved from U.S. Department of Justice, National Criminal Justice Reference Service website: http://www.ncjrs.gov/pdffiles1/ojjdp/188947.pdf

Balfanz, R., Bridgeland, J. M., Fox, J. H., DePaoli, J. L., Ingram, E. S., Maushard, M. (2014). *Building a grad nation: Progress and challenge in ending the high school dropout epidemic.* Retrieved from http://diplomasnow.org/wp-content/uploads/2014/04/BGN-Report-2014_Full.pdf

Balfanz, R., & Byrnes, V. (2012). *Chronic absenteeism: Summarizing what we know from nationally available data.* Retrieved from Johns Hopkins University Center for Social Organization of Schools website: http://new.every1graduates.org/wp-content/uploads/2012/05/FINALChronicAbsenteeismReport_May16.pdf

Balfanz, R., & Byrnes, V. (2013). *Meeting the challenge of combating chronic absenteeism: Impact of the NYC mayor's interagency task force on chronic absenteeism and school attendance and its implications for other cities.* Retrieved from Johns Hopkins School of Education website: http://new.every1graduates.org/wp-content/uploads/2013/11/NYM-Chronic-Absenteeism-Impact-Report.pdf

Becker, W. C., & Engelmann, S. (1971). *Teaching: A course in applied psychology.* Columbus, OH: Science Research Associates.

Brophy, J. E. (1980). *Teacher praise: A functional analysis.* East Lansing, MI: Institute for Research on Teaching.

Brophy, J. E. (1986). Teacher influences on student achievement. *American Psychologist, 4*(10), 1069–1077.

Brophy, J. (1987). Synthesis of research on strategies for motivating students to learn. *Educational Leadership, 45*(2), 40–48.

Bruner, C., Discher, A., & Chang, H. (2011). *Chronic elementary absenteeism: A problem hidden in plain sight.* Retrieved from http://www.attendanceworks.org/wordpress/wp-content/uploads/2010/04/ChronicAbsence.pdf

Cameron, J., & Pierce, W. D. (1994). Reinforcement, reward, and intrinsic motivation: A meta-analysis. *Review of Educational Research, 64*(3), 363–423.

Chang, H., & Romero, M. (2008). *Present, engaged, and accounted for: The critical importance of addressing chronic absence in the early grades.* New York, NY: National Center for Children in Poverty.

Collins, J. (2001). *Good to great: Why some companies make the leap . . . and others don't.* New York, NY: HarperCollins Publishers.

Colvin, G. (Writer/Producer). (1992). *Managing acting-out behavior: A staff development program* [video]. Longmont, CO: Sopris West.

Colvin, G. (2004). *Managing the cycle of acting-out behavior in the classroom.* Eugene, OR: Behavior Associates.

Cooper, J. O., Heron, T. E., & Heward, W. L. (2007). *Applied behavior analysis* (2nd ed.). Upper Saddle River, NJ: Pearson.

Cotton, K. (1990). *Schoolwide and classroom discipline* (Close-Up #9). Portland, OR: Northwest Regional Educational Laboratory.

Donovan, M. S., & Cross, C. T. (Eds.) (2002). *Minority students in special education and gifted education.* Washington, DC: National Academy Press.

Emmer, E. T., & Evertson, C. M. (2012). *Classroom management for middle and high school teachers* (9th ed.). Upper Saddle River, NJ: Pearson.

Esler, A., Godber, Y., & Christenson, S. (2008). Best practices in supporting school-family partnerships. In A. Thomas & J. Grimes (Eds.), *Best practices in school psychology V* (pp. 917–936). Bethesda, MD: National Association of School Psychologists.

Evertson, C. M., & Emmer, E. T. (2012). *Classroom management for elementary teachers* (9th ed.). Upper Saddle River, NJ: Pearson.

Fabelo, T., Thompson, M. D., Plotkin, M., Carmichael, D., Marchbanks, M. P. III, & Booth, E. A. (2011). *Breaking schools' rules: A statewide study of how school discipline relates to students' success and juvenile justice involvement.* Retrieved from http://csgjusticecenter.org/wp-content/uploads/2012/08/Breaking_Schools_Rules_Report_Final.pdf

Feather, N. T. (1982). Expectancy-value approaches: Present status and future directions. In N. T. Feather (Ed.), *Expectations and actions: Expectancy-value models in psychology.* Hillsdale NJ: Erlbaum.

Furlong, M., Felix, E. D., Sharkey, J. D., & Larson, J. (2005). Preventing school violence: A plan for safe and engaging schools. *Principal Leadership, 6*(1), 11–15. Retrieved from http://www.nasponline.org/resources/principals/Student%20Counseling%20Violence%20Prevention.pdf

Get Schooled and Hart Research (2012). *Skipping to nowhere: Students share their views about missing school.* Retrieved from https://getschooled.com/system/assets/assets/203/original/Hart_Research_report_final.pdf

Glossary of Education Reform for Journalists, Parents, and Community Members. Retrieved from http://edglossary.org/school-culture/

Gottfredson, D. C., Gottfredson, G. D., & Hybl, L. G. (1993). Managing adolescent behavior: A multiyear, multischool study. *American Educational Research Journal, 30*(1), 179–215.

Jensen, E. (2009). *Teaching with poverty in mind: What being poor does to kids' brains and what schools can do about it.* Alexandria, VA: Association for Supervision and Curriculum Development.

Jenson, W., Rhode, G., & Reavis, H. K. (2009). *The Tough Kid tool box.* Eugene, OR: Pacific Northwest Publishing.

Kerr, J., & Nelson, C. (2002). *Strategies for addressing behavior problems in the classroom* (4th ed.). Englewood Cliffs, NJ: Merrill/Prentice Hall.

Kerr, J., Price, M., Kotch, J., Willis, S., Fisher, M., & Silva, S. (2012). Does contact by a family nurse practitioner decrease early school absence? *Journal of School Nursing, 28,* 38–46.

Kim, C. Y., Losen, D. J., and Hewitt, D. T. (2010). *The school-to-prison pipeline: Structuring legal reform.* New York, NY: New York University Press.

Klem, A. M., & Connell, J. P. (2004). Relationships matter: Linking teacher support to student engagement and achievement. *Journal of School Health, 74*(7), 262–273.

Kounin, J. S. (1977). *Discipline and group management in classrooms.* Huntington, NY: Krieger Publishing.

Losen, D. J. (2011). *Discipline policies, successful schools, and racial justice.* Boulder, CO: National Education Policy Center. Retrieved from http://nepc.colorado.edu/publication/discipline-policies

Losen, D. J., & Martinez, T. E. (2013). *Out of school & off track: The overuse of suspension in American middle and high schools.* Retrieved from http://civilrightsproject.ucla.edu/resources/projects/center-for-civil-rights-remedies/school-to-prison-folder/federal-reports/out-of-school-and-off-track-the-overuse-of-suspensions-in-american-middle-and-high-schools/OutofSchool-OffTrack_UCLA_4-8.pdf

Maag, J. (2001). *Powerful struggles: Managing resistance, building rapport.* Longmont, CO: Sopris West.

Marzano, R. J. (2003). *Classroom management that works: Research-based strategies for every teacher.* Alexandria, VA: Association for Supervision and Curriculum Development.

Maslow, A. H. (1962). Some basic propositions of a growth and self-actualization psychology. In A. W. Combs (Ed.), *Perceiving, behaving, becoming: A new focus for education* (pp. 34–49). Washington, D.C: Association for Supervision and Curriculum Development.

McNeely, C. A., Nonnemaker, J. A., & Blum, R. W. (2002). Promoting school connectedness: Evidence from the National Longitudinal Study of Adolescent Health. *Journal of School Health, 72*(4), 138–146.

National Association for Sport and Physical Education (2006). *Recess for elementary school children* (Position Statement). Retrieved from http://www.eric.ed.gov/PDFS/ED541609.pdf

National Center for Education Statistics (2012). *Digest of Education Statistics* (NCES 2014-015). Retrieved from http://nces.ed.gov/programs/digest/d12/ and http://nces.ed.gov/programs/digest/d12/tables/dt12_122.asp

O'Leary, K. D., & O'Leary, S. G. (1977). *Classroom management: The successful use of behavior modification* (2nd ed.). New York, NY: Pergamon Press.

O'Neill, R. E., Horner, R. H., Albin, R. W., Storey, K., & Sprague, J. R. (1996). *Functional assessment and program development for problem behavior: A practical handbook* (2nd ed.). Belmont, CA: Cengage.

Payne, C. (2008). *So much reform, so little change: The persistence of failure in urban schools.* Boston, MA: Harvard Education Press.

Purkey, W. W., & Novak, J. M. (2005). *Inviting school success: A self-concept approach to teaching, learning, and democratic practice in a connected world* (4th ed.). New York, NY: Wadsworth Publishing.

Ready, D. (2010). Socioeconomic disadvantage, school attendance, and early cognitive development: The differential effects of school exposure. *Sociology of Education, 83*(4), 271–289.

Rhode, G. R., Jenson, W. R., & Reavis, H. K. (2010). *The Tough Kid book: Practical classroom management strategies* (2nd ed.). Eugene, OR: Pacific Northwest Publishing.

Sheets, R. H., & Gay, G. (1996). Student perceptions of disciplinary conflicts in ethnically diverse classrooms. *NASSP Bulletin, 80*(580), 84–94.

Skiba, R. J., Horner, R. H., Chung, C.-G., Rausch, M. K., May, S. L., & Tobin, T. (2011). Race is not neutral: A national investigation of African American and Latino disproportionality in school discipline. *School Psychology Review, 40*(1), pp. 85–107.

Skiba, R. J., Michael, R. S., Nardo, A. C., & Peterson, R. L. (2002). The color of discipline: Sources of racial and gender disproportionality in school punishment. *Urban Review, 34*(4), 317–342.

Skiba, R., & Peterson, R. (2003). Teaching the social curriculum: School discipline as instruction. *Preventing School Failure, 47,* 66–73.

Sparks, S. D. (2010). Districts begin looking harder at absenteeism. *Education Week, 30*(6), 1, 12–13.

Spinks, S. (n.d.). Adolescent brains are works in progress. *Frontline.* Retrieved from http://www.pbs.org/wgbh/pages/frontline/shows/teenbrain/work/adolescent.html

Sprague, J. R., & Walker, H. M. (2005). *Safe and healthy schools: Practical prevention strategies.* New York, NY: Guilford Press.

Sprague, J. R., & Walker, H. M. (2010). Building safe and healthy schools to promote school success: Critical issues, current challenges, and promising approaches. In M. R. Shinn, H. M. Walker, & G. Stoner (Eds.), *Interventions for achievement and behavior problems in a three-tier model including RTI* (pp. 225–258). Bethesda, MD: National Association of School Psychologists.

Sprick, R. S. (1995). School-wide discipline and policies: An instructional classroom management approach. In E. Kame'enui & C. B. Darch (Eds.), *Instructional classroom management: A proactive approach to managing behavior* (pp. 234–267). White Plains, NY: Longman Press.

Sprick, R. S. (2009a). *CHAMPS: A proactive and positive approach to classroom management* (2nd ed.). Eugene, OR: Pacific Northwest Publishing.

Sprick, R. S. (2009b). *Stepping in: A substitute's guide to managing classroom behavior.* Eugene, OR: Pacific Northwest Publishing.

Sprick, R. S. (2009c). *Structuring success for substitutes.* Eugene, OR: Pacific Northwest Publishing.

Sprick, R. S. (2012). *Teacher's encyclopedia of behavior management: 100+ problems/500+ plans* (2nd ed.). Eugene, OR: Pacific Northwest Publishing.

Sprick, R. S. (2014). *Discipline in the secondary classroom: A positive approach to behavior management* (3rd ed.). San Francisco: Jossey-Bass.

Sprick, R. S., & Garrison, M. (2000). *ParaPro: Supporting the instructional process.* Eugene, OR: Pacific Northwest Publishing.

Sprick, R. S., & Garrison, M. (2008). *Interventions: Evidence-based behavior strategies for individual students* (2nd ed.). Eugene, OR: Pacific Northwest Publishing.

Sprick, R. S., Howard, L., Wise, B. J., Marcum, K., & Haykin, M. (1998). *Administrator's desk reference of behavior management.* Longmont, CO: Sopris West.

Sprick, R. S., Swartz, L., & Glang, A. (2005). *On the playground: A guide to playground management* [CD program]. Eugene, OR: Pacific Northwest Publishing and Oregon Center for Applied Sciences.

Sprick, R. S., Swartz, L., & Schroeder, S. (2006). *In the driver's seat: A roadmap to managing student behavior on the bus* [CD and DVD program]. Eugene, OR: Pacific Northwest Publishing and Oregon Center for Applied Sciences.

Sugai, G., Horner, R. H., Dunlap, G., Hieneman, M., Lewis, T., Nelson, C. M., & Wilcox, B. (2000). Applying positive behavior support and functional behavioral assessment in schools. *Journal of Positive Behavioral Interventions, 2,* 131–143.

U.S. Department of Education. (2000). *Safeguarding our children: An action guide.* Retrieved from http://www2.ed.gov/admins/lead/safety/actguide/action_guide.pdf

U.S. Department of Health and Human Services, Centers for Disease Control and Prevention (2009). *Fostering school connectedness: Improving student health and academic achievement.* Retrieved from http://www.cdc.gov/healthyyouth/protective/pdf/connectedness_administrators.pdf

U.S. Department of Health and Human Services, Centers for Disease Control and Prevention. (2012). *Youth violence: Facts at a glance.* Retrieved from http://www.cdc.gov/violenceprevention/pdf/yv_datasheet_2012-a.pdf

U.S. Department of Health and Human Services, Centers for Disease Control and Prevention. (2013a). *Asthma and schools.* Retrieved from http://www.cdc.gov/healthyyouth/asthma/index.htm

U.S. Department of Health and Human Services, Centers for Disease Control and Prevention. (2013b). *State and program examples: Healthy youth.* Retrieved from http://www.cdc.gov/chronicdisease/states/examples/pdfs/healthy-youth.pdf

U.S. Department of Justice, Office of Justice Programs, Office of Juvenile Justice and Delinquency Prevention. (2006). *Statistical briefing book.* Retrieved from http://www.ojjdp.gov/ojstatbb/offenders/qa03301.asp

University of Utah, Utah Education Policy Center. (2012). *Research brief: Chronic absenteeism.* Retrieved from Utah Data Alliance website: http://www.utahdataalliance.org/downloads/ChronicAbsenteeismResearchBrief.pdf

Wald, J., & Losen, D. J. (2003). Defining and redirecting a school-to-prison pipeline. *New Directions for Youth Development, 99,* 9–15. doi:10.1002/yd.51

Walker, H. (1995). *The acting-out child: Coping with classroom disruption.* Longmont, CO: Sopris West.

Walker, H. M., Colvin, G., & Ramsey, E. (1995). *Antisocial behavior in school: Strategies and best practices.* Pacific Grove, CA: Brooks/Cole.

Walker, H., Ramsey, E., & Gresham, F. M. (2003–2004a). Heading off disruptive behavior: How early intervention can reduce defiant behavior—and win back teaching time. *American Educator, Winter,* 6–21, 45–46.

Walker, H., Ramsey, E., & Gresham, F. M. (2003–2004b). How disruptive students escalate hostility and disorder—and how teachers can avoid it. *American Educator, Winter,* 22–27, 47–48.

Walker, H. M., Ramsey, E., & Gresham, F. M. (2004). *Antisocial behavior in school: Evidence-based practices* (2nd ed.). Belmont, CA: Cengage Learning.

Walker, H. M., Severson, H. H., & Feil, E. F. (2014). *Systematic screening for behavior disorders* (2nd ed.). Eugene, OR: Pacific Northwest Publishing.

Walker, H., & Walker, J. (1991). *Coping with noncompliance in the classroom: A positive approach for teachers.* Austin, TX: Pro-Ed.

Wentzel, K. R., & Brophy, J. E. (2013). *Motivating Students to Learn* (4th ed.). New York, NY: Taylor & Francis.

Wise, B. J., Marcum, K., Haykin, M., Sprick, R. S., & Sprick, M. (2011). *Meaningful work: Changing student behavior with school jobs.* Eugene, OR: Pacific Northwest Publishing.

Wright, A. (n.d.). Limbic system: Amgdala. In J. H. Byrne (Ed.). *Neuroscience online.* Retrieved from http://neuroscience.uth.tmc.edu/s4/chapter06.html

APPENDIX A
Foundations Implementation Rubric and Summary

The rubric is a relatively quick way for the Foundations Team to self-reflect on the implementation status of each of the modules. If you are just beginning *Foundations*, you might use this rubric toward the end of your first year of implementation. Thereafter, work through the rubric each year in the spring and consider using it in mid- to late fall to guide your work during the winter.

Each column—Preparing, Getting Started, Moving Along, and In Place—represents a different implementation status. The text in each row describes what that status looks like for each *Foundations* presentation. For each presentation, read the four descriptions from left to right. If the statements in the description are true, check the box. Each description assumes that the activities preceding it in the row have been attained. Stop working through the row when you reach a description that you cannot check off because you haven't implemented those tasks.

Notice that the descriptions for the In Place status include a section about evidence, which suggests where to find objective evidence that the described work is truly in place. If no documentation exists, think about whether the work has really been thoroughly completed. Throughout *Foundations*, we recommend archiving all your work so that policies and procedures are not forgotten or lost when staff changes occur.

When you've worked through every row, summarize your assessment on the Rubric Summary. If any items are rated as less than In Place, or if it has been more than 3 years since you have done so, work through the Implementation Checklist for that module. Of course, if you know that you need to begin work on a module or presentation, you can go directly to the corresponding content.

> Print the summary and rubric (Form B-01) from the Module B CD.

For Module B, evaluate (separately) the common areas and schoolwide policies that you have implemented—that is, you've structured them for success and taught students the behavioral expectations. Use the rows labeled Other for your school's common areas and schoolwide policies that do not appear on the rubric by default.

Figure A-1 shows a summary form completed by an imaginary school in the spring of their second year of *Foundations* implementation. They have highlighted the checkboxes to create a horizontal bar graph, giving the evaluation an effective visual component. They've done a great job on most of Module A, the common areas they've prioritized so far (hallways and cafeteria), and Welcoming New Staff, Students, and Families (C7). They need to work a bit more on staff engagement and unity (A5) and most of Module C, which they began in Year 2. Modules D, E, and F are blank because they plan to work on them in future years.

Figure A-1   *Sample Foundations Rubric Summary*

Date _____

Foundations Implementation Rubric and Summary (p. 8 of 8)

	Preparing (1)	Getting Started (2)	Moving Along (3)	In Place (4)
Module A Presentations				
A1. Foundations: A Multi-Tiered System of Behavior Support	X	X	X	X
A2. Team Processes	X	X	X	X
A3. The Improvement Cycle	X	X	X	X
A4. Data-Driven Processes	X	X	X	X
A5. Developing Staff Engagement and Unity	X	X		
Module B Presentations				
Hallways	X	X	X	X
Restrooms				
Cafeteria	X	X	X	X
Playground, Courtyard, or Commons				
Arrival				
Dismissal				
Dress Code				
Other:				
Other:				
Other:				
Other:				
Module C Presentations				
C2. Guidelines for Success	X	X	X	
C3. Ratios of Positive Interactions	X	X		
C4. Improving Attendance	X	X	X	
C5 & C6. School Connectedness and Programs and Strategies for Meeting Needs	X	X		
C7. Welcoming New Staff, Students, and Families	X	X	X	X
Module D Presentations				
D1. Proactive Procedures, Corrective Procedures, and Individual Interventions				
D2. Developing Three Levels of Misbehavior				
D3. Staff Responsibilities for Responding to Misbehavior				
D4. Administrator Responsibilities for Responding to Misbehavior				
D5. Preventing the Misbehavior That Leads to Referrals and Suspensions				
Module E Presentations				
E1. Ensuring a Safe Environment for Students				
E2. Attributes of Safe and Unsafe Schools				
E3. Teaching Conflict Resolution				
E4. Analyzing Bullying Behaviors, Policies, and School Needs				
E5. Schoolwide Bullying Prevention and Intervention				
Module F Presentations				
F2. Supporting Classroom Behavior: The Three-Legged Stool				
F3. Articulating Staff Beliefs and Solidifying Universal Procedures				
F4. Early-Stage Interventions for General Education Classrooms				
F5. Matching the Intensity of Your Resources to the Intensity of Your Needs				
F6. Problem-Solving Processes and Intervention Design				
F7. Sustainability and District Support				

Additional information about the rubric appears in Module F, Presentation 7, Task 1.

Thanks to Carolyn Novelly and Kathleen Bowles of Duval County Public Schools in Florida. We modeled the Foundations Implementation Rubric on a wonderful document they developed called the School Climate/Conditions for Learning Checklist. Thanks also to Pete Davis of Long Beach, California, for sharing samples of rubrics and innovation configuration scales.

School Name _____ Date _____

Module A

Foundations Implementation Rubric and Summary (p. 1 of 8)

Directions: In each row, check off each description that is true for your *Foundations* implementation. Then summarize your assessment on the Rubric Summary form. For Module B, evaluate each common area and schoolwide policy separately, and use the rows labeled Other for common areas and schoolwide policies that do not appear on the rubric by default. *Note:* Each block assumes that the activities in previous blocks in the row have been attained.

Presentation	Preparing (1)	Getting Started (2)	Moving Along (3)	In Place (4)
A1 Foundations: A Multi-Tiered System of Behavior Support	☐ Staff are aware of the *Foundations* approach and basic beliefs, including that *Foundations* is a process for guiding the entire staff in the construction and implementation of a comprehensive approach to behavior support.	☐ *Foundations* multi-tiered system of support (MTSS) processes are coordinated with academic MTSS (RTI) processes, and team organization has been determined (e.g., one MTSS Team with a behavior task force and an academic task force).	☐ Staff have been introduced to the STOIC acronym and understand that student behavior and motivation can be continuously improved by manipulating the STOIC variables: Structure, Teach, Observe, Interact positively, and Correct fluently.	☐ A preliminary plan has been developed for using the *Foundations* modules. For a school just beginning the process, the plan includes working through all the modules sequentially. For a school that has implemented aspects of positive behavior support, the team has self-assessed strengths, weaknesses, and needs using this rubric. **Evidence:** Foundations Implementation Rubric
A2 Team Processes	☐ Foundations Team members have been identified. They directly represent specific faculty and staff groups, and they have assigned roles and responsibilities.	☐ Foundations Team attends trainings, meets at school, and has established and maintains a Foundations Process Notebook and Foundations Archive.	☐ Foundations Team members present regularly to faculty and communicate with the entire staff. They draft proposals and engage staff in the decision-making process regarding school climate, behavior, and discipline.	☐ Foundations Team is known by all staff and is highly involved in all aspects of climate, safety, behavior, motivation, and student connectedness. **Evidence:** Staff members represented by Foundations Team members and presentations to staff are documented in the Foundations Process Notebook.
A3 The Improvement Cycle	☐ Foundations Team is aware of the Improvement Cycle and keeps staff informed of team activities.	☐ Foundations Team involves staff in setting priorities and in implementing improvements.	☐ Foundations Team involves staff in using multiple data sources to establish a hierarchical list of priorities and adopt new policies. Team members seek input from staff regarding their satisfaction with the efficacy of recently adopted policies and procedures.	☐ All staff actively participate in all aspects of the Improvement Cycle, such as setting priorities, developing revisions, adopting new policies and procedures, and implementation. Foundation Team presents to staff at least monthly. **Evidence:** Memos to staff and PowerPoint presentation files are documented in the Foundations Process Notebook.
A4 Data-Driven Processes	☐ Administrators and Foundations Team review discipline data and establish baselines.	☐ Common area observations and student, staff, and parent climate surveys are conducted yearly.	☐ Discipline, climate survey, and common area observation data are reviewed and analyzed regularly.	☐ Based on the data, school policies, procedures, and guidelines are reviewed and modified as needed (maintaining the Improvement Cycle).
A5 Developing Staff Engagement and Unity	☐ Foundations Team regularly communicates with staff through staff meetings, scheduled professional development, memos, and so on.	☐ Foundations Team members understand that they play a key role in staff unity. They periodically assess whether any factions of staff are disengaged and how they can develop greater staff engagement in the *Foundations* process.	☐ A building-based administrator attends most *Foundations* trainings and plays an active role in team meetings and in assisting the team in unifying staff.	☐ For districts with more than five or six schools, a district-based team meets at least once per quarter to keep the *Foundations* continuous improvement processes active in all schools. **Evidence:** Meeting minutes and staff presentations are documented in the Foundations Process Notebook.

If any items are rated as less than In Place or if it has been more than 3 years since you have done so, work through the Module A Implementation Checklist.

Foundations Implementation Rubric and Summary (p. 2 of 8)

Common Area	Preparing (1)	Getting Started (2)	Moving Along (3)	In Place (4)
Hallways	☐ Common area observations are conducted and data from multiple sources are collected and analyzed.	☐ Current structures and procedures have been evaluated and protected, modified, or eliminated.	☐ Lesson plans have been developed, taught, practiced, and re-taught, when necessary.	☐ Common area supervisory procedures are communicated to staff and monitored for implementation. **Evidence:** Policies, procedures, and lessons are documented in the Foundations Archive and, as appropriate, in the Staff Handbook.
Restrooms	☐ Common area observations are conducted and data from multiple sources are collected and analyzed.	☐ Current structures and procedures have been evaluated and protected, modified, or eliminated.	☐ Lesson plans have been developed, taught, practiced, and re-taught, when necessary.	☐ Common area supervisory procedures are communicated to staff and monitored for implementation. **Evidence:** Policies, procedures, and lessons are documented in the Foundations Archive and, as appropriate, in the Staff Handbook.
Cafeteria	☐ Common area observations are conducted and data from multiple sources are collected and analyzed.	☐ Current structures and procedures have been evaluated and protected, modified, or eliminated.	☐ Lesson plans have been developed, taught, practiced, and re-taught, when necessary.	☐ Common area supervisory procedures are communicated to staff and monitored for implementation. **Evidence:** Policies, procedures, and lessons are documented in the Foundations Archive and, as appropriate, in the Staff Handbook.
Playground, Courtyard, or Commons	☐ Common area observations are conducted and data from multiple sources are collected and analyzed.	☐ Current structures and procedures have been evaluated and protected, modified, or eliminated.	☐ Lesson plans have been developed, taught, practiced, and re-taught, when necessary.	☐ Common area supervisory procedures are communicated to staff and monitored for implementation. **Evidence:** Policies, procedures, and lessons are documented in the Foundations Archive and, as appropriate, in the Staff Handbook.
Arrival	☐ Common area observations are conducted and data from multiple sources are collected and analyzed.	☐ Current structures and procedures have been evaluated and protected, modified, or eliminated.	☐ Lesson plans have been developed, taught, practiced, and re-taught, when necessary.	☐ Common area supervisory procedures are communicated to staff and monitored for implementation. **Evidence:** Policies, procedures, and lessons are documented in the Foundations Archive and, as appropriate, in the Staff Handbook.
Dismissal	☐ Common area observations are conducted and data from multiple sources are collected and analyzed.	☐ Current structures and procedures have been evaluated and protected, modified, or eliminated.	☐ Lesson plans have been developed, taught, practiced, and re-taught, when necessary.	☐ Common area supervisory procedures are communicated to staff and monitored for implementation. **Evidence:** Policies, procedures, and lessons are documented in the Foundations Archive and, as appropriate, in the Staff Handbook.
Other: _____	☐ Common area observations are conducted and data from multiple sources are collected and analyzed.	☐ Current structures and procedures have been evaluated and protected, modified, or eliminated.	☐ Lesson plans have been developed, taught, practiced, and re-taught, when necessary.	☐ Common area supervisory procedures are communicated to staff and monitored for implementation. **Evidence:** Policies, procedures, and lessons are documented in the Foundations Archive and, as appropriate, in the Staff Handbook.
Other: _____	☐ Common area observations are conducted and data from multiple sources are collected and analyzed.	☐ Current structures and procedures have been evaluated and protected, modified, or eliminated.	☐ Lesson plans have been developed, taught, practiced, and re-taught, when necessary.	☐ Common area supervisory procedures are communicated to staff and monitored for implementation. **Evidence:** Policies, procedures, and lessons are documented in the Foundations Archive and, as appropriate, in the Staff Handbook.

If any items are rated as less than In Place or if it has been more than 3 years since you have done so, work through the Module B Implementation Checklist.

Foundations Implementation Rubric and Summary (p. 3 of 8)

Schoolwide Policy	Preparing (1)	Getting Started (2)	Moving Along (3)	In Place (4)
Dress Code	☐ Foundations Team has discussed the clarity and consistency of the current schoolwide policy.	☐ Data from multiple sources about the efficacy of the policy have been gathered and analyzed.	☐ The policy has been analyzed for clarity, efficacy, and consistency of enforcement.	☐ Schoolwide policies, lessons, and procedures have been written and are reviewed as needed with staff, students, and parents. **Evidence:** Policies, lessons, and procedures are documented in the Foundations Archive and, as appropriate, in the Staff Handbook.
Other: _____	☐ Foundations Team has discussed the clarity and consistency of the current schoolwide policy.	☐ Data from multiple sources about the efficacy of the policy have been gathered and analyzed.	☐ The policy has been analyzed for clarity, efficacy, and consistency of enforcement.	☐ Schoolwide policies, lessons, and procedures have been written and are reviewed as needed with staff, students, and parents. **Evidence:** Policies, lessons, and procedures are documented in the Foundations Archive and, as appropriate, in the Staff Handbook.
Other: _____	☐ Foundations Team has discussed the clarity and consistency of the current schoolwide policy.	☐ Data from multiple sources about the efficacy of the policy have been gathered and analyzed.	☐ The policy has been analyzed for clarity, efficacy, and consistency of enforcement.	☐ Schoolwide policies, lessons, and procedures have been written and are reviewed as needed with staff, students, and parents. **Evidence:** Policies, lessons, and procedures are documented in the Foundations Archive and, as appropriate, in the Staff Handbook.
Other: _____	☐ Foundations Team has discussed the clarity and consistency of the current schoolwide policy.	☐ Data from multiple sources about the efficacy of the policy have been gathered and analyzed.	☐ The policy has been analyzed for clarity, efficacy, and consistency of enforcement.	☐ Schoolwide policies, lessons, and procedures have been written and are reviewed as needed with staff, students, and parents. **Evidence:** Policies, lessons, and procedures are documented in the Foundations Archive and, as appropriate, in the Staff Handbook.
Other: _____	☐ Foundations Team has discussed the clarity and consistency of the current schoolwide policy.	☐ Data from multiple sources about the efficacy of the policy have been gathered and analyzed.	☐ The policy has been analyzed for clarity, efficacy, and consistency of enforcement.	☐ Schoolwide policies, lessons, and procedures have been written and are reviewed as needed with staff, students, and parents. **Evidence:** Policies, lessons, and procedures are documented in the Foundations Archive and, as appropriate, in the Staff Handbook.
Other: _____	☐ Foundations Team has discussed the clarity and consistency of the current schoolwide policy.	☐ Data from multiple sources about the efficacy of the policy have been gathered and analyzed.	☐ The policy has been analyzed for clarity, efficacy, and consistency of enforcement.	☐ Schoolwide policies, lessons, and procedures have been written and are reviewed as needed with staff, students, and parents. **Evidence:** Policies, lessons, and procedures are documented in the Foundations Archive and, as appropriate, in the Staff Handbook.
Other: _____	☐ Foundations Team has discussed the clarity and consistency of the current schoolwide policy.	☐ Data from multiple sources about the efficacy of the policy have been gathered and analyzed.	☐ The policy has been analyzed for clarity, efficacy, and consistency of enforcement.	☐ Schoolwide policies, lessons, and procedures have been written and are reviewed as needed with staff, students, and parents. **Evidence:** Policies, lessons, and procedures are documented in the Foundations Archive and, as appropriate, in the Staff Handbook.
Other: _____	☐ Foundations Team has discussed the clarity and consistency of the current schoolwide policy.	☐ Data from multiple sources about the efficacy of the policy have been gathered and analyzed.	☐ The policy has been analyzed for clarity, efficacy, and consistency of enforcement.	☐ Schoolwide policies, lessons, and procedures have been written and are reviewed as needed with staff, students, and parents. **Evidence:** Policies, lessons, and procedures are documented in the Foundations Archive and, as appropriate, in the Staff Handbook.

If any items are rated as less than In Place or if it has been more than 3 years since you have done so, work through the Module B Implementation Checklist.

School Name _____

Date _____

Foundations Implementation Rubric and Summary (p. 4 of 8)

Presentation	Preparing (1)	Getting Started (2)	Moving Along (3)	In Place (4)
C2 Guidelines for Success (GFS)	☐ All staff understand what Guidelines for Success (GFS) are and why they are important.	☐ Foundations Team has drafted proposals and engaged all stakeholders in the decision-making process of developing GFS.	☐ GFS have been finalized and posted and are reviewed regularly.	☐ GFS are embedded into the culture and are part of the common language of the school. **Evidence:** Procedures for teaching and motivating students about GFS are documented in the Foundations Archive, Staff Handbook, and Student and Parent Handbook.
C3 Ratios of Positive Interactions	☐ Staff have been taught the concept of 3:1 ratios of positive interactions and the importance of creating a positive climate and improving student behavior.	☐ Staff have been taught how to monitor ratios of positive interactions and are encouraged to evaluate their interactions with students.	☐ Administrator plans for teachers to observe and calculate other teachers' classroom ratios of interactions; the teachers involved meet to discuss outcomes.	☐ Observation data show that most staff at most times strive to interact with students at least three times more often when students are behaving responsibly than when they are misbehaving. **Evidence:** Procedures for teaching and motivating staff are documented in the Foundations Archive and Staff Handbook.
C4 Improving Attendance	☐ Average daily attendance is monitored to view long-term trends and patterns. Faculty and staff have been made aware of the importance of encouraging regular attendance by all students.	☐ All students with chronic absenteeism (absent 10% or more of school days) are identified at least quarterly; Foundations Team determines whether universal intervention is warranted.	☐ Each student with chronic absenteeism is identified and assigned one school-based support person who monitors whether additional support is needed. Foundations Team has analyzed attendance data and analyzed policies for clarity and efficacy.	☐ Every student with chronic absenteeism that has been resistant to universal and Tier 2 supports becomes the focus of a multidisciplinary team effort. **Evidence:** Data on average daily attendance and chronic absenteeism as well as efforts to improve attendance (e.g., parent newsletters) are documented in the Foundations Process Notebook.
C5 & C6 School Connectedness and Programs and Strategies for Meeting Needs	☐ Foundations Team has analyzed the degree to which current programs and practices meet the needs of all students (outstanding, average, and at risk).	☐ Foundations Team has developed proposals for programs and practices that might help meet unmet needs of students (e.g., the average student's need for purpose and belonging).	☐ Faculty and staff have implemented programs and practices designed to meet basic needs of all students (e.g., Mentorship, Student of the Week, Meaningful Work).	☐ Programs to meet students' basic needs are in place and analyzed at least once per year to determine their effectiveness and assess whether the needs of any student groups are not being met. **Evidence:** Analysis is documented in the Foundations Process Notebook, and programs and practices for meeting needs are documented in the Foundations Archive.
C7 Welcoming New Staff, Students, and Families	☐ Foundations Team has reviewed the welcoming aspects of the school, such as signage, website, and phone and front office procedures, and has suggested improvements.	☐ Foundations Team has analyzed procedures and suggested improvements for welcoming and orienting new students and families at the beginning of the school year. (New students include those in a new grade-level cohort [e.g., ninth graders in high school] and students who are not part of that cohort.)	☐ Foundations Team has analyzed procedures and suggested improvements for welcoming new students and families who arrive during the school year. Improvements might include written information about rules, procedures, GFS, and so on.	☐ Foundations Team has analyzed procedures and suggested improvements for welcoming new staff members, both professional and nonprofessional, at the beginning of the year. New staff members are oriented to essential procedures and the culture and climate defined by the school's behavior support procedures. **Evidence:** All policies and procedures for welcoming and orienting staff, students, and families are documented in the Foundations Archive.

If any items are rated as less than In Place or if it has been more than 3 years since you have done so, work through the Module C Implementation Checklist.

Foundations Implementation Rubric and Summary (p. 5 of 8)

Presentation	Preparing (1)	Getting Started (2)	Moving Along (3)	In Place (4)
D1 Proactive Procedures, Corrective Procedures, and Individual Interventions	☐ Foundations Team is aware of data and staff opinions about consistency in correcting misbehavior, including clarity of staff roles in discipline compared with administrative roles.	☐ Staff understand the potential limitations of office referral as a corrective procedure and avoid using it whenever possible.	☐ Staff have been made aware of the limited benefits and potential drawbacks (including disparate impact) of out-of-school suspension (OSS) as a corrective consequence.	☐ Staff avoid pressuring administrators to use OSS. Staff perceptions of consistency and administrative support for disciplinary actions are documented in staff survey results. **Evidence:** Discussions on these topics are documented in the Foundations Process Notebook.
D2 Developing Three Levels of Misbehavior	☐ Staff are aware of the concept of three levels of misbehavior: Level 1 (mild), Level 2 (moderate), and Level 3 (severe) misbehavior.	☐ Annually, staff discuss and agree on what behavior *must* be sent to the administrator, what can be sent to the administrator, and what should be handled in the setting in which the infraction occurred (3-level system for responding to misbehavior).	☐ A referral form that reflects the agreed-upon definition of Level 3 misbehavior has been developed. A notification form that reflects the agreed-upon definition of Level 2 misbehavior has been developed. (Alternatively, both Level 2 and Level 3 may be on one form.) Accurate data are kept and analyzed quarterly for all Level 2 and Level 3 misbehaviors and consequences.	☐ Data are collected on the implementation of the 3-level system for responding to misbehavior and on staff and administrator satisfaction with the system. **Evidence:** All aspects of the policy are documented in the Foundations Archive and Staff Handbook.
D3 Staff Responsibilities for Responding to Misbehavior	☐ Staff have generated and administrators have approved a menu of corrective consequences for use in common areas.	☐ Staff have generated and administrators have approved a menu of corrective consequences for use in classrooms.	☐ Staff have been trained in how to use Level 2 notifications as a process for moving toward collaborative planning for severe or chronic behavior problems.	☐ Staff have been trained in writing objective and appropriate office referrals for Level 3 misbehavior. **Evidence:** Menus and procedures are documented in the Foundations Archive and Staff Handbook.
D4 Administrator Responsibilities for Responding to Misbehavior	☐ Procedures have been developed for responding to Level 2 notifications to ensure that the reporting staff member receives timely feedback and that administrators and support staff take appropriate actions.	☐ Office procedures for dealing with students sent to the office have been analyzed and streamlined. Students do not get too much attention from office staff or staff members who visit the office	☐ Administrators are familiar with the game plan for dealing with Level 3 incidents. The game plan includes a menu of alternative consequences to out-of-school suspension.	☐ If the school has an ISS program, that program has been analyzed and revised as needed to ensure that it is highly structured and includes an instructional component. **Evidence:** All procedures for Level 2 and Level 3 infractions are documented in the Foundations Archive.
D5 Preventing the Misbehavior That Leads to Referrals and Suspensions	☐ Foundations Team has examined data on Level 2 and Level 3 infractions to determine what misbehaviors get students into trouble.	☐ Foundations Team has reviewed the lessons in Module D (how to interact appropriately with adults) and discussed whether they might reduce misbehaviors that get students into trouble.	☐ To avoid duplication, the Foundations Team has compared the Module D lessons with other social skills or social-emotional curricula currently in use. Staff have agreed on a plan for when and how to teach expected behaviors to all students.	☐ Foundations Team has discussed whether re-teaching the Module D lessons (or similar) in ISS or detention settings would be beneficial; if so, the team has planned when and how to re-teach. **Evidence:** Lesson plans and teaching logistics and schedule are documented in the Foundations Archive.

If any items are rated as less than In Place or if it has been more than 3 years since you have done so, work through the Module D Implementation Checklist.

School Name _____ Date _____

Foundations Implementation Rubric and Summary (p. 6 of 8) *Module E*

Presentation	Preparing (1)	Getting Started (2)	Moving Along (3)	In Place (4)
E1 Ensuring a Safe Environment for Students	☐ Team members are aware of their responsibilities for overseeing school safety efforts. The team coordinates with other teams or task forces that may be doing similar work and avoids duplicating other efforts.	☐ Foundations Team has viewed or read Module E and has compared that content with the school's current efforts toward safety, managing conflict, and bullying prevention. The team has developed a proposal for closing any gaps in the current efforts.	☐ Foundations Team has made staff aware of the importance of a comprehensive view of safety that includes preparing for outside attackers as well as the more common occurrences of playground injuries, student fights, bullying, and so on.	☐ Foundations Team has assessed problems with safety, conflict, and bullying within the last 3 years. If problems exist, a plan for using or adapting information from this module and integrating them with current curriculum or procedures has been completed. **Evidence:** Data analyses are documented in the Foundations Process Notebook, and final policies and procedures are documented in the Foundations Archive.
E2 Attributes of Safe and Unsafe Schools	☐ Team members and other staff directly involved with safety concerns have viewed or read Presentation 2 and have completed (individually) the form Understanding the Attributes of Safe and Unsafe Schools.	☐ Foundations Team has compiled individual responses to Understanding Attributes of Safe and Unsafe Schools and correlated those data with safety assessments completed in the last 3 years. Information about strengths and concerns has been shared with staff, and priorities have been set.	☐ Foundations Team and other staff involved with safety concerns have completed the form Assessing Emergency Preparedness, evaluated current plans for natural disasters and man-made emergencies, revised any weak procedures, including training on policies regarding seclusion and restraint.	☐ Foundations Team has completed the form Lessons to Increase Safety and Belonging, reviewed the Module E sample lessons, and evaluated whether current problems and policies address all features of the sample lessons. If there are gaps, a plan to teach some or all of the *Foundations* lessons is established. **Evidence:** Lesson plans and procedures are documented in the Foundations Archive.
E3 Teaching Conflict Resolution	☐ Foundations Team has assessed whether the school has a conflict resolution strategy that students and staff use when necessary. If so, document the effective procedures in the Foundations Archive (and skip the rest of this row).	☐ Foundations Team has reviewed the concepts and lessons in the Stop-Think-Plan (STP) approach and has prepared an implementation plan for staff.	☐ With staff input, lessons have been revised, an implementation plan has been established, and a process is in place for training all staff in how to encourage students to use the conflict-resolution strategy.	☐ Foundations Team has established a process for evaluating the effectiveness of STP by analyzing multiple data sources. The policy and lessons are revised and staff are retrained when necessary, and successes are celebrated. **Evidence:** Data analyses are documented in the Foundations Process Notebook, and lessons and teaching procedures are documented in the Foundations Archive.
E4 Analyzing Bullying Behavior, Policies, and School Needs	☐ Foundations Team is aware of the content of this presentation and can compare it with current policies and procedures related to bullying.	☐ Foundations Team has completed the form School-Based Analysis of Bullying Data and has identified whether new or revised procedures need to be implemented to enhance the current use of data related to bullying.	☐ Foundations Team has completed the form School-Based Analysis of Bullying Policies and has identified whether new or revised policies need to be implemented to enhance current policies related to bullying.	☐ Quarterly, the Foundations Team reviews data related to bullying. Annually, the team uses those data to answer each of the questions in the form STOIC Analysis for Universal Prevention of Bullying (or an equivalent process), and improvement priorities are established. **Evidence:** Data analyses are documented in the Foundations Process Notebook.
E5 Schoolwide Bullying Prevention and Intervention	☐ Foundations Team has completed the form Staff Training in Preventing and Responding to Bullying and has developed and implemented a plan to fill in any identified gaps in current practices.	☐ Foundations Team has completed the form Student Training in Preventing and Responding to Bullying. As part of a previously adopted bullying curriculum or through the *Foundations* lessons, students are taught about bullying prevention.	☐ Foundations Team has completed the form Family Training in Preventing and Responding to Bullying and has developed an implementation plan to fill in any identified gaps in current practices.	☐ Foundations Team has completed the form Active Engagement for the Prevention of Bullying and has developed an implementation plan to fill in any gaps in current practices. Bullying issues are a regular part of the team's work and are integrated into staff development efforts. **Evidence:** Ongoing discussions are documented in the Foundations Process Notebook. Established programs to enhance student engagement are documented in the Foundations Archive.

If any items are rated as less than In Place or if it has been more than 3 years since you have done so, work through the Module E Implementation Checklist.

Foundations Implementation Rubric and Summary (p. 7 of 8)

Module F

Presentation	Preparing (1)	Getting Started (2)	Moving Along (3)	In Place (4)
F2 Supporting Classroom Behavior: The Three-Legged Stool	☐ A research-based model for classroom management has been adopted at the building or district level. All teachers have access to training, and teachers new to the building or district receive the same training.	☐ School and district personnel are identified as resources for teachers who would like observations, feedback, and coaching. An effort is made to actively market the benefits of coaching support.	☐ The administrator has communicated clear outcomes and goals of effective classroom management: • 90% engagement • 95% respectful interactions • 95% of behavior matches posted expectations	☐ The model creates a common language among teachers, support staff, coaches, and administrators for problem solving and intervention. Data are collected and analyzed to evaluate classroom management efforts. **Evidence:** Information on the model, administrative walk-through visits, and coaching supports is included in the Foundations Archive and Staff Handbook.
F3 Articulating Staff Beliefs and Solidifying Universal Procedures	☐ Foundations Team has reviewed sample staff beliefs about behavior management.	☐ In faculty and staff meetings, faculty and staff have examined and discussed sample staff beliefs about behavior management.	☐ All staff have developed and adopted a set of written staff beliefs regarding discipline and behavior, and ensured that it aligned with the school's mission statement.	☐ To solidify the culture of the school and to guide the ongoing development of school policies and procedures, staff beliefs are reviewed, discussed, and revised as needed at least annually. **Evidence:** Staff beliefs and the review process are documented in the Foundations Archive and Staff Handbook.
F4 Early-Stage Interventions for General Education Classrooms	☐ Foundations Team and support staff (counselor, school psychologist, and so on) understand the concept of early-stage intervention.	☐ Foundations Team, support staff, and principal (or district administrators) agree on the interventions that should be included in the early-stage protocol.	☐ All teachers and support staff have been trained on the interventions in the school or district early-stage protocol, including how and why to keep records of each intervention.	☐ Data Collection and Debriefing (or an equivalent) is adopted as a required intervention for most chronic behavioral problems. Data must be charted before assistance is requested from support staff or problem-solving teams. **Evidence:** Expectations about when and how to get assistance are included in the Foundations Archive and Staff Handbook.
F5 Matching the Intensity of Your Resources to the Intensity of Your Needs	☐ Foundations Team and support staff (counselor, psychologist, and so on) have identified a set of red-flag criteria and (if possible) have conducted universal screening to identify students who may need individual behavior support.	☐ Foundations Team, support staff, and principal (or district administrators) agree on who can serve as advocates for students who need additional support.	☐ The advocates meet regularly to discuss progress and case studies to ensure that each student's needs are being met. Patterns of need are communicated to the Foundations Team so prevention efforts can be implemented.	☐ All support staff and problem-solving teams have written brief job descriptions that outline the services they can provide. The documents are shared with staff to inform them about available resources. **Evidence:** Suggestions for accessing these services are in the Foundations Archive and Staff Handbook.
F6 Problem-Solving Processes and Intervention Design	☐ Foundations Team understands that it will not conduct staffings (team-based problem solving) on individual students, but the team should examine current processes for supporting students and staff.	☐ Foundations Team and support staff (counselor, school psychologist, and so on) have discussed the range of problem-solving support (individuals and teams) currently available to students and staff.	☐ Foundations Team and support staff have discussed the problem-solving processes suggested in *Foundations* (e.g., the 25-Minute Planning Process), and have determined whether the processes would strengthen current practices.	☐ A flowchart or description of how the school meets the needs of students and staff has been created. It clarifies how the intensity of student needs matches the intensity of both problem-solving processes and intervention design and implementation. **Evidence:** This information is documented in the Foundations Archive and summarized in the Staff Handbook.
F7 Sustainability and District Support	☐ Foundations Team archives data, in-process work, and all completed policies and procedures, and builds on this work each year.	☐ Foundations Team orients new staff and re-energizes returning staff about all policies and procedures, and emphasizes unity and consistency.	☐ Foundations Team uses the rubric annually and the Implementation Checklists as individual modules near completion and every 3 years thereafter. The team uses this information to guide staff in setting improvement priorities.	☐ In larger districts (more than four schools), a district-based team works on sustainability. The team reminds schools about important milestones (e.g., surveys, year-end tasks, etc.) and ongoing staff development opportunities on behavior support. **Evidence:** This information can be found in district communications (e.g., emails) to schools and agenda items for principals' meetings.

If any items are rated as less than In Place or if it has been more than 3 years since you have done so, work through the Module F Implementation Checklist.

Foundations Implementation Rubric and Summary (p. 8 of 8)

	Preparing (1)	Getting Started (2)	Moving Along (3)	In Place (4)
Module A Presentations				
A1. Foundations: A Multi-Tiered System of Behavior Support				
A2. Team Processes				
A3. The Improvement Cycle				
A4. Data-Driven Processes				
A5. Developing Staff Engagement and Unity				
Module B Presentations				
Hallways				
Restrooms				
Cafeteria				
Playground, Courtyard, or Commons				
Arrival				
Dismissal				
Dress Code				
Other:				
Other:				
Other:				
Other:				
Module C Presentations				
C2. Guidelines for Success				
C3. Ratios of Positive Interactions				
C4. Improving Attendance				
C5 & C6. School Connectedness and Programs and Strategies for Meeting Needs				
C7. Welcoming New Staff, Students, and Families				
Module D Presentations				
D1. Proactive Procedures, Corrective Procedures, and Individual Interventions				
D2. Developing Three Levels of Misbehavior				
D3. Staff Responsibilities for Responding to Misbehavior				
D4. Administrator Responsibilities for Responding to Misbehavior				
D5. Preventing the Misbehavior That Leads to Referrals and Suspensions				
Module E Presentations				
E1. Ensuring a Safe Environment for Students				
E2. Attributes of Safe and Unsafe Schools				
E3. Teaching Conflict Resolution				
E4. Analyzing Bullying Behaviors, Policies, and School Needs				
E5. Schoolwide Bullying Prevention and Intervention				
Module F Presentations				
F2. Supporting Classroom Behavior: The Three-Legged Stool				
F3. Articulating Staff Beliefs and Solidifying Universal Procedures				
F4. Early-Stage Interventions for General Education Classrooms				
F5. Matching the Intensity of Your Resources to the Intensity of Your Needs				
F6. Problem-Solving Processes and Intervention Design				
F7. Sustainability and District Support				

APPENDIX B
Module B Implementation Checklist

The Implementation Checklist is a detailed checklist of the processes and objectives in each *Foundations* module. The Module B checklist (Form B-02) appears in this appendix and can be printed from the Module B CD.

As you near completion on the module, use the Implementation Checklist to ensure that you have fully implemented all recommendations. If you've decided not to follow some recommendations—you've adapted the procedures for your school—indicate the reason on the checklist. If data show problems later, this record of what you implemented and what you chose not to implement could be helpful in deciding how to address the problem.

In addition to using the checklists as needed, plan to work through all *Foundations* checklists every 3 years or so. See the sample schedule below. Additional information about Implementation Checklists appears in Module F, Presentation 7, Task 1.

Sample Long-Term Schedule: Improvement Priorities, Data Review & Monitoring

Year 1	Work on:
	• Modules A and B (continuous improvement process, common areas and schoolwide policies) • Cafeteria • Guidelines for Success
	In late spring, work through the Foundations Implementation Rubric for Modules A, B (cafeteria), and C2 (Guidelines for Success).
	Use the Modules A and B Implementation Checklists to assess status as you near completion of those modules.
Year 2	Work on:
	• Module C (inviting climate) • Hallways
	In the fall, evaluate cafeteria data.
	In late spring, work through the Foundations Implementation Rubric for Modules A, B (cafeteria and hallways), and C.
	Use the Module C Implementation Checklist to assess status as you near completion of Module C.

Year 3	Work on:
	• Module D (responding to misbehavior) • Playground
	In the fall, evaluate hallway data.
	In late spring, work through the Foundations Implementation Rubric for Modules A, B (cafeteria, hallways, and playground), C, and D.
	Use the Module D Implementation Checklist to assess status as you near completion of Module D.
Year 4	Work on:
	• Module E (safety, conflict, bullying prevention) • Arrival and dismissal
	In the fall, evaluate playground data.
	In late spring, work through the Foundations Implementation Rubric for Modules A, B (cafeteria, hallways, arrival and dismissal), C, D, and E.
	Use the Module E Implementation Checklist to assess status as you near completion of Module E.
	Monitor Year 1 priorities:
	• Module A Implementation Checklist • Module B Implementation Checklist for cafeteria • Module C Implementation Checklist for Guidelines for Success (C2 only)
Year 5	Work on:
	• Module F (classroom management and sustaining *Foundations*) • Assemblies • Guest teachers
	In the fall, evaluate arrival and dismissal data.
	In late spring, work through the Foundations Implementation Rubric for Modules A, B (playground, arrival and dismissal, assemblies, guest teachers), C, D, E, and F.
	Use the Module F Implementation Checklist to assess status as you near completion of Module F.
	Monitor Year 2 priorities:
	• Module B Implementation Checklist for hallways • Module C Implementation Checklist

Year 6	In the fall, evaluate assemblies and guest teacher data.
	Work through the Foundations Implementation Rubric for all modules.
	Monitor Year 3 priorities:
	• Module B Implementation Checklist for playground
	• Module D Implementation Checklist
Year 7	In the fall, work through the Foundations Implementation Rubric for all modules and all common areas and schoolwide policies.
	Monitor Year 4 priorities:
	• Module A Implementation Checklist
	• Module B Implementation Checklist for arrival, dismissal, and cafeteria
	• Module C Implementation Checklist for Guidelines for Success (C2 only)
	• Module E Implementation Checklist
Year 8	In the fall, work through the Foundations Implementation Rubric for all modules and all common areas and schoolwide policies.
	Monitor Year 5 priorities:
	• Module B Implementation Checklist for assemblies, guest teachers, and hallways
	• Module B Implementation Checklist for hallways
	• Module C Implementation Checklist
	• Module F Implementation Checklist
Year 9	In the fall, work through the Foundations Implementation Rubric for all modules and all common areas and schoolwide policies.
	Monitor Year 6 priorities:
	• Module B Implementation Checklist for playground
	• Module D Implementation Checklist

Module B Implementation Checklist (p. 1 of 3)

Date of Discussion: _____

Annually, the Foundations Team as a group should evaluate the three items below.

Implementation Actions	Completed Y/N	Evidence of Implementation	Evidence Y/N
1. All staff have been involved in completing a list of the school's common areas (settings and situations) and schoolwide policies.	✓ ☐	Foundations Process: Current Priorities	✓ ☐
2. All staff have been involved in ranking the common areas and schoolwide policies from most to least urgent and deciding which area or policy (and how many) to work on.	☐	Foundations Process: Current Priorities	☐
3. Each year, multiple data sources (surveys, observations, incident referrals, and injury reports) are used to assess strengths and concerns about each common area and schoolwide policy. Areas of concern are identified to eventually become priorities for improvement.	☐	Foundations Process: Data Summaries	☐

The following checklist is an abbreviated version of the Revision Checklist and STOIC Worksheet (Form B-06). You do not need to work through the STOIC portion of the checklist for each common area or schoolwide policy each year. It is most useful for common areas and schoolwide policies that have been targeted as a priority for improvement. For example, as you are preparing to present a revision proposal to the staff for adoption, the checklist can help you evaluate whether you have addressed all essential issues. For areas and policies that you've already revised, we recommend you work through this checklist as a team every 3 years (anytime during the year) to determine whether the policies and procedures are still working well, need tweaking, or need to become a priority for improvement (for example, when observations show major safety issues).

Over time, every common area and schoolwide policy should be analyzed and revised as needed, and the procedures documented in the Foundations Process Notebook

Common Area or Schoolwide Policy: _____

Implementation Actions (Using STOIC Framework)	Completed Y/N	Evidence of Implementation	Evidence Y/N
1. (S) Structure	✓ ☐	Foundations Process: Current Priorities	✓ ☐
A. Considerations for improving the structural and organizational features of the prioritized common area or schoolwide policy have been considered, including (but not limited to) whether and how the following might be contributing to student behavior problems: • Physical setting and materials • Entry and exit procedures • Scheduling • Overcrowding • Procedures		*When policies are final, file them in the Foundations Archive:*	
B. Current behavioral expectations for the prioritized common area or schoolwide policy have been evaluated and revised as needed to ensure that the expectations are: • Clear • Age appropriate • Sufficiently detailed • Reasonable and humane (for example, students are not expected to do nothing) • Known by all supervising staff members and other adults who might be in the setting or situation	☐	Foundations Archive: Schoolwide Policies, Common Area Policies and Procedures	☐
C. Elementary schools have determined whether schoolwide policies for behavior with specialists are needed.	☐	Foundations Archive: Schoolwide Policies	☐
D. Current supervision arrangements for the prioritized common area or schoolwide policy have been evaluated and, if needed, revised to ensure that the following measures are in place: • There are enough supervisors. • The supervision schedule is adequate. • Supervisors are strategically placed throughout the setting or situation. • Supervisors circulate unpredictably throughout the setting or situation. • Emergency communication procedures are established for supervisors to use. • Supervisors are trained in established emergency communication procedures. *(continued)*	☐	Foundations Archive: Schoolwide Policies	☐

Implementation Actions (Using STOIC Framework)	Completed Y/N	Evidence of Implementation	Evidence Y/N
	✓		✓
(continued) **(S) Structure** E. Develop job descriptions for supervisors of particularly complex settings, such as playgrounds and cafeterias.	☐	Foundations Archive: Job Descriptions for Common Area Supervisors	☐
2. (T) Teach expectations. One or more lessons have been developed to teach students the expectations for behavior in the prioritized common area and related to the schoolwide policy. An implementation plan for the lessons has been developed and includes: • Who will teach the lessons • A schedule for teaching the lesson(s) to students and communicating essential information to parents (e.g., dress code) • A plan for when and how lessons will be re-taught	☐	Foundations Archive: Lesson Plans for Teaching Common Area and Schoolwide Policy Expectations	☐
3. (O) Observe and supervise. Staff who have supervisory responsibilities for the prioritized common areas and schoolwide policies have been trained in active supervision. If there is a job description, staff have been trained in all the details.	☐	Foundations Process: Presentations/Communications With Staff Foundations Archive: Job Descriptions for Common Area Supervisors	☐
4. (I) Interact positively with students. Staff who have supervisory responsibilities understand and follow through on: • Using noncontingent interactions such as greetings. • Using age-appropriate positive feedback. • Maintaining 3:1 ratios of positive interactions.	☐	Staff Handbook: Roles and Responsibilities	☐
5. (C) Correct fluently. Staff who have supervisory responsibilities understand and follow through on correcting misbehavior: • Consistently • Calmly • Immediately • Briefly • Respectfully	☐	Staff Handbook: Roles and Responsibilities	☐

APPENDIX C
Guide to Module B
Reproducible Forms and Samples

The CD provided with this book contains many materials to help you implement *Foundations*. A thumbnail of the first page of each form, figure, or sample on the CD appears in this appendix. Most forms can be completed electronically. See the "Using the CD" file on the CD for more information about using fillable forms. Unless otherwise noted, all files are in PDF format.

Folders included on the CD are:

- Forms (B-01 through B-12)
  ◦ Fillable Forms
  ◦ Print Forms
- Other Resources (B-13 through B-16)
- Sample Expectations (B-17 through B-29)
- Sample Job Descriptions (B-30 through B-33)
- Sample Lesson Plans (B-34 through B-45)
- Sample Lesson Templates (B-46 through B-50)
- Sample Policies (B-51 through B-62)
- PowerPoint Presentations (B1 through B7)
  ◦ B1 Introduction.pptx
  ◦ B2 Structure.pptx
  ◦ B3 Expectations.pptx
  ◦ B4 Supervision CA-Part 1.pptx
  ◦ B5 Supervision CA-Part 2.pptx
  ◦ B6 Supervision All Staff.pptx
  ◦ B7 Monitoring.pptx

Forms

(B-01 to B-12)

B-01 *Foundations Implementation Rubric and Summary (8 pages)*

B-02 *Module B Implementation Checklist (3 pages)*

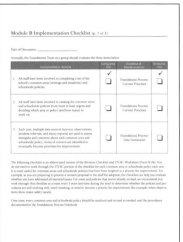

Form B-03 *Common Area Observation and Instructions (5 pages)*

Form B-04 *Common Area Concerns Worksheet*

B-05 *Schoolwide Policy Concerns Worksheet*

B-06 *Revision Checklist and STOIC Worksheet (5 pages)*

B-07 *Red Card*

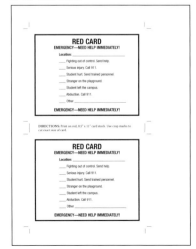

B-08 *Supervisory Skills Checklist (4 pages)*

B-09 *Behavior Improvement Form, Version 1*

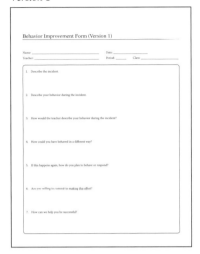

B-10 *Behavior Improvement Form, Version 2*

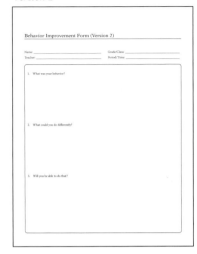

Form B-11 *Adoption and Implementation Checklist for Common Areas and Schoolwide Policies*

Form B-12 *Monitoring Checklist for Common Areas and Schoolwide Policies*

Other Resources

(B-13 to B-16)

B-13 *Evaluation Flowchart*

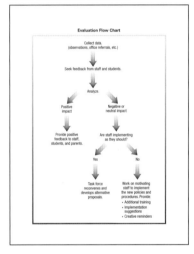

B-14 *Foundations Continuum Graphic*

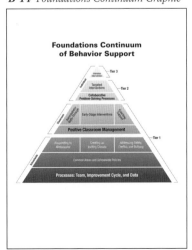

B-15 *Playground and Lunchroom Supervision (adapted from PowerPoint; 6 pages)*

B-16 *Voting Rubrics (4 versions)*

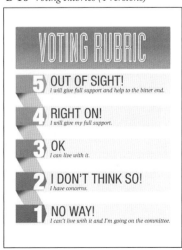

Sample Expectations
(B-17 to B-29)

B-17 *Bus Loop*

B-18 *Cafeteria (2 pages)*

B-19 *Dress Code, Poster 1*

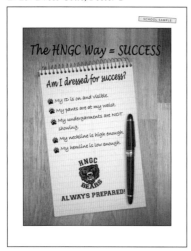

B-20 *Dress Code, Poster 2 (2 versions)*

B-21 *Electronic Device Expectations*

B-22 *Expectations Posters (Elementary): Hallways, Lunch Room, Playground, Rest Rooms (5 pages)*

B-23 *Hallways (2 pages)*

B-24 *Indoor Recess*

B-25 *Interacting With Adults: How to Respond to Verbal Reminders (adapted from PowerPoint; 3 pages)*

B-26 *Interacting With Adults: Mutual Respect Poster*

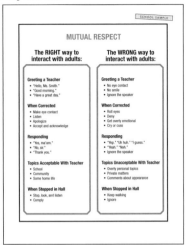

B-27 *Proper Use of Playground Equipment (3 pages)*

B-28 *Playground (adapted from PowerPoint; 12 pages)*

B-29 *Restrooms*

Sample Job Descriptions
(B-30 to B-33)

B-30 *Cafeteria (2 pages)*

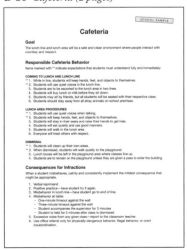

B-31 *The Art of Supervising Secondary School Hallways*

B-32 *Playground, Sample 1*

B-33 *Playground, Sample 2 (2 pages)*

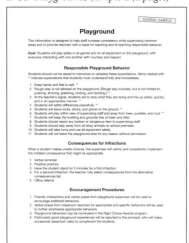

B-34 *After-School Procedures*

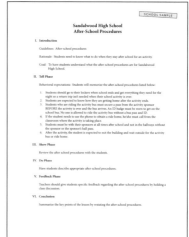

Sample Lesson Plans

(B-34 to B-45)

B-35 *Assemblies*

B-36 *Before and After School (2 pages)*

B-37 *Cafeteria, Sample 1 (2 pages)*

B-38 *Cafeteria, Sample 2*

B-39 *Cafeteria, Sample 3 (K–6)*

B-40 *Hallways/Movement, Sample 1 (3 pages)*

B-41 Hallways/Movement, Sample 2

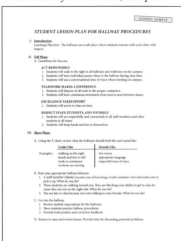

B-42 Playground (K–6)

B-43 Restrooms (K–3)

B-44 Secondary 10-day Plan (Attendance, Electronics, Dress Code, etc.; 30 pages)

B-45 Substitute Teachers

Sample Lesson Templates
(B-46 to B-50)

B-46 Lesson Template, Sample 1 (2 pages)

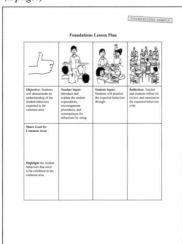

B-47 Lesson Template, Sample 2

B-48 Lesson Template, Sample 3

B-49 Lesson Template, Sample 4
(Social Skills)

B-50 Lesson Template, Sample 5

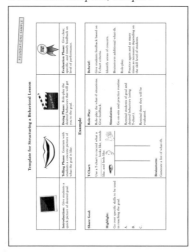

Sample Policies
(B-51 to B-62)

B-51 Assemblies, Sample 1

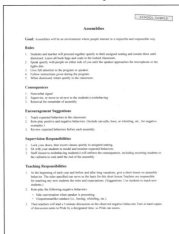

B-52 Assemblies, Sample 2

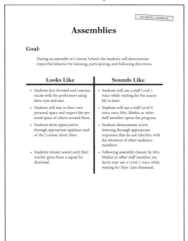

B-53 Cafeteria, Sample 1 (2 pages)

B-54 Cafeteria, Sample 2

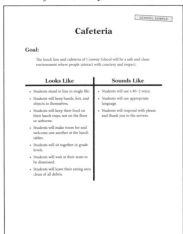

B-55 Personal Electronics Policy
(2 pages)

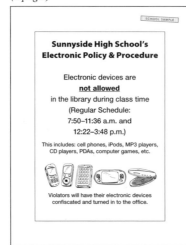

B-56 Extracurricular Good
Conduct Policy (2 pages)

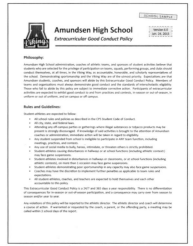